Rhetoric as Social Imagination

RHETORIC AS SOCIAL IMAGINATION

Explorations in the Interpersonal
Function of Language

GEORGE L. DILLON

INDIANA UNIVERSITY PRESS · BLOOMINGTON

Manufactured in the United States of America

Library of Congress Cataloging-in-Publication Data

Dillon, George L., 1944–
Rhetoric as social imagination.

Bibliography: p.
Includes index.
1. Language and languages. 2. Interpersonal relations. 3. Social interaction. I. Title.
P106.D46 1986   415   85-45069
ISBN 0-253-35011-5

1   2   3   4   5   90   89   88   87   86

For Kukie

CONTENTS

PREFACE

Your mission, reader, if you choose to accept it, will take you on a strange journey, a journey pursuing theory through the racks of Crown Books, from Derrida to Dale Carnegie, from Barthes to Benjamin Spock. Why such a trek should be undertaken is nowhere better expressed than in this book's prologue, introduction, and along the road. The usual map of the book can be found at the end of the introduction.

You may be encouraged in this undertaking to know that various scouts and ingenious persons have preceded you over portions of the trail, have wielded the machete, and left clearer markings. The trail begins in my Critical Linguistics seminar at the University of Maryland in 1982, and special thanks go to Meg Chandler, Carolyn Hill, Eve Shapiro, Nancy Runion, and Chuck Wilkinson for pointing out the interest of some of the texts discussed here. The Graduate Research Board of the University of Maryland provided some modest funds to establish a base camp. Further down the trail, several friends and colleagues, notably Fred Kirchhoff, Gene Hammond, Linda Coleman, Avon Crismore, Jeanne Fahnestock, Mike Agar, Michael Marcuse, and Temma Berg, read and commented on chapters in the draft. Finally, a special acknowledgment is due to Lynne Hamilton Dillon, who taught me much about hard rhetoric—more, in fact, than I wanted to know.

Rhetoric as Social Imagination

PROLOGUE

In a passage at once programmatic and enigmatic, Jacques Derrida proposes to describe the scene of writing without the "sovereign solitude of the author" as a key element in its structure:

> In order to describe the structure, it is not enough to recall that one always writes for someone; and the oppositions sender-receiver, code-message, etc., remain extremely coarse instruments. We would search the "public" in vain for the first reader: i.e., the first author of a work. And the "sociology of literature" is blind to the war and the ruses perpetrated by the author who reads and by the first reader who dictates, for at stake here is the origin of the work itself. The *sociality* of writing as *drama* requires an entirely different discipline.[1]

What sort of critique or reorientation of traditional rhetorical thinking is foreshadowed here? One can extrapolate two theses.

A. Writing is the origin of the self, not vice versa.

For a self to exist as an object of thought, it must have some permanence, some inscription, as in the medium of language; it must be available to itself to be read, edited, interpreted. The self is a theme of consistency: there must be some text before us so that we can write its continuation. But to write is to employ codes that one did not originate; it is to create an artifact, an appearance in a public role; it is to wear clothes off the rack (but to be invisible without them).

This is no new discovery. It is radical primarily in its return to roots. The study of rhetoric distinguishes itself by its indifference to the personal self; Aristotle's concept of *ethos* in the *Rhetoric*, for example, is not a principle of inwardness, but the deliberate orchestration of codes and gestures. Aristotle is discussing the spoken word (*Rhetoric*, 1356a), though the speaking is deliberate and the circumstances are the highly codified and conventionalized ones of formal oratory. We see here that it is not the physical act of writing that is at issue: the self of the orator is also an interpretation mediated by codes.

'Writing' must be understood broadly, for speech is not exempt from mediation and hence interpretation through codes. It is true that in face-to-face conversation, interpretations are largely negotiated on the

1

spot, guided by the specific purposes of the exchange, and hence that one rarely experiences irresolvable uncertainty in midstream (though one may do so later, upon reviewing the talk, in memory, as a text). On review, talk may become, as Paul de Man has it, 'rhetorical.' It is true also that the conversing (or monologuing) self lacks the permanence of an artifact. The language is not intended for wider dissemination, reading, and rereading by other selves at other times and places, but while it can be less self-conscious and deliberate than writing, one's talk is also provisional, less committed, less self and more formula, not always fully invested but a pastiche of voices shot through with degrees of reservation and dissociation; it is arguably more code-ridden than writing, not less. As M. A. K. Halliday says, "In real life, most sentences that are uttered are not uttered for the first time. A great deal of discourse is more or less routinized."[2]

The editor—the self reading and rewriting itself—is hard to set aside (except when one is 'beside oneself'). Analysis of casual, unplanned monologues reveals "initial scanning . . . followed by the expression of supplemental focuses"[3]—the speaker reviewing her own text and amplifying it, improving the sound of it, the speaker as first commentator, the commentary begun before the sentence closes. The self is always written, always interpreted, always 'rhetorical.'

B. Writing is the source of the scene of writing.

Sociolinguists describe selection of words and constructions according to the external, social relations that obtain between speaker and addressee (e.g., relative status, familiarity, membership in a common group). But the imagined footing may fluctuate and change between them without anything changing in the social relation in which they stand. So John Gumperz concludes: "Rather than claiming that speakers use language in response to a fixed, predetermined set of prescriptions, it seems more reasonable to assume that they build on their own and their audience's abstract understanding of situational norms, to communicate metaphoric information about how they intend their words to be understood."[4] So, for example, using language associated with 'them' rather than 'us' may signal that the speaker is warning rather than appealing to the addressee, or making a casual remark as opposed to an expression of personal feeling—all while maintaining the same social relationship. When we read a text, we may read a situation out of it, but that situation could not be fully specified before the writing. It did not give the writing shape; rather, the writing gave it shape.

INTRODUCTION
WRITING/READING AS INTERACTION

> Speakers interact with their audiences,
> writers do not.
>
> Wallace Chafe[1]

Many would suppose that writing is not the best place to begin an investigation of the interpersonal function of language. It is often alleged that writing is a cool or even impersonal medium. This assumption seems relatively appropriate for the special kind of writing principally or wholly devoted to conveying mere information without evaluation—writing, that is, that does not seek to engage the reader in action, writing whose persuasive impulse is only to get the reader to augment his store of knowledge in specific ways. But a great deal of writing seeks to engage the reader as a human agent and 'interlocutor,' and this move toward engagement of the reader brings about the intrusion of the writer that M. A. K. Halliday and Ruqaiya Hasan take to be the mark of the interpersonal function:

> The interpersonal component is concerned with the social, expressive and conative functions of language, with expressing the speaker's "angle": his attitudes and judgments, his encoding of the role relationships into the situation, and his motive in saying anything at all. We can summarize these by saying that the ideational component represents the speaker in his role as observer, while the interpersonal component represents the speaker in his role as intruder.[2]

A roughly similar distinction between conveying content and interacting with the reader or hearer has been drawn by many writers ranging from Karl Bühler to Roland Barthes.[3] A slightly curious feature of the Halliday and Hasan account is its emphasis on the speaker's activity in establishing the interpersonal dimension; surely the hearer is impli-

3

cated as well, as in the case of questions, imperatives, ironies, and sometimes even direct address with *you*. The relation of writing/reading may be dramatized as a communicative event, as it were, even before the question of action is raised—as it characteristically is in an exploratory essay—but there is very little persuasive writing without it. It is human subjects who persuade and are persuaded.

It is possible for writing to engage the reader in action but still remain impersonal; such is the mode of official rules and regulations, notices, contracts, and the like. Here the writer is nothing more than the spokesman for constituted collective authority. To be sure, rules and regulations are composed of imperatives and other sentences having the force, roughly, of commands, so that one might say there is an interpersonal drama implicit in them, but this drama remains latent, partly because the writer is rarely the origin of the 'mands' and the reader is involved only as a member of the regulated public. It would not be exaggerating to say that such writing has neither a Writer nor a Reader, or only a minimally realized Reader (note that the writing is typically unsigned). In John Lyons's terms, it exhibits objective (rather than subjective) deontic modality.[4] There is, then, a rhetoric of official notices, but no interpersonal encounter—a situation that is not to the liking of every linguist or layman.[5] Such writing, however, is only slightly persuasive, since it does not depend on itself for its own effect but rather on either a general tendency of people to obey rules or, ultimately, some schedule of institutional sanctions for misbehavior. Persuasion begins where compulsion leaves off, and with persuasion the interpersonal function comes to life; in comes jaw-boning, arm-twisting, flattery, intimidation, inveiglement, innuendo—the whole lexicon of interaction.

To study the interpersonal function of writing, then, it seems sensible to begin with writing that is both persuasive and personal, establishing thereby a set of benchmarks against which more marginal, complicated interactions (such as those in some fiction) can be measured. For this study, I have chosen a body of largely contemporary American advice writing—a genre that supports a very sizable part of the publishing industry, regularly dominates the nonfiction best-seller lists, and is as much a staple of the American diet as big-budget movies and bleached flour. And it is consumed in much the same way, as an experience with minimal historical affiliations. Rather than being organized into traditions or extending outward into a network of intertextuality—advice books rarely refer to other, previous works—they appear on the stands *sui generis*, with one proviso: they aspire to be the origin of revised editions and sequels. Americans without question like to be advised, and, as Dwight MacDonald noted twenty-five years ago, they entertain advice on a range of topics that stretches credulity, extending into areas once thought too trivial or too private to read a book about.[6] This enormous market may reflect a desire to professionalize living or reduce it to a series of techniques, as MacDonald suggested, or a breakdown in the transmission of traditional wisdom—but the interest of the present study is not external, with advice as a phenomenon, but internal, taking it as a series of cases in which the interpersonal dimension of writing can be rather closely examined. It is a dimension in which these books show great inventiveness: since the amount of new information is usually slight, and the number of advice books is large, the key to success is inventiveness in packaging, in the way the 'scene of advising' is conceived and executed. Only in advertising and some avant-garde fiction do we find comparable foregrounding of the reading/writing relationship.

If one wishes to maintain the position that 'real' writing breaks free of the interpersonal function, then one might observe that advice writing occupies a sort of middle ground between 'real' writing and face-to-face conversation. One could argue that it is displaced or imitated interaction, and even that the whole notion of interpersonal engagement is a kind of metaphor when applied to writing and is parasitic on face-to-face encounters for its effect. And this argument could be extended to all persuasive writing.

A consequence of this position, however, would seem to be that one is denying or concealing or obfuscating the impersonal reality of writing when 'intruding' in a text written for an unknown other—pretending, that is, that there is some personal relationship with the reader when in fact the text is a communication between strangers who do not face each other: the 'I' writes with only the hope of a 'you'; the 'you' infers a necessary but insubstantial 'I.' On each end one blooded person and one ghost. Here the two theses of my prologue come into play. Exchanges with both parties physically present are not in any clear way fuller or more real. The interpersonal can unfold and determine itself more amply, perhaps, in writing. It is true that we may read with the sense that the writer is talking to us, but that is in fact an illusion.

In short, the 'personalizing is pretense' view follows from the general notion that writing is *unsituated* discourse, an observation so frequent these days as to need (or bear) little explication.[7] But advice writing as it were compensates for the lack of shared time, place, and personal knowledge of the other. It situates itself: it postulates or projects a scene of advising—a Reader with needs, concerns, and responses; a

Writer with some sort of authority and responsiveness to the Reader; and a Footing between them. And this projection is not window-dressing. The first objective is to describe how particular choices writers make build up these scenes, composing themselves and their readers simultaneously in the writing of advice.

Many rhetoric textbooks approach writing from an almost exactly opposite perspective, stressing the way the actual communicative situation imposes constraints on the writer's choices: one adjusts (or accommodates) one's language to the subject, the audience, the purpose of the writing, and so on. Here too the primary model seems to be a speaking (or substitute speaking—a memo or letter) in the context of a pre-existing, predefined relationship in which the audience is knowable (if not thoroughly known) outside of the act of speaking. Now of course it is well recognized that in much writing, the audience isn't obviously there in any very useful way, but rhetoricians respond by saying that it should be—that one should imagine or 'take account of' one's audience, much as an advertiser targets a segment of the population identifiable in social, economic, or cultural terms. This conception of audience (or readership) has very little to do with the notion of Reader as one pole of a projected interaction: it doesn't tell the Writer how to treat the Reader—that remains the writer's choice. Put another way, we see writing directed at the same readership (e.g., that of *Newsweek* or *Critical Inquiry*) treating the Reader in a wide variety of ways.

We conclude, then, that the notion of writing as displaced interaction is partly right. It is displaced, but not faked. Rather, it is set free to develop itself according to the special conditions and possibilities of writing.

A similar argument might be made concerning the colloquial or informal language that most writers of advice use. While it is far from actual speech (or a transcript of speech), it still functions, broadly, to evoke a voice speaking, and in that sense could be said to be a pretense and denial of the actual facts of composition (planning, calculation, editing, revision). But again, the functions of colloquialism in speech are by no means as simple and clear as they have been made out to be.[8] Colloquial language can suggest various attitudes:

—warmth, good nature, hence solidarity with the reader
—spontaneity, lack of calculation, hence sincerity
—seriousness, urgency, hence commitment to what is said
—suggestiveness (versus conclusiveness)
—exaggeration and play (versus weighted deliberation)

The colloquial ties into many codes of interaction, and this potential for complex articulation is particularly evident when the language is fixed in print as part of an orchestrated strategy.

Just as it is important to avoid reducing written interaction to face-to-face exchanges, so is it crucial to avoid the reduction to external, social relations. Roger Fowler, among others, has repeatedly argued that the notions of choice and selection by the writer postulate a naive freedom from determination by social institutions and forces. He finds this "bourgeois individualism" in interactionist social psychology: "It suggests that the individual constructs himself, the discourse he utters, and the texts he reads, under weak general constraints such as 'appropriateness,' 'cues,' etc. Thus discourse is regarded as freely chosen, and structured by the speaker or writer according to his assessment of what is suitable for the situation."[9] His principal objection is that language is codified and commits writers to positions on scales of status, power, and authority; it evokes social realities. The codes of interaction are part of the social structure. To interpret Fowler by means of an example from advice writing, when a writer says, 'Many patients have told me,' he is claiming a status of authority within social structures known by all parties. Even when a writer claims a stance that is outside recognized, institutional roles, this stance is socially defined precisely in that it is the stance of an 'outsider.'

Fowler is quite right, I think, in pointing out that self-presentation in language is always conditioned by the way selves are defined in a culture at that point in its history. Indeed, I would amplify his argument by saying that writing constantly alludes to models (stereotypes) of interaction floating around in the collective consciousness (or repertoire of cultural knowledge) at the time. This is why it can prove difficult for a modern reader to grasp the interpersonal nuances of writing from several centuries ago—when, for example, someone is being unusually 'pert' or 'saucy' (though some writing heavily encodes the relevant norms and expectations—the 'manners' of the era).[10] What we do *not* need to know is how people actually talked or behaved. Of course, the culture of a period is never homogeneous. There is always a plurality of milieus, some emerging; some widespread; some old-fashioned; some associated with particular region, class, or ethnic background; and members of the culture may be expected to differ in their perceptions of which is 'current,' 'classy,' and so on. Suppose 'husband' and 'wife' name roles in a prototype of intimacy. Do 'master of the house' and 'the little woman' likewise refer to the same relation? The later phrases call up a milieu that might be regarded as not only old-fashioned but a sorry substitute for real intimacy, at least in certain urban and academic environments. When one realizes that the roles of 'husband' and 'wife' are differently defined in various more or less contemporary milieus, it should be clear that even such a basic and apparently self-evident notion as 'intimacy' is also culturally constructed.

It is necessary to draw a much sharper distinction than Fowler does, however, between *culture* and *society*. The crucial issue is how the codes of interaction work. Fowler takes the Marxist position that the codes implicate (however obliquely) social reality. Social reality, however, he does not conceive of as constituted by codes but by the material ("objective") social relations that do in fact obtain. The users of the language may not be conscious of the realities underlying the language, but it is the mission of "critical linguistics" to lay them bare. Similarly, Manfred Bierwisch argues that connotations of linguistic choices, such as familiarity, status, and formality, must ultimately be explained in terms of "discernible aspects of the social structure of the speech community," the categories of this analysis being taken from a theory of social structure, and the whole project resulting in "a principled analysis of the conditions of communication in close connection with the analysis of the conditions of production initiated by Marx."[11] One sample of analysis conducted along these lines can be found in *Language and Control*, a collection of essays by Fowler, Bob Hodge, Gunther Kress, and Tony Trew that give accounts of the interpersonal function of language in various contemporary British texts by exposing it as controlling and manipulating the reader according to the interests of the ruling class.[12] Culture, in the sense of the network of codes, is ideology, and its function is to negotiate and enact control.

It has been argued, however, that any account of 'real' social relationships is itself a text, and so the reduction of the cultural code to social 'reality' is only the cross-referencing of texts, not a move outside the text to the world.[13] If we ask, "What's really going on in this relationship?" the only answer is in terms of another codification of reality. We do not in this way get outside of the culture; we only articulate the workings of one code with another. There is no reality of interpersonal relations that the text more or less accurately reflects. 'Elitist snob' does not refer to anybody out there, though it can be cross-referenced to 'class enemy.' Now, there may be good practical, political, or pedagogical reasons for privileging a text, say the psychoanalytic or Marxist one, and perhaps taking it to be the 'real,' but that results in our being worked by the text to some degree, illustrating it, rather than observing the workings of texts. It is useful to approach the study of writing/reading as interaction with as few preconceptions as possible about how relationships really do work, and to shed them as quickly as one can.

Marxists are not the only ones who treat the codes of social identity and relations as grounded in social facts to which they more or less obliquely refer. This issue has also been discussed in relation to gender, namely, whether there is a women's way of talking distinct from men's, particularly whether men characteristically relate to others more impersonally and distantly than women do. Such is the code, or stereotype, Robin Lakoff claims, and it must reflect the actual behavior of men and women: "It is important to remember at the outset that, when two types of behavior are put in contrast by a society, they will tend to be polarized—to be perceived and stereotyped as more different than they probably are. But these exaggerated stereotypes must, to be intelligible, be based on real differences."[14] Here Lakoff gives an account of origin based on some sort of social division of behavior, but why could things not be the other way around, with the polarization arising from the codifying act itself, from its notable proclivity for binary opposition and dichotomy? Why must code imitate life, and not life, code? Why, above all, must the code refer to "real differences" in order to be intelligible? Lakoff herself demonstrates just the opposite, explicating the codes in terms of other codes (of personality types, neurotic patterns, movie-star images, national stereotypes), not in terms of "real" differences with all the complexities and qualifications that would entail. Perhaps Lakoff means that it is hard to imagine how one could learn and apply the stereotypes without observing them in one's experience—but the necessary experience in this regard may be not observation of people but movies, TV, books, magazines, parents, teachers, friends, and other transmitters of the codes themselves (i.e., already fabricated).[15]

Lakoff's second pass at the relation of codes to reality is no more successful in explaining how the codes are grounded in reality. She is discussing the stereotype that men have of women arising from applying a man's norm of discoursing (accurately and impersonally)—namely, that women are manipulative and deceitful, and do not say what they mean:

> But the crucial question is whether there lurks a reality behind the stereotype. For stereotypes are important to study only insofar as they are representations of reality. And I would argue further that societies only create and maintain those stereotypes that their members feel hold a mirror up to reality—though it be a fun-house mirror. (p. 70)

This seems to mean that the only important codes are the ones people take to be true (as opposed to silly, ignorant, prejudiced, exaggerated). If so, however, the word *representation* has lost all referential force; one might as well substitute *imagination* or *vision*. Even Lakoff seems to be conceding that we cannot interpret the codes in terms of a reality known independently of them. The codes function to project a 'social reality' with only the roughest links to the actual behavior of individuals.

Culture, in the sense to be explored in this book, is thus a code or conglomeration of codes that are not codes *for* anything; language refers, but always to another piece of codified reality, to more language. Culture is nothing other or more than the codes and stereotypes themselves. In analyzing the codes, we are led to other codes, endlessly tracing a network. An advice book counseling you on how to manage your spouse alludes to a code (or bundle of codes) that pertains to relations between 'Men' and 'Women,' to 'Marriage,' 'Breadwinner,' 'Head of Household,' 'Home,' 'Family,' and so on. It is misleading to speak of marriage as an institution, and it leads one to write articles on the divorce rate that yield no insight whatsoever.

Barthes says, "The codes are simply associative fields, a supra-textual organization of notations which impose a certain idea of structure; the instance of the code is, for us, essentially cultural: the codes are certain types of 'déjà-lu', of 'déjà-fait': the code is the form of this 'déjà', constitutive of all the writing in the world."[16] At the same time, writing recreates the codes; they exist only by being evoked. Writing—advice writing—is simply a form of culture-making, not just the reflection of some pre-existent thing, Culture. Press either view to the extreme, and you lose the delicate balance of evocation. John Sturrock, for example, takes Barthes to task for treating the codes as preformulated:

> When Balzac talks of "the kind of frenzy which only disturbs us at that age when desire has something terrible and infernal about it", Barthes allots this dismissively to "the psychology of age" as if it were unthinkable that it might be the fruit of observation or experience. Under his dispensation it is hard to see how the common stock of knowledge or belief could ever be modified.[17]

But it should be noted that the codes are modified not merely by "observation or experience" but by writing in and with codes as Balzac does; note that Balzac presents the observation as 'already known' ("at *that* age . . .")—observed, perhaps, but also observed by others. Barthes's example in fact precisely reflects the mode of operation of the codes, of which the action of stereotyping is the core, not reference to some canonical set of stereotypes.

Likewise, this notion of code should not be equated with that of *schema* as developed in the theory of language comprehension (i.e., of the encoding/decoding of content, which is the core of the ideational function). A schema is a knowledge structure, a representation of something we know whereby we can categorize and integrate, summarize and abstract, what we read, specify further plausible understandings and derive inferences, and make predictions about what is to come.[18] Codes, as they mediate the sociality of writing, have not a determining function but a loose-textured, open-ended quality of allusion; they are echoes, suggestions rather than comprehensions. Essentially, they are part of what was traditionally called connotation—connotations, specifically, of relational models and norms.[19]

Consider this set of words for describing and evaluating an attitude toward the other: cool, deferential, diffident, modest, reserved, respectful, restrained, unassuming. The connotations that differentiate these terms are not just 'positive' and 'negative' but rather tie in to subtle assumptions about norms and models. *Reserved* suggests keeping something valuable to oneself; *restrained* suggests keeping forces within oneself under control; *deferential* suggests a struggle to please a potentially hostile, competitive other; *diffident* suggests lack of involvement or force, perhaps from timidity; and so on. The same is true of words to describe relationships (engagement, entanglement, exchange, interaction, involvement) or to describe a certain felicity in a relationship (camaraderie, closeness, familiarity, friendliness, intimacy, mutuality, rapport). The lexicon of interaction is huge and articulated by many subtle threads and interconnections, discriminations, and evaluations that people may make as they listen or read.

It is clear, therefore, that the study of writing/reading as interaction will carry us into models of 'social reality'—accounts, texts, codifications of how relationships generally do work and should work in the world. It is not a purely linguistic inquiry, but one that has always an eye on the culture that defines and is defined by the writing. On the other hand, it is certainly linguistic, since it deals with the meanings and workings of questions, adverbs, pronouns, and a host of other grammatical and rhetorical features.

To investigate reading/writing as the imagining of interaction, two procedures suggest themselves. The sociality of particular acts of writing develops in a field of assumptions about human subjectivity and action; the interaction of Writer and Reader outlined in chapter 1 is but a single immediate instance of the possibilities as the text conceives them. Our first procedure will be to examine texts that are explicit about their axioms of personal and social interaction. One major branch of advice pertains to personal relationships and thus spells out the principles for treating others that are illustrated in the handling of the reader. Such advice on how to 'relate' will be the subject of chapter 2. In 'relating' books, action and interaction are conceived in 'personal' (or dyadic) terms ('I' and 'you'), as atomistic exchanges governed by forces of attraction and repulsion. Other advice books, such as those covering good usage or child rearing, however, develop their axioms of interaction in terms of larger collectivities and forces; the scene of writing/reading is played out in terms of 'us' and 'them' against a social, political, and historical backdrop. Such writing will be the subject of chapter 3.

The second procedure exploits the practice of bringing out revised editions, which are rarely stimulated by an access of new knowledge (i.e., by a new relation to the subject matter). Rather, revision reflects an alteration in the cultural milieu, or in the writer's relation to the milieu, that stimulates her to recast her relation to the reader. Revision study will be useful in many chapters, but will be especially central to chapter 4, where change is examined as the basis of antiauthoritarian rhetorics.

In the course of articulating the cultural codes operative in advice, it will be handy to employ a number of oppositions such as colloquial/ literary (spoken/written), sincerity/pose, aggressive/ingratiating, spontaneous/calculated, author/work, serious/play, literal/figurative, personal vision/traditional wisdom, implied/real (writer and reader). There is an acute problem of metalanguage in so doing, however, for these oppositions are thoroughly entangled in common sense, which is to say they are themselves part of the codes to be examined. More complicated yet, the bases of opposition are not self-evident and prove more illuminating when brought into question. The later chapters of this book will take up texts that render many of these familiar pairs problematic. Chapter 4 will take up the oppositions of real/implied writer and personal vision/traditional authority; chapter 5 will bring into question literal/figurative, sincerity/pose, and serious/play as it discusses the forces of representation, gesture, and figuration in crisis advice books; and chapter 6 will scrutinize the distinction of implied/ real as it has been applied to readers. To place these distinctions in question is not to destroy them, but rather to deprive them of self-evidentness, to release the insights they block without discarding the ones they make possible. We must be tender with the codes, for they finally are the codes of our identities. And one cannot bring all common-sense notions into question at once. The basic concepts—writer, purpose, reader—though rife with complexities, will be employed in a fairly uncritical way in the early chapters but will then themselves become the object of scrutiny and reconsideration in the later chapters as the implications of the two theses of the prologue gradually unfold. We should finally arrive at an understanding of what it means to say that verbal interaction is fundamentally and irreducibly rhetorical.

The exploration of language pursued in this book pushes the resources of English punctuation to their limits. It is necessary to set off certain words and phrases in at least five ways, but currently printed English only gives three distinctions, so some doubling up is necessary. (1) Italic type face indicates the 'word qua word' or word in its material reality (e.g., *quasi* is a prefix borrowed from Greek; *quasi* is a hedge or 'weasel' word). (2) Double quotation marks (") are used either to indicate the sense (or reading) of a word or phrase (e.g., *kill* means "cause to cease to be alive") or for verbatim citation of an individual text (e.g., Sonnet 94 begins, "They that have power to hurt and will do none"). (3) Single quotation marks (') are used in two cases of mention, first (3a) for phrases in the air, as it were, from which the writer wishes to dissociate himself somewhat. Thus in my example for (1), I set off 'word qua word' and 'weasel'—the first because it seemed a bit of nearly opaque jargon, the second as slightly too colloquial to be used in a learned discourse. Single quotation marks are also used (3b) for words and phrases characteristically employed by a particular writer or speaker, but not cited from any particular point in a text (e.g., one of Dr. Spock's favorite sentence openers is 'I think'). These last mentions could be called generic quotations or citations—what one or more people typically say—and should not send the reader off searching for a page reference. The general function of the single quote offset, then, is to bracket some piece of language as discourse. All texts are woven out of codifications of the ways other people talk; the parts of the text we want to displace or call attention to, we set off in single quotes. In a sense, this is the fundamental analytic move in this book.

Similarly, I have used capitalization to call out certain words that are meant to be taken in a technical or semitechnical way, that is, as defined in this study both explicitly and by recurring use. This convention of scholarly discourse, especially heavily used in pragmatics, attempts to freeze or limit the connotative skid of words in free circulation, and it is one of the theses of this book that such attempts are perverse, with the same prospect of success as applying the topiary art to a kudzu vine. Worse, this use of capitalization is intoxicating in its suggestion of even a temporary hegemony over words: one finds oneself capitalizing more and more. Not the least of the services provided by Judy Allensworth, the copy editor of this book, however, was to prune this proliferation and return many words to the wilds of general usage whence they sprang.

I

FOOTING
THE CODES OF ENGAGEMENT

> A *style* is not simply a response to a
> particular kind of subject-matter, nor is it
> entirely a matter of the writer's situation
> and his presumed audience. It is partly a
> matter of sheer individual will, a desire for
> a particular kind of self-definition no
> matter what the circumstances.
>
> Walker Gibson[1]

I.

Traditional rhetorical analysis views situations as constraints on a writer's choices, *situation* being used broadly to include the particular purpose of the discourse (or writer), the subject matter, and the intended audience. Style in Gibson's sense is what remains undetermined after purpose, subject matter, and audience have been given their due, and his position is that there is always room for individual self-definition. That is, purpose, matter, and audience do not completely determine the selections of the writer; they only define the external outline of the situation within which the writer must fashion roles for himself and his reader and a relation between them. In practical terms, the situation constrains choices in writing when the purpose of writing is to further personal interaction—when there is an external situation that the writing serves instrumentally (e.g., as in an office memo, termination-of-coverage letter, etc.). The writer partly interprets that situation, of course, by his choices—he can tune the solemnity and the lightness of his touch, for example—but the situation is 'there' in independently ascertainable ways, and the writing is intended to affect some aspect of it. Choices are made with regard to what is appropriate to the situation as generally understood by all parties, and the choices may be judged to be effective (persuasive) insofar as they affect the situation in the desired way. The selves of writer and reader relevant to the interaction are institutionally predefined to a considerable degree.

When the text is not instrumental to furthering a pre-existing relationship, however, as in advice writing, the writer has a scope to create roles and relations that is almost as large as that in literature. In this case, Gibson's notion of style as what is left over after the situationally determined choices are subtracted doesn't seem very useful, since the definition of the situation is also to a large degree a choice of the writer. Indeed, we might reverse the priority in these cases and say that the style determines the situation: it is because the style is what it is that we know the writer conceives of the situation as he does. Comparing parallel passages from advice books highlights the degree to which the externally defined audience and purpose do not determine the style. Writing (and reading) a relatively unsituated text is an act of social imagination: projection or construction of a self, an other, and a footing between them, out of bits of social and linguistic codes.[2] The writer must do more than select from a repertoire of 'varieties' (or registers) the style suitable for the intended readership: his style functions 'metaphorically' (it is sometimes said) to convey the situation as the writer defines it. If one writes to the teenage reader, for example, one is to some degree working from preconceptions about teenagers as a group (they are antagonistic to authority, watch certain TV shows, etc.), but one is also constituting the Teenager-as-advisee. That is to say, the choices are generally not made in order to accommodate to any particular teenagers, and even a detailed formulation of 'The Teenager' would not dictate how the writer should handle the transaction. Failure to recognize that the relation to an audience involves projection as well as accommodation is the source of many vacuous 'explanations' of writers' choices in terms of 'the audience,' for, if we infer the intended audience from the pattern of choices that writers have made, then we have said no more than that the writers have made their choices to shape or project the Model Reader. As Hans Robert Jauss says:

> Whoever reduces the role of the implied reader to the behaviour of an explicit reader, whoever writes exclusively in the language of a specific stratum, can only produce cookbooks, catechisms, party speeches, travel brochures, and similar documents. He will not excel in these genres either, as may be seen from eighteenth-century cookbooks which aimed at universal good taste and not at limited structures of pre-understanding.[3]

(Hereafter I will capitalize Reader and Writer when referring to implied, textual entities, use lower case for 'real' writers and readers, and occasionally use "Model Reader" for emphatic contrast to "reader.")

The roles of Writer and Reader, and the Footing between them, are not just set once in advance, but are adjusted constantly as the discourse proceeds and may be altered for various reasons. Frequently in advice writing, the Writers move in closer to Readers when the text dramatizes a situation or process of thinking in which the reader might find herself. In these passages, contractions, colloquialisms ("If your fantasy is bizarre, really wild, I mean, don't let it worry you," says Hamilton, p. 34), nonreference pronouns, reader's terminology, present tense, and of course lots of *you* abound. Sometimes the shifts of Footing can be rapid and wide, as in the following paragraph from *Changing Bodies, Changing Selves*:

> We have so many expectations, so many fantasies about what IT will be like. It seems like everything we've heard or seen or learned about sex is all pointing in one direction: toward sexual intercourse—which, in slang, people call fucking, humping, screwing, home base, going all the way, making it. The importance of intercourse has been so exaggerated in books and magazines and movies that people forget it is only one part of lovemaking. Teenagers also get so little information about it that they often don't know what to expect. Even teens who have had intercourse say there's a lot that they don't know. The teenagers who advised us about this chapter said, "Be straight about it. Tell what it is, who does what, the different ways people might feel, the problems and what to do about them." (p. 101)

The initial *we* is one of shared viewpoint with the teenage Reader (solidarity). The shift via the list of slang terms into the impersonal didactic ("The importance of intercourse has been so exaggerated . . .") is fairly abrupt. Then *teenagers* emerges as a class contrasting with *us*, so that the *we* no longer encodes solidarity with the Reader. It is as if the writer, having adopted the virgin's ignorance and diffuse excitement, must scramble to regain some authoritative distance and perspective. Shifts of Footing are quite common in advice writing, but rarely are they so awkwardly executed.

Just as the other of the Reader is not fully preformulated, so the self addressing it is partially a result of its address to the Reader. Richard Lanham, following Kenneth Burke, contrasts two extremes of the self we may encounter in reading:

> Style as personality implies an agonistic relationship, a contest. We must feel the force of this great man, like it or not. By his style as by his

presence, we are to be overpowered. But style as ingratiation offers an alternative to competition. It aims at the gentlest kind of persuasion, the attempt to make oneself over in the form most agreeable to the other.[4]

Lanham is not talking about particular styles here but about conceptions of how language functions as social interaction. It is clear where Gibson stands:

In the very act of addressing someone we acknowledge a wish to push him around, and in our zeal to push a little harder, it is no wonder our voices begin to sound strident. It is with style that we try to behave like a decent person, one who ruefully concedes his drive for power while remaining aware of his reader's well-chosen resistance. (Gibson, p. 110)

It is a harsh, Hobbesian world that lies behind such a statement: Gibson seems to be saying that speaking to people inherently threatens what Penelope Brown and Stephen Levinson call their Negative Face Wants—desires for "freedom of action and freedom from imposition."[5]

But people have something to gain from social interaction as well as something to fear. We engage in social relations because of the desire to be "ratified, understood, approved of, liked, or admired" (Brown and Levinson, p. 67). These are Positive Face Wants, and we might conceive of styles as ways of bringing these potentially discordant impulses into harmonious concord. Brown and Levinson capture one aspect of this reconciliation in their notion of 'redressive action': if you are going to threaten someone's face wants, use language that compensates her by pulling back or gratifying other wants. More deeply, however, it is better to view these 'selves' (pushy, ingratiating, or what have you) not as personal self-definition but as strategically motivated constructs or roles that cast the Reader in the corresponding role.

Although in the balance of this discussion, I will proceed from the encoding of Readers to the encoding of Writers and Footings, each really emerges in relation to the other two. What the Burke/Lanham/Gibson tradition has in common with Brown and Levinson is the view of the relation of Writer and Reader as analyzable into somewhat metaphorical vectors of approach and distance or aggression and ingratiation. Footings vary over several dimensions, however, and I have found it useful not to squeeze them all into a single opposition, but to differentiate at least five complexly related dimensions, which in tabular form are:

impersonal/personal
distant/solidary (meets positive face wants)
superior, authoritative/equal, limited (respects negative face wants)
direct, confrontive/oblique (respects positive face wants)
formal/informal

The term 'intimate' does not even appear in this table. It presupposes extensive personal knowledge between parties and is thus metaphorical when applied to unsituated writing, and it is so powerfully attractive that it seems to make further discriminations superfluous. Intimacy easily becomes a term for 'presence' (namely, copresence) and is then subject to Derridean critique. Martin Joos, for example, says that the language of intimacy is that spoken by husband and wife at the dinner table (alone, presumably).[6] But of course husbands and wives sometimes speak in nonintimate ways to each other at the dinner table. One would not want to tape-record dinner-table conversations and then analyze the results for the traits of intimacy, unless one meant by that simply the language of people who are in a conventionally 'intimate' relation. Intimacy is not predictably present in any given circumstance, and hence it is not *observable*. It is a name for felicity, a vanishing point on the horizon of expectation. According to my understanding, intimate talk would likely be personal, solidary, equal, relatively direct, and informal, but I can imagine variation in the areas of equality and directness, and all of these might obtain without intimacy being present. Intimacy is an achievement—or a blessing—it is not a relationship, a Footing, or a style. In any case, Reader and Writer are never really related this way in advice writing; at most, the Writer can suggest or allude to such a face-to-face relation. Somewhat the same thing could be said about the term *rapport*, which seems to have edged its way into English in the modern, very positive sense via its association with mesmerism (namely, the bond between hypnotist and subject—see the *Oxford English Dictionary*).

In the next section, I will differentiate these five scales, illustrating some of their components with short examples from a corpus of advice writing, and in the third section I will give somewhat more extended examples of how the five scales work together to project a Reader, a Writer, and a Footing between them.

A few preliminary observations about method, however, are in order. Within the framework of current rhetorical theory, Footings would probably be treated as a part of *tone*, where tone is defined as the writer's attitude toward the reader (as distinguished from her *stance* toward the material). Tones are commonly described impressionistically as authoritarian, intimate, parental, friendly, dogmatic, stuffy, condescending, wheedling, etc. There is nothing wrong with this practice, but in relation to the present project three points suggest themselves. First, these terms are used quite variably: people disagree about which adjectives to use for a particular passage and use the same adjective for rather different passages. This is especially the case for *authoritarian, intimate,* and *parental.* Second, the terms sometimes appear to overlap and sometimes to contrast, and it often seems that they are applied primarily to express liking or disliking rather than to make subtle discriminations. In short, they could do with some analysis that relates them to traits and features of language. Third, they seem to express responses that are based both on Footings (textual strategies) and on content, so that a vehement and sweeping assertion of a controversial opinion will be felt to be much more dogmatic than similar vehemence used to assert a commonplace. I think it is useful to distinguish Footings from total effects, but it should be borne in mind that an abstraction from response is involved. It is desirable to have a descriptive, analytic vocabulary that is relatively neutral in evaluation, since evaluation always brings in implicit frames of expectation about how the writer should behave. *Engagement,* for example, is a wonderfully neutral term, with implications ranging from engaging to marry to engaging in combat. There are limits, however, to how much clarity one can find or impose in this area, for descriptions of tones are not referentially oriented toward things in the world of common experience but toward expressing and sharing impressions and experience that a reader has.

Insofar as Footings involve allusions to cultural codes, a question arises about the amount and nature of variation we might expect to find among readers. A particular gesture might be quite rude in one cultural context but not in another, and it is possible that readers might bring different conventions and expectations to a text. Brevity and directness might signal 'plainspokenness' and hence sincerity in one milieu, but hostility and churlishness in another.[7] There are many codes, however, not only linguistic but cultural, that are very widely shared, and one's cultural competence includes the knowledge that certain codes exist and may be employed even if one does not personally operate with them. Language evoking the role of 'tough drill sergeant' or casting the Reader as 'male head of family' ties into concepts in the public domain, regardless of how sceptical individual readers may be of their application in real life. Codes and expectations do vary according to genre, of course, so that what seems very directive or heavy-handed in an advice book may seem much less so in a school textbook or Army training manual. Indeed, it is only against a background of prevailing practices that writers make tactical and strategic choices. Only when conventions of impersonality are rather rigidly in force, for example, is it daring to use *I*. Certain linguistic choices have an effect in advice writing that may be muted in another genre, though I believe that in many cases the effect will be in the same direction. Understanding does not always beget tolerance, of course—or liking— and some readers might find a particular writer offensively blunt and pushy or annoyingly oblique and deferential. These are matters of taste in personal styles that doubtless do color our responses when we read. Our concern here, however, is with what they are responses *to*.

Yet another complexity arises from the possibility that a reader will regard a particular Footing as a pose that may simulate its opposite. Treating the other as an equal, for example, may be read as reflecting an upper-class security in one's superiority: one need not raise one's voice. The confrontive voice of the tough drill sergeant may suggest to some a deeper, kindly regard for the reader's real sensitivities and well-being. The main means of generating these 'reversed' effects is the dichotomy 'conventional/real' with the conventional pose understood as covering an opposite actual attitude; the reversal is thus almost a textbook example of ironical reading. This process, however, can cycle on itself, never reaching the 'real' with certainty. Could one not, for example, imagine an insecure person treating the reader as an equal, hoping to be taken for a secure mandarin? Or a tough drill sergeant who consciously produced that role hoping to be thought kindhearted, to the point of interpolating a few hints of kindheartedness in the role? Although some fairly baroque involutions are conceivable arising from reversals, the process does not send readers all over the map. And one must first describe the pose before exploring the complexities of how it may be taken.

These observations limit the privilege claimed for the analytic framework developed below. It is not a scientific or objective or causative account of why we respond as we do to various texts, for it is not directly an account of responses, mine or others'. Rather, it is a sketch of the frameworks that writers offer us within which actual responses occur. It does not make all the difference in the world whether a writer uses *we* in a certain way or not, but it does make some difference in the way the Writer's and Reader's involvements are scripted. It is important to inquire into the responses of real readers and to remember that our responses to the passages cited below are colored by an analytic interest; we do not read them with the purpose for which they were intended. We may imagine ourselves reading them with the intended purpose, but our response is then to some degree an imaginary one or one based on an imaginary premise—as perhaps more of our responses are than we think.

II.

1. Impersonal/Personal

'If I were you'—this formula reminds us that advice is characteristically offered not as the best course in general but as best in relation to the purposes and values of the addressee as these are known to the speaker. It is common for advice writing to encode (or 'inscribe') Writer and Reader with the first- and second-person pronouns. *You* without *I* is unusual, characteristic only of highly directive kinds of advice. Grammatical theory treats personal/impersonal as a simple dichotomy, as for example of pronouns or constructions. Impersonal alternatives for the Writer's *I* are passives and impersonal constructions ('it is evident that'); alternatives for the *you* of the Reader include *one*, general class terms (*people, parents, students, investors*—in these cases the public addressed), and some passives. Grammatically, personal/impersonal would constitute a scale in only a quantitative sense—so many personal forms and constructions, so many impersonal ones. But counting forms would miss the point in a number of ways. A writer moves the Footing toward the personal by dramatizing (or scripting) his and the reader's involvement in the discourse. That is, a personal pronoun introduces subjectivity, but this subjectivity can be developed to various degrees. It is easy to see that personal forms may be necessary but are not in and of themselves sufficient to dramatize an interpersonal engagement.

The pronouns *I, you,* and *we* do not always personalize the discourse, for they are sometimes used with a 'generic' or impersonal sense, as most obviously in these examples:

If you try hard, you will get ahead. ("If one tries hard, one will get ahead.")
When we are depressed, we sometimes cannot control our tempers.

The case is similar for *I* when the writer is citing herself as an example:

As a member of this society, I am responsible for the decisions our government makes.

These impersonal or (unsubjective) uses are especially common in hypothetical contexts:

If I keep a book out too long, I have to pay a fine.

Involvement begins to be scripted when *I* means Writer and *you* means Reader, but as long as these pronouns refer only to the sender and addressee postulated by any communication, the *I* and *you* represent what Umberto Eco calls mere "textual strategies" or "ghosts" in the text.[8] The *I*, for example, can perform only the 'ordering function,' as in sign posts, such as 'First I shall take up the causes . . . .' But the *I* (and to a lesser extent, the *you*) can be developed as individuals as well, if the Writer discusses his own experiences and sketches his assumptions about the Reader's interests, motives, and responses. As the *I* talks more about itself, we begin to have what Wayne Booth calls the "dramatized author"—the text includes information that could be used for a biography.[9] Similarly, emotive and evaluative language and markers of certainty develop the *I* as an engaged subject (these are discussed in subsequent sections). Nonetheless, even more specified, individualized *I*s should still be regarded as 'strategic' and an implication of the text, composed of codes; they are still "nothing other than the instance saying *I*."[10]

We may speak of the Reader being scripted by such devices as *you* and (implicitly) by imperatives and questions. Classical rhetoric distinguishes several types of 'rhetorical questions' that script the Reader's role in various ways. The least degree of involvement occurs with the deliberative question ('How did these myths arise?'), which is not necessarily presumed to originate with the Reader but is simply posed by the Writer (fig.: *ratiocinatio*).[11] The standard 'rhetorical' question presupposes its answer (e.g., Penelope Leach concludes a section of advice on putting your toddler to bed: "How can the child come to believe that it is perfectly all right to be left to go to sleep if you suggest that he is right to mind? And how can he be expected to accept that bedtime is the end of his day if he has nightly proof that his day will go on if he cries?" p. 300). The writer doesn't answer this sort of question, nor is the reader expected to. (The example here is actually of *epiplexis*: "asking questions to reproach or upbraid"; the prototype is *erotesis*: "rhetorical question implying strong affirmation or denial.") Rhetorical questions do not acknowledge the response of the Reader—in effect, they so surely predict it that they move in the direction of Superiority. However, they do presuppose Solidarity, insofar as the Reader can be expected to know and assent to the assumed answer.

More important as a scripting of the Reader are questions, presumably posed by the Reader, that the text then proceeds to answer (fig.: *sermocinatio* or *anthypophora*). There seems to be a subtle range in advice texts here from direct encoding ("Can I Enjoy the Water Without Getting in Over My Head?"—a chapter title from a sex education book) to indirect (Spock's "Parents sometimes ask. . . . " in *Baby and Child Care*). In their sex advice for teenagers, Lieberman and Peck walk a tightrope, starting with the chapter-titling questions "What's Normal? What's Moral?" In their text, however, the questions are posed quasi-impersonally, so that it is sometimes unclear who is posing them ("there is still the question," "but the question then is"). (The use of *the* here seems a little superior to me—they not only know the answers, they know the questions too, which are independent of any asker.) Occasionally entire books are structured as question and answer (Dr. Lee Salk in the child-rearing area and Dr. David Reuben's famous *Everything You Always Wanted to Know. . .*). Question and Answer must be handled very deftly to avoid the superiority of posing the Reader's questions for him. It works best when the questions are genuine, out-of-the-blue sounding (Reuben's first question: "How big is the normal penis?"). Some writers, however, rebuke foolish or badly phrased questions, making the Reader a patsy, or they invent earnest questions about the previous answer ("Does that mean I should. . . ."), casting the Reader in the role of plodding, cooperative straight man, or, as Rudolf Flesch puts it, Charlie McCarthy to Edgar Bergen's cues.[12]

These limitations point to a general problematic in 'personalizing' the discourse from the reader's end. Using *you*, rhetorical questions, and questions from the audience are sometimes praised as ways of engaging or involving the reader in the text.[13] However, insofar as they formulate a role for the reader, they may be resented as controlling or manipulative, or involve the reader in some complex role-playing, such as imagining oneself as a member of a plural audience—i.e., other people are asking the stupid questions, not me. This effect may suit a writer's purposes, if he wants to dramatize the discourse as a stage or talk-show appearance, or as an extension of an advice column in the newspaper (as Dr. Salk does). Curiously enough, such an approach sacrifices the privacy of reading, the potential for the illusion that the writer is addressing me and me alone, but it is just this illusion that lies close to the heart of what one might well mean by 'personal involvement.'

2. Distant/Solidary

If *I* and *you* anchor the personal scale, *we* encodes solidarity with the Reader, though much depends on the shared values, terminology, and point of view. The *we* of 'we humans' is not very solidary. Similarly, the *we* (plus present tense) that means 'writer and reader' bases its solidarity in the act of writing/reading and hence is a mere textual function, though writers are sometimes advised to avoid using it because of this very slight presumption of solidarity. A text moves toward solidarity as it recognizes the Reader's knowledge, concerns, values, and responses, but it does not really enact solidarity until it endorses and adopts that point of view. The Reader's knowledge of background information can be presupposed or explicitly encoded (personally, e.g., "Most of you have probably heard of. . . ," or impersonally, via common beliefs and myths or general classes—"Investors/people seem to think. . ."). Presupposing is a kind of implicit encoding of the Reader—we infer a Model Reader who would know the identity or relevant facts of the subject mentioned. It does *not* follow that if we do not know a piece of information, we will be put off by the assumption that we do. Indeed, by assuming a shared piece of specialized knowledge, the Writer moves toward solidarity with the Reader, and a reader may respond to that gesture by pretending to know the presupposed information, as one sometimes does in conversation.

More important than factual knowledge, however, are the Reader's attitudes to and terms for the matter under discussion or for related matters. Rarely does a Writer script and endorse the Reader's view as overtly as this:

> You are reading this book because you are perceptive enough to sense that something is terribly wrong out there and you are one of millions of Americans with a growing sense of unease about the future. The institutions you always trusted are now giving you a queasy feeling, you are making more money but you seem to have less, and you know all is not well. I congratulate you on your insight. I share your feelings.[14]

Despite the apparent directness, the passage is something of a rhetorical trick. The feelings on which the solidarity is based here are simply the premises of the book; they *define* the concern to which the book is addressed, rather than adopting the personal point of view of the Reader.

The standard treatment, which requires shared knowledge and attitude as preconditions for interaction, is part of the general social-realistic view of writing that was placed in question in the introduction. Discussing 'Intersubjectivity,' Stephen Tyler argues that it is because we are communicating that we look for and will find commonality with our interlocutor: "intersubjectivity is a presupposition which is subjectively sustained in acts of communication."[15] The notion of pretense is really much too crude for what goes on when a piece of knowledge, an opinion, attitude, or thought that he does not have is attributed to the Reader, since the reader in most cases does not have to pretend he has it. That is, the very act of writing/reading presupposes solidarity. As with personalizing, we might distinguish two stages of more marked or foregrounded solidarity—first, when the beliefs and attitudes are represented (encoded), as in the examples so far, and second, when that encoding extends beyond the immediately obvious premises of the discourse. A liking (or disliking) for dogs, starry nights, coffee, baseball, or Chopin, when encoded, offers such 'extra' bases of solidarity. The zero grade of solidarity (distance) would make no such representations of either kind.

But if the very act of writing/reading presupposes commonality, it also presupposes difference of knowledge and perspective on the part of the Reader—minimally, the ignorance or folly the advice is directed to. Let us assume that a passage's point of view can stand in one of three relations to Writer and Reader: it may be that of the Writer as distinct from the Reader (older, wiser, more experienced, more learned, etc.); it may be shared with the Reader (this is solidary); or it may be the Reader's but not the Writer's. Some theorists claim this third point of view is not possible, arguing that since it is represented in the text by the Writer, the Writer must obviously be able to share that point of view.[16] Yes, but the passage can still appear in the text as an alien voice—i.e., a kind of mimicry or indirect citation of the voice of the other. One example of this is the passage from *Changing Bodies, Changing Selves* cited early in this chapter, where the Writer tries to adopt the perspective of the virgin. When the Reader's attitudes and terminology are presumed to be markedly different from those of the Writer (as in advice to teenagers or composition students) a gap opens between Writer's terms and Reader's, and a choice may be necessary between Writer's terms ("a woman's sex organ"—hardly a teenager's mode of reference) and (presumed) Reader's terms ("intercourse can be great if you want to be doing it and like the person you're doing it with—and awful if you don't"—all words following *intercourse* seem to be the Reader's). Clichés are one sort of lingua franca to bridge the gap and can be a quite powerful (if anti-intellectual) means of demystifying and evoking a sort of guileless sincerity: "I also believe the nation will survive, and if enough of us do the right things, we may come out of this stronger than we went into it. I doubt if this book will transform the world, even if it sells a zillion copies, but maybe it can change just enough people's attitudes to tip the scales in a close case" (Ruff, p. 17).

Jargon similarly is insider language and confers membership in the club, even if the reader has to learn it from the book. Stipulating a new term special to the discourse is a tactic that establishes Writer and Reader as a new in-group with its own jargon, as when Hamilton substitutes *autoeroticism, self-gratification,* and *self-pleasuring* for *masturbation,* or Berthoff calls the exercises and assignments in her composition book "assisted invitations." These are both instances of deliberate euphemism, of course, but ones in which the Reader is invited to cooperate.

Similes and analogies may also function to bridge the gap. In advice writing, they generally do not explain the unfamiliar in terms of the familiar; rather, they do *evaluative* duty by likening the explicandum to something the reader presumably has more interest in or definite judgments about ("As in romancing, so in writing: you're most effective when your heart is in it."—Trimble, passage cited as "T"). Since comparisons may involve incongruous likenings of great things to small, they can be a source of humor.

Humor reflects and establishes solidarity in that it presupposes a shared sense of incongruity, expectation, and response. Used at the expense of a third party, humor helps to set up an 'us versus them' dynamic. Irony, as Wayne Booth points out, builds solidarity and in addition is somewhat flattering to the Reader, who is assumed able to get the point without having to have it spelled out.[17] Exaggeration and parody of foolish behavior are effective as long as they are directed at a third party; directed at *you,* they are risky, as the following passage by Kelly illustrates: "Or maybe you're one of the lucky ones. You've never had any trouble with writing. You say it's just a matter of good grammar and spelling and punctuation and psyching out the teachers, finding out what they want and giving it to 'em. In every paper."[18] Although Kelly uses 'you' terms here, she does not adopt them, but rather employs them for ironic mimicry. Because of the irony, *you* doesn't really address the intended Reader here; the "lucky ones," after all, exempt out, and the irony is intended to trigger repudiation of facile, inauthentic teacher-pleasing—i.e., we strugglers are better people. Developing solidarity in this fashion involves a kind of politicizing of the world—solidarity by exclusion or opposition.

The Reader's response to the experience of reading the text is also occasionally scripted (as in *Tom Jones,* except that the Reader is not fictive). One user's manual for a printer says, at the end of the chapter describing switching on the machine, "*WHEW!* That's enough for this chapter. Take a short walk to vent the exhilaration."[19] The voices of Writer and Reader merge in the first sentence, but the mimicry has a genial double irony: we recognize both that "exhilaration" is an exaggerated response to turning on our machine and that the response is natural and common. The Writer makes a slight fool of himself along with us. Lieberman and Peck encode the Reader's response to old, foolish beliefs and practices with exclamation points ("A few centuries ago 'experts' argued as to whether a man's blood or his seminal fluid was the more essential to long and vigorous life!" [p. 208]).

It has been suggested to me that solidarity is very close to Kenneth Burke's notion of "identification," the sharing of values, attitudes, and interest on the part of the writer and reader, without which there can be no persuasion.[20] In Burke's use, however, identification is a broad term that encompasses a huge variety of means, including agonistic struggle, mystification, ritual, and appeals to unconscious fantasies.[21] Solidarity in the sense described here is but one of the simplest and most overt ways of claiming identity of interest—i.e., by claiming or presupposing identity of values, attitudes, terminology, and point of view. A lofty distance could equally well serve as the basis of "identification" if we should come to admire its philosophical calm and sweeping perspective, deeper insight and more precise language, and so on. Identification can overcome difference by means other than collapsing or denying it, and inherent in advice is some difference, which may be minimized at times, but must reassert itself—dialectically, as it were, as part of the higher identity. So I think it would be a mistake to equate solidarity with identification, and find little use for identification as a descriptive or analytic concept in this study.

3. Superior/Equal

Although the giver of advice may be presumed to be wiser and more knowledgeable about the matter at hand than the advisee, the Writer can choose whether to highlight or minimize this difference by controlling the vehemence and explicitness of his assertions and by various equalizing moves.

Degree of assertion and vehemence are linguistically marked by adverbs of certainty/uncertainty (e.g., *perhaps* means 'I am not sure if') and in the modal verbs (*must, may,* etc.) both when operating as markers of certainty (or hedges) and of obligation/necessity (i.e., 'You must do this' means 'I feel very strongly that you should do this'). Strong, non-negotiable claims of superior knowledge or self-evident fact are expressed by the adverbs *clearly, certainly,* etc.; by the universal quantifiers and adverbs (*all, none, only, never, always*); and by negation (generally, of some stupid or foolish belief or practice from which the Reader needs to be weaned). Sweeping value judgments also characterize the superior end of the scale: the Writer *knows*, and he does not hesitate to say so. He does not often provide evidence or reasons or explain the process that led to the beliefs, which are therefore grounded effectively on his say-so. If a Writer is generally very certain, sweeping, and vehement, we are not on an equal Footing, or one that invites us to use our own judgment and information. If he admits limits to his certainty and the scope of his expertise, he approaches the Reader more as an equal. On this end of the scale are hedges and 'downtoners,' such as *sometimes, generally, usually, seems, tends, somewhat, rather, a little,* and *perhaps.* Such hedges, Joseph Williams observes, "let us sound small notes of civilized diffidence"[22] (*restraint* might be better, depending on how you read the code 'civilized diffidence'). Equality or limited scope is not the same as solidarity—one can keep one's distance while admitting one's limits. On the opposite extreme, superiority that is personal and informal (with *you*, imperatives, colloquialisms, etc.) can produce an effect we might call 'parental' in that the parental voice mixes familiarity with superior knowledge and authority. It seems best not to view these words and features as markers that accumulate their effect incrementally, for it is important to see in each instance what the writer is asserting or hedging. Note that superiority as defined here is not associated with the 'stuffy' or 'official' style, which is widely condemned for the Writer's lack of commitment to what is written. The superior Writer is fully committed.

In addition to categorical vehemence in assertion, a superior stance is marked by a tendency to spell out the implications of what is said, rather than leave them for the reader to draw. To be sure, when the concepts are abstract or technical, the standard textbook technique of first stating them and then translating them into simpler terms (and often more colloquial language) has much to recommend it, not the least of which is that a certain amount of rest and repetition is welcome when the terrain is unfamiliar. Another pattern of explication is 'Do this. Don't do that.' If, however, this spelling out is carried too far, readers may feel that they are being treated as utterly mindless. Consider for example the following piece of advice on breast-feeding from a Washington, D.C. hospital: "Glucose water *should not* be given in the place of nursing the baby. After you have nursed the baby you may offer him 1/2 to 1 ounce of glucose water if he still seems hungry. Give the baby just enough water to satisfy him for the time being; do not give so much that he won't wake up within 3 or 4 hours." Although exceedingly explicit, this passage is not pellucid, step by step, since the last clause suggests a process of trial and error.

Superiority is thus a composite of several factors usually discussed separately: by vehemence, I mean to include what is sometimes called modality (specifically, subjective epistemic modality[23]—the degree of certainty with which material is asserted), but also to include strong quantifiers and sweeping categorizations, to point out the interpersonal consequences of vehemence: the Reader has most of the work done for him and is not invited into the act to form his own conclusions on the matter at hand. That is why the writer's attitude toward the subject matter spills over to become an attitude toward the Reader, and why explicit spelling out works with vehemence to establish a Footing of superiority. It is important to note that devices that leave something for the reader to do, such as rhetorical questions and irony, may reflect intellectual or moral superiority on the part of the Writer, but not rhetorical superiority toward the Reader. Rather, the Reader is being treated as a fellow shrewd person.

Some of what I would call equalizing, Robin Lakoff refers to as "deferential." This is a term somewhat unfortunate in suggesting abasement of Writer to Reader; we could use the term *modest* (as in, "My claims to expertise in this area are modest") to convey this effect of implying "that decisions as to the interpretation and outcome of the exchange are in the hands of the addressee."[24] The term *deference* conveys the assumption that exchanges are in fact struggles for power or status. A framework for describing Footings, however, will be the more useful insofar as it avoids commitments to what the underlying reality is.

Various devices can be used to engage the Reader as a more equal partner in the exchange. A Writer's reference to his own performance can be equalizing in that he accepts the Reader's judgments and right to criticize (Ruff: "If you care to understand why bonds are a lousy investment for widows and orphans, you need to understand how the bond market works. I'll keep it simple and try not to go down deep and come up dry" [p. 69]). The 'let me say a few words about' formula for introducing a topic is not uncommon, as is the hedged assertion, 'I would say that. . . .' Self-deprecatory humor is an obvious equalizing move and is as likely to misfire in a text as in life: such moves obliquely emphasize the difference they purport to level. Safire uses parenthetical inserts to comment on his own performance, showing both that he is monitoring his effect and that he can drop the public role to be even more unbuttoned: "We are not fuddy-duddies: If we want to carefully and deliberately split an infinitive, we do so with zest, knowing that the most fun in breaking a rule is in knowing what rule you're breaking. (That's why I can get away with all these parentheses.)" (p. xii). The parentheses evoke other codes of self-consciousness: the stage aside or lecturer's 'subsidiary comments' on his presentation.[25] The interaction is quite complicated, since we are made aware that the writer is playing a role by his very stepping out of it. We may be gratified by being taken into his confidence but reminded also that he is managing us with his comments. Such commentaries on what one is doing, especially if apologetic ('I hate to sound old-fashioned on this point, but . . .'), can come off as manipulative—they both acknowledge the reader's possible critical responses and attempt to control them.

To use 'I' statements, personal experience, and self-conscious commentary 'redressively' to step down from the pedestal of superiority runs yet another risk: self-dramatization easily becomes self-glorification. The personal anecdote that illustrates the point has 'folksy' associations, but it also usually illustrates what a wise and noticing person the Writer is. Personalization is not equality is not solidarity.

4. Confrontive/Oblique

The fundamental premise of advice writing, that the Writer knows better than Reader about the matter at hand, is usually managed so as not to put the Reader on the spot. The writer gives his credentials, his authorities, and his reasons, and the reader decides whether to accept them. It is not uncommon to present oneself as a Communicator rather than an Authority. Negative examples (foolish behavior) are usually ascribed to third parties. Diet books seem to be something of an exception, as perhaps are others dealing with addictive and self-defeating behavior. Dr. Morton Glenn's *How to Get Thinner Once and For All* is directly confrontive. Here is a sample:

> And so I will be as direct and blunt with you: I will start off by asking if you are adult enough to meet a challenge. Before you answer, let me warn you that this book cannot do for you what you are unwilling to do for yourself. I can show you how to take weight off permanently, as thousands of others have done, but I personally do not take one ounce from you! Your success will require more than a desire to be thinner—it will demand you willingness to follow instructions. (p. 14)

Telling the Reader what he thinks and feels and why he behaves badly is near the extreme of confrontiveness and is of course a direct denial of the Reader's desire to be thought well of (positive face wants). But presumably readers of diet books think poorly of themselves already and do not expect to be told that fat is beautiful.

On the other hand, one may decide that the weak-willed reader

needs just the opposite treatment—sympathy, support, and no scolding—and the nicest, kindest, least confrontive book I have ever read is
JoAnn Ploeger's *Slim Living Day By Day*. She writes from the perspective of a fellow food addict, not the authoritarian who gets results. This
contrast illustrates in the most dramatic way that a writer's preconcep-
tion of the reader does not dictate the Footing he should establish,
since both Glenn and Ploeger assume a reader addicted to eating. This
does not mean that the writer's choices are in fact motivated solely by
strategies special to the discourse. Morton Glenn explicitly links the
way he will treat his reader to the way he treats his patients, and the
authority he claims is ultimately based in the M.D. degree held by the
historical person Morton Glenn; that is, Glenn's choices presumably
reflect to some degree his preconceptions of himself.

Confrontive should not be confused with superior, for one can claim
complete and certain knowledge without putting the Reader on the
spot. In fact, exactly this combination is the core of the 'new method of
communicating with children' associated with Drs. Ginott and Gordon
(the latter of Parental Effectiveness Training fame): messages should
preserve the child's as well as the parent's self-respect. Ginott's formula
for doing this is to speak impersonally and nonconfrontively while not
conceding one iota of superiority. He writes to parents that way too:

> In reacting to a child who violates a limit, the parent must not become
> argumentative or verbose. He must not be drawn into a discussion
> about the fairness or unfairness of the limit. Neither should he give a
> long explanation for it. It is unnecessary to explain to a child why he
> must not hit his sister, beyond saying that "people are not for hurting,"
> or why he must not break a window, beyond saying that "windows are
> not for breaking." (p. 121)

This uses the general class term *parent* to set up third rather than
second person, and *you* is also avoided via impersonals, infinitives, and
gerunds ("It is unnecessary to explain . . . beyond saying . . ."). The
writing is impersonal and superior, but not confrontive.

5. Formal/Informal

Informality of language tends to correlate with solidarity (and personalization), but we may share values, terminology, and point of view
without being on a relaxed Footing. The choices range from formal
diction and patterned prose (isocolon; balance; antithesis; complex,
periodic sentences) to contradictions, dashes, fragments, nonreference
pronouns (especially *this, it, which*), freely sprinkled parenthetical com-

ments, and colloquialisms. Partly because the formal/informal markers are so identifiable, it is easy to observe mixes and shifts in formality.

Formality/informality in language alludes to general codes of social interaction on the one hand, and, via them, to codes governing the behavior of speakers.[26] Choices characteristically function as 'frame' markers to signal whether the discourse is 'serious' or 'playful,' and in what way, to what degree. As Martin Joos observed decades ago, formal, 'correct' writing connotes responsibility on the part of the speaker: "Responsible language does not palter. It is explicit. It commits the speaker. The responsible speaker is under a sort of almost morbid compulsion to leave himself no way out of his commitment. The responsibility-dialect does not mumble; its grammar does not contradict itself; its semantics doesn't weasel."[27]

Informality in behavior allows the suspension of normal rules of social distance with strangers or superiors; it allows greater freedom in the selection and treatment of conversational topics; it is an invitation to be less careful of the prerogatives and personal territory of the other. It is likewise associated with spontaneity, warmth, and lack of calculation. Statements may be less precise, and the speaker less responsible for them as his well-considered, well-grounded opinion. In short, informality alludes to the codes sometimes called Utterance, orality, or casual conversation (hence to casualness, sincerity, and so on)—a densely woven network. Because much writing is governed by a decorum of formality, informality can suggest a refreshing, egalitarian thrust at stodgy, 'upper' aloofness—but not always, as for example when it is combined with superiority and confrontiveness to give one version of the 'parental' Footing.

There seem then to be at least five distinct scales of stances or Footings where only one (distant/intimate) has traditionally been assumed:

impersonal/personal
distant/solidary (meets positive face wants)
superior, authoritative/equal, limited (respects negative face wants)
direct, confrontive/oblique (respects positive face wants)
formal/informal

These are not wholly independent variables; complex combinations are possible. Shared values and point of view seem central to the solidary end of things, and devices such as humor seem to accelerate in that direction. Knowing and using the Reader's terms establishes a basis for solidarity, but unless Writer actually adopts them, a difference remains that can sour into condescension. Claiming to know and share the Reader's feelings works the same way (recall, "We have so many expectations, so many fantasies about what IT will be like."). If this backfires, it does so in the direction of condescending superiority: 'I know how you feel (though of course I do not in fact feel that way now.') We have seen that personal can combine with superior, and the other crisscross (impersonal and equal) should occur as well. This last is 'decorous' after the fashion of academic writing and is not usually sustained throughout an advice book.

III.

The purpose of distinguishing these five dimensions has been to provide a more adequate vocabulary for describing the Footings that writers can set up. It remains to show how these choices along these dimensions combine and interact in real texts. In this section, I will illustrate the application of these categories to matched small samples from child-rearing, sex education, and composition books. These samples do not represent extremes on the scales; they simply illustrate the way various bundles of values make up actual styles.

The first two texts (B and S) are written by medical doctors and address the question of how to put small children to bed. Text B begins with a narrative about a couple called the Tuckers, who were unable to put their daughter Kara to bed to stay until she had become exhausted and her parents' evening spoiled. The commentary then commences:

[B]   To the observer, this is patently absurd. The child has had to disintegrate before the adults could make a decision which so obviously should be theirs to make. This kind of parental indecision is less common now than it was in the permissive era, thank goodness. It certainly wasn't easy for the children involved. Although parents would give all sorts of excuses—such as "We can't stand to let her scream," "It's too hard on the neighbors," "She must need something we haven't given her"— there is no adequate excuse. These are all rationalizations for underlying reasons. Why should she want to give up at the end of the day if there is this much ambivalence to play on?

     In the case of the Tuckers, it may be partly based on experiences of their own in which separation from parents was hard, or on unresolved fears, or on any number of other personal reasons. I do see this commonly when both parents work, and leave the baby during the day. No amount of reassurance can relieve the Tuckers of an underlying fear that the child has been neglected or mistreated during the day—

and that they are at fault. They probably also feel unsatisfied about their all too brief contact with Kara at the end of the day and, without knowing it, feel they should keep her near them to make up for it. But these guilty feelings do *not* help Kara. In fact, they incapacitate the parents to [sic] play an important role for her—that of helping her learn the limits and learn how to separate without disintegrating in the process. Somehow it seems to me that being allowed to continue with this behavior will do Kara more harm than any effects of being separated from her parents during the day. She will soon realize that they feel inadequate as parents.[28]

This is quite vehement and Superior, as indicated by the adverbs *patently, obviously, certainly,* and *in fact*; the heavy use of *all, any, must, no,* and *not*; and the sweeping value judgments (*disintegrate, incapacitate*). The qualifying beginning of the penultimate sentence ("Somehow it seems to me") is quickly forgotten as the sentence continues with its prediction of doom and comes off as a finger-wagging gesture rather than a mitigation of the superiority. But the passage is also oblique: we are discussing the folly of the Tuckers, and the Reader, so far from being put on the spot, can join in scolding them. The language is quite formal, the only slight informalities being the one contraction, the dashes, and the exclamation "thank goodness!" (which also presupposes a value in common with the Reader). It is personal insofar as it uses *I*, but the *I* enters to generalize the problem of the Tuckers on the basis of clinical experience (apparently); the *I* dramatizes itself implicitly as an expert, not simply as the one conducting the discourse. That is, I = doctor, not I = Writer. This voice is quite intimidating, for only the obliqueness stands between us and its strong and sweeping assessments; if it should get *us* in its sights, instead of the Tuckers . . . .

The other text bears the heading "545. Mild bedtime difficulties"—a far cry from rationalization, ambivalence, inadequacy, and guilt—and follows a section entitled "How to help a fearful 2-year-old child."

[S]   I don't want to leave the impression that every 2-year-old who objects to being put to bed should be sat with. Far from it. Severe separation anxiety is rare, but mild reluctance to be separated is very common. There are two varieties. The first consists of trying to keep the parent in the room. A boy will urgently say, "Wee wee!" though he went to the bathroom just a few minutes ago. This puts the parent in a quandary. She knows it's an excuse, but on the other hand she wants to encourage cooperation from the child by being cooperative herself. So she says, "Once more." As soon as he's back in bed and she starts to leave, he cries, "Drink of water!" looking as pathetic as a person dying of thirst. If his parent complies, he keeps alternating these two requests all evening.

I think that such a child is feeling just slightly worried about being left alone. Usually the best and most practical way for the parent to reassure him is to remind him in a friendly, firm, and breezy tone that he's just had a drink and been to the bathroom, and then to say good night and leave the room without hesitation. If parents allow themselves to be detained or look troubled and uncertain, it's as if they were saying, "Well, maybe there is something to be nervous about." Even if a child whimpers or cries for a few minutes, I think it is wiser not to go back. It's much easier on the child to learn the lesson right away with a little unhappiness than to have the struggle drag on for weeks.[29]

The assertions in this passage are limited by various devices, such as "I think the child is feeling just slightly worried," "Usually the best and most practical way," "I think it is wiser not to go back," and, later in the section, "I think it's sensible." This passage is also oblique, though the narrative is a 'habitual' or 'frequentative' one ('children will do this') rather than the specific, if somewhat fictionalized, third-person account of the Tuckers. The passage ranges widely on the formal/informal scale from contractions, 'nonreference' *it* and *this*, colloquial fragments and diction (*right away*) to formal diction (*complies, detained*) and the magisterial, crafted sentence, "Severe separation anxiety is rare, but mild reluctance to be separated is very common." Although the passage is personal with *I* (one almost wants a term 'first-personal'), *you* is avoided, sometimes via passives, as in the first and last sentences; this is just the opposite of textbookese *you* with no *I*. And *I* here is different from the *I* of the first passage: the initial *I* ("I don't want to leave the impression") is the *I* of the Writer, monitoring his performance. Solidarity with the Reader is cultivated with humor and adoption of the parent's point of view ("the struggle")—the focus falls on the manipulativeness of the child, not the weakness or gullibility of the parents. In general, the passage exemplifies its own prescription for a "friendly, firm, and breezy tone." It is characteristic of *all* the child-rearing books I have examined that they address the reader in the same way that they advocate talking to children—this is called modeling, I believe.

The second pair of texts are taken from two successful, widely adopted sex-education books for teenagers. They deal with masturbation, specifically with whether you can do it too much. The first passage begins a section headed "Myths About Masturbation":

[H]   Boys and girls hear all sorts of intimations of the dire consequences of masturbation. They are false. There are no dire consequences except the consequence of feeling unnecessarily guilty. We all suffer if we feel guilty. Perhaps when you understand what a positive act autoeroticism is—how it contributes to your sexual development rather than the reverse—you will dissolve whatever guilty feelings you have acquired. I hope so.

One very common misstatement found in some books on sex and morals is this one: "Masturbation is all right if you don't do it too much."

Such a statement sets up a lot of anxiety because every intelligent person then begins to wonder "How much is too much?" The correct answer is that autoeroticism is self-limiting. This means that each person determines his or her own normal frequency by his or her own needs. In a way it is like eating. If you eat too much, you feel uncomfortable. If you masturbate too much, it ceases to be gratifying, at least until you have worked up a hunger for it again.

Furthermore, there are enormous differences between individuals. Some seem to burst with sexual energy that simply shouts for release every day in the week—sometimes several times a day. Others can be happily satisfied by a once-a-month experience. Frequency of need for self-gratification also depends on what else is going on in your life. If you are enormously involved in some engrossing activity that captivates all your attention, the result may be temporary shoving aside of your sexual urges.

But this is only temporary. By and large, when you are not afraid of your own sexuality, it will emerge in its own good time to the degree that is in harmony with your own nature and your own energy.[30]

This passage takes two positions on the superior/equal scale. When it is dispelling myths, we find plenty of universal quantifiers and categorical judgments. The language is considerably more qualified when discussing people's needs and frequency of masturbation (*some, others, by and large*). It is quite confrontive, telling you to dissolve those guilty feelings and get over being afraid of your own sexuality. It falls somewhere in the medium range of formality/informality in that it does not use contractions, but does use nonreference *this* and dashes and mixes an occasional colloquialism (*a lot*) with some relatively learned words (*intimations, captivates*) and an occasional academic (or bureaucratic) heavy subject ("Frequency of need for self-gratification"). The passage is very personal, though more you- than I-centered, but not as solidary as one might expect: the central categories are those of social and educational psychology (*positive, sexual development, anxiety*), and unlikely to be completely familiar to the intended reader. As anyone associated with the schools knows, these terms can turn judgmental in a hurry. On the previous page occurs the sentence "I would also caution both boys and girls not to let the ease of autoeroticism deter you from

the more difficult, more highly evolved task of developing social relationships" (p. 35). The Writer may have substituted the psychological
for traditional moral categories to suggest a new Footing of counselor/
counselee, but in the school setting, this is still the language of control.

The parallel passage is from another book that has enjoyed considerable success:

[J]   Then there are those who say that masturbation may not be so bad if
       you don't do it too much—whatever that means. It's really impossible to
       masturbate too much because when your body has had enough it will no
       longer respond to such efforts to have an orgasm. However, given the
       strong feelings most people have about the privacy of sex, it is wise to
       masturbate only in private. Little children don't know this, which partly
       explains why they get punished for a harmless activity.
           I think it will be useful for me to state some facts about masturbation,
       just to help remove any fears you or your parents may have. Masturba-
       tion is harmless to the body. It does not cause mental illness (although it
       can be followed by a damaging sense of guilt and shame in people
       brought up to fear it); it does not lessen a person's later capacity to enjoy
       sex in marriage. The stories about its causing pimples, circles under the
       eyes, weakness, or various diseases are just plain myths and not to be
       taken seriously.[31]

This is neither sweeping nor heavily hedged, though there is some
hedging in "it is wise" and "partly explains." It is quite oblique: there
are senses of guilt and shame, but these are in "people," not in you, nor
need you cast them out for the sake of your development. The passage
lies toward the informal end of the scale, with contractions, colloquial
really and *just*, non-reference *this* and *which*, and the *get* passive. It is
quite personal, with the authorial *I* commenting on his own performance; *you*, however, is not chosen at every opportunity ("when your
body has had enough it will not respond to such efforts"; "it is wise to
masturbate only in private"), and some general category words (*person,
people*) are used where we could have *you*. Solidarity is not cultivated at
all—there is no claim to know what the Reader is thinking, and the
writer keeps his distance with terms like 'boys and girls,' and 'the
young,' which occur elsewhere in this passage and underline difference. This is plain language indeed, all the way down to sentence
structure, and it is not surprising that the writer teaches in a school
associated with the Society of Friends.

The last two passages are drawn from composition books and give
advice on how to choose a paper topic to a basically teenage student

audience not entirely unlike that of the previous pair. The first passage follows the heading "Recommendations" in the chapter "Getting Launched":

[T]   My first recommendation is so simple as to seem puerile, but I can't recall a piece of good prose that didn't reflect it so I am persuaded that it deserves top billing. The recommendation is this: Pick a subject that *means* something to you, emotionally as well as intellectually. As in romancing, so in writing: you're most effective when your heart is in it. If you can't say of your topic, "Now *this* is something I really think is important," you're a fool to write on it, and you really don't need me to tell you. Make yourself a cup of coffee and give yourself a few more minutes to ponder what you would genuinely enjoy tangling with. Eventually you'll come up with a subject, or a new angle of the old subject, that ignites your interest.

If you feel in good spirits, you might consider writing what's called an "appreciation"—of a person, an event, a character, a book, a locale, or whatever. Share your sense of his or its magic; let yourself sing. If, on the other hand, you feel in a negative mood, you might consider writing a salty denunciation after the model of Mark Twain or H. L. Mencken. But whatever you do, *turn your feelings to account*—work in harmony with them and actively tap them. If you ignore your real feelings, which is perilously easy to do, or if you try to write with just your head, the inevitable result will be phony, bloodless prose. Also, the labor of writing will be excruciating. You'll have the nagging, wearying sense that you are simply practicing an intellectual minuet.

But all this is too abstract. We need examples—models of prose that crackles with emotional electricity. A fount of such examples is Pauline Kael, celebrated film critic for *The New Yorker*. Ms. Kael is one writer who never fails to turn her feelings to account. She is that rare creature: someone who thinks passionately. Her reviews—always gutty and dead honest—virtually smoke with emotion.[32]

This text is decidedly superior: the value judgments are strong, un-hedged, and the quantifiers sweeping ("never fails," "inevitable result," "eventually you'll ignite"). He knows, and if you don't do it his way, it's disaster. This is also a very confrontive passage: you are on the spot, not just for considering writing about something you don't care about, but for being out of touch with your true feelings. There are many informal touches—contractions, dashes, initial *Buts*, nonreference *this*, and various colloquialisms ("gutty and dead honest," "phony," "whatever"), but mixed with these are learned terms ("puerile," "appreciation," "salty denunciation after the model of Mark Twain or H. L. Mencken," "perilously," "intellectual minuet"). The breeziness of the colloquialisms may to some degree mask (or redress) the rather artful barrage of figurative language carried even to the point of a somewhat submerged conceit of fire/heat (*ignites, crackles, smokes*). The text is highly personal, and the *I* quite self-consciously criticizes his own performance and articipates the reader's response to it. The author has in mind a face-to-face model for this discourse, for he subtitled the book *Conversations on the Art of Writing*. This self-consciousness may be an attempt to redress the superiority and confrontiveness, but for me the effect is somewhat stagy. There seem to be some attempts to cultivate solidarity via exaggeration, the coffee business, the curious term *romancing*, and the merging of *I* and *you* into *we*.

The final passage is a parallel piece of advice from a recent, weightier, and more decorous composition text. It is an entire section entitled "Choose a Topic You Really Want to Think About":

[HL]   If you're free to choose your own topic, pick one in which you are genuinely interested and about which you want to know more. You have to know something about any topic you write on, but writing is not just an act of transmitting information. It should also be an act of learning.

If you're free to choose any topic at all, you might well try to find something from your own experience, something that will let you explore yourself, perhaps something that you have never fully described or analysed to anyone, even to yourself. The richest moments of our experience are often born out of conflict. Suppose you recall a time when you were made or asked to do something you did not want to do. When and where did it happen? How did you feel about having to act against your will? How did you feel about the person who asked you to do so? What did you learn from the episode?

Raising questions will help you to think more about any subject. If you know something about ceramics, say, or kayaking, you might ask a specific question about that. What makes kayaking so different from rowing a boat or paddling a canoe? Does centering a clay pot on a wheel have anything to do with finding the center of your own existence? It's always an advantage to write about what you know. But if you start writing on the assumption that you know it all, you drain the life out of the writing process.[33]

This is mildly superior—"It's always an advantage," "writing is not just an act of transmitting information," and so on. It is much less confrontive than the previous sample: it doesn't accuse you of writing without caring, and it doesn't dilate upon the awful consequences of doing so; its advice is couched in the hedged "you might (well)" format. It is more formal than T, with just a few contractions and no distinctively colloquial diction. This is our only example of exclusively second-personal writing, one of the pillars of textbookese. It is also quite distant—no jokes, no shared values or point of view—and interlarded with lofty apothegms, such as "The richest moments of our experience are often born out of conflict" and "Raising questions will help you to think more about any subject." Contrast the *we (our)* in the "Richest moments of our experience" sentence with the *we* in T: here it is the *we* of human-kind. The Writer's engagement in the exchange is the slightest of that in all the passages we have examined. Perhaps this has to do with the book's being a text for college composition classes.

Composition books do stand in a special relation to their audience: normally they are required reading for a course and are used in the familiar institutional setting. Their 'advice' puts the Reader in jeopardy, since she may be graded down for not following it. Even though this setting means that the writing is not entirely unsituated, I think it is clear that these books do have considerable scope to project roles and a Footing. The composition class, after all, is the least prestructured of all the course formats, and to choose a textbook is to choose roles for everybody. The 'audience' for these books is peculiarly bi- or trifur-cated into Teacher and Reader, Model and real. It is very likely that the Model Reader for these books (the one who knows of Twain's and Mencken's salty denunciations, worries about doing intellectual min-uets, and is pursuing a center for his existence) approximates only a very small percentage of the actual readers of these books. There is probably a hidden agenda in this mismatch, a 'Be thou him,' and the student who will not at least pretend to be him should get the message that he does not 'belong in college.' Put another way, real solidarity is an almost impossible Footing in a generally required course. We may meet students halfway, but only halfway. Any serious attempt to go all the way to meet the student where he is will be anti-institutional after the models of Ken Macrorie and Lou Kelly (which is still not to say that it will be successful).

Fundamentally, the problem of solidarity in instructional writing generally arises because the Writer does not face the same problem the Reader does. In much advice, the Writer, though more on top of the problem than the Reader, still has to deal with it—is affected by it—and this is the most intrinsic shared basis for a solidary *we* (we all are affected by inflation; we all have to get along with people; we all hate to clean house, want to eat healthily and reasonably; etc.). But if the Reader's problem is essentially one of ignorance/innocence or his sta-tus that of a novice, then the *we* becomes problematic. This I think is one source of the difficulties in the passage cited from *Changing Bodies,*

Changing Selves at the beginning of this chapter. The writer(s) are mature adults, not teenage virgins full of vague if eager expectations "about what IT will be like." The writers probably adopted *we* because the book is a publication of the Boston Women's Health Book Collective, a feminist group that employs the *we* very heavily to claim solidarity with the reader on the basis of interest and experience. The *we* in composition books is also hard to swallow, since the Writer is obviously a professional, and that seems a long way off to the freshman writer.

These definitions and analyses of Footings have combined categories of grammatical form, such as pronouns, adverbs and quantifiers, parentheses, and contractions, with categories of use, such as irony, self-deprecation, Reader's terms, exaggeration, and spelling out. The former could conceivably be counted by machine; the latter could not, unless a human were to do a lot of interpreting for the machine. Furthermore, mere counts would not be very revealing, since for an item such as *I* it is crucial to determine what kind of I (I as expert, I as Writer, I as typical person, and so on) is being dramatized. Similarly, a high incidence of *you* does not tell us how personal the Writer is being or how confrontive, since *you* is not always effectively "addressee." And again, a passage with sweeping, unhedged assertions and evaluations may enact a superior Footing, or it may be in the mode of *exaggeration* and hence more playful than overbearing (a common marker of the 'exaggeration frame' is informal language). My point is that the Reader's sense of what Footing she is on with the Writer involves a synthesis of many different sorts of indicators and much experience in human interchange within a particular cultural milieu. The mode of responding involved is a kind of personal knowledge and is analogous to the perception of faces, which does not seem to be produced by a summation of features. The analogy is imperfect, inasmuch as rhetorical response is mediated by codes of signification by which we link attitudes toward other people (and toward us) to particular verbal features and configurations of features. Hence a better analogy would be to physiognomy. There would seem to be an asymmetry in the syntheses of writer and reader, in that the writer projects a Reader without any clues or traces, but the reader synthesizes a Writer who is treating her a certain way via the traces on the page. Nonetheless, it remains extremely one-sided to view writing as the self-definition of the writer, since the self that is defined is a Self-on-a-footing-with-an-Other. One could as well describe writing as an imagination of a relationship.

There is a further misleading implication of the notion of writing as reflecting a will to self-definition—or, for that matter, the notion of imagination of a relationship—namely, that the terms *will* and *imagination* sound autonomous and free of wider motivation. But it is reasonable to ask, "Why should a writer select one Footing instead of another at any given point? What assumptions is he making about how relationships work? What does he think the relationship to the reader is, and hence what will work best on the reader?" In some works, we have to infer the answers to these questions from the pattern of actual choices made and other occasional clues, but advice books on relationships make it easy, since how relationships work is their theme. That is, advice books dealing with personal and social interaction ('coping,' 'relating,' 'self-presentation'), for example, articulate theories of social psychology, though they tend to be ahistorical and apolitical, treating identity and power in personal rather than collective or social terms. Other writing, such as books on usage and on child rearing, sketch more elaborated social visions, and in that sense give us the widest context in which to view the rhetorical options of writers, or the fullest illustration of the ideological implications of particular styles. These expanding contexts will be the subjects of the following two chapters, with the narrower coming first.

II

HARD AND SOFT RHETORICS
THE CODES OF PERSONAL RELATIONSHIPS

As noted in chapter 1, human interaction may be thought of as either competition, contention, and combat, or as cooperation, participation, and enactment of social bondedness. As Walter Ong has noted, the rhetorical tradition has always leaned heavily toward the former side, rooted as it is in disputation and litigation; 'persuading' seems very close to 'prevailing'—over the audience as well as the antagonist.[1] One can imagine a rhetoric that aimed at collective negotiation of a common resolve: there are hints of it in Kenneth Burke's evocation of "congregational" ways of "being right" that involve acquiescence rather than conquest.[2] This second conception is prominent also in feminist circles, where cooperation, camaraderie, and deference are said to be women's means and goals in interaction as opposed to the thrusting and isolating contentions of men. And similarly, Asians are often said to value harmonious and indirect exchanges more than brusque, rude Americans do.[3]

As part of a code, however, 'cooperation,' 'avoidance of conflict,' etc., suffer a division of means and goals, appearance and reality. The code describes the means, the 'style,' of interacting, not the goals of individual participants, which may be as selfish or competitive as those of speakers employing a code less concerned with the enactment of social harmony. There is something Edenic or redemptive about Burke's vision of the congregation, based as it seems to be on a mutual harmony of motives and wills (not just gestures), or a unification of motive and gesture. Similarly, the approach now called Rogerian rhetoric begins with Carl Rogers's essay "Communication: Its Blocking and Its Facilitation," which advocates employment of empathetic understanding and

43

reduction of threat to aid in solving problems. As it becomes method-
ized by Anatol Rapaport as persuasion strategy and reduced to textbook advice by Becker, Young, and Pike, however, questions about the
rhetoric as a manipulative technique begin to be voiced.[4] The questions
arise because Rogerian rhetoric presents the writer's attempt to change
the reader as an effort on the writer's part to engage in a cooperative,
mutually advantageous endeavor. Rogers advises people to be less
critical of the other person's side of the issue, less defensive, and to
make more of an effort to understand that person's perspective. Via
Rapaport and Becker, Young, and Pike, this becomes advice on what *to
say* (and not say), how to approach an issue, and a reader, so as to
convince the reader that one is open-minded and cooperative. To be
sure, Becker, Young, and Pike urge that the writer really hold the
attitude conventionally conveyed by the gestures—they advocate
Rogerian rhetoric as "reasonable, generous, and honest behavior"
(p. 283)—but they acknowledge that "Machiavellian" uses of these
gestures of openness and trust are possible. They really do not confront the problem that there can be no self-validating gesture because
they exhort the student writer to be sincere.

The vast bulk of (secular) advice about personal relationships
assumes the fallen condition of man and presupposes the simple view
of society as the arena in which individuals compete to get their own
way. This does not mean that these writers ignore gestures of solidarity
and the desires of others for approval and endorsement. Indeed, one
may describe a distinct school advising what I shall call a 'soft' rhetoric
in dealing with others, a mode that avoids overt verbal aggressiveness,
such as sarcasm and criticism, even "arguing" itself, and that advocates
indirection and self-effacement. Counterposed to this, however, is a
mode of 'hard' rhetoric that frankly acknowledges its desire for mastery. (Note: I am using *aggressiveness* here and throughout with no
necessary implication of malice, according to the note in Merriam-
Webster's *Seventh Collegiate Dictionary*: "*aggressive* implies a disposition
to dominate often in disregard of others' rights or in determined and
energetic pursuit of one's own ends." Some social psychologists, such as
Elliot Aronson, employ a narrower and more pejorative definition that
requires the intention to hurt the other—malice, in short.)

Because soft rhetoric employs an equal, solidary, oblique Footing as
a means of persuading, it has attracted some suspicion from the time of
its appearance in Greek theorizing—Artistotle's sketch of how the
orator, especially the political orator, can establish an ethos of "friendly
feeling" (*Rhetoric*, II.4). Aristotle stresses the satisfying of 'positive face
wants' in the audience: we like those who desire what we desire; who

praise our good qualities (especially those we are not sure we possess); who admire, believe in, and enjoy us for qualities we value in ourselves; who do not threaten our self-esteem by criticizing or reproaching us; and who are not themselves sarcastic or heavily critical of others (are not "evil speakers"). We also like those who are honest with us to the point of disclosing their own weaknesses—all of this in the service of getting one's political counsel adopted. That adoption is not necessarily disadvantageous to the audience, of course; one may sincerely believe it to be in the audience's best interests. The uneasiness arises at gestures that may be taken as ends in themselves being employed for an ulterior purpose, or at least at our *consciousness*, when reading Aristotle's comments, that 'friendliness' may be employed for selfish ends. Aristotle makes it clear that a speaker or writer should cultivate her "friendly disposition" precisely to establish her good will—i.e., to project her belief that her recommended course of action *is* advantageous to the audience (because she is the sort of person who does have their best interests at heart)—this is how solidarity enhances persuasiveness.

Our assumption in this study is that there is no standard or conventionalized model for what the relation of writer/reader should be. Indeed, this relation is typically "laminated" out of various models of participation, to use Erving Goffman's term. As he says of conversation, "In something like the ethological sense, we quite routinely ritualize participation frameworks; that is, we self-consciously transplant the participation arrangement that is natural in one social situation into an interactional evironment in which it isn't. In linguistic terms, we not only embed utterances, we embed interaction arrangements."[5] The writing draws from a storehouse of codes and possibilities, weaving particular items into a pattern for which, in most cases, a rationale can be discerned. Since these advice books describe how relationships work and how they should be managed, one would expect their dealings with their readers to illustrate their own advice—that they would use the very devices they counsel the reader to use. It is true that advice books might simply privilege the relationship of writer/reader, setting it outside and above the sorry realities of life in the world, but in fact they do not miss the chance to make the book an example of their methods applied, just as child-care books talk to parents as they would have parents talk to children. They become also the most immediate *proof* of their methods if they can win the reader's assent. In the case of soft rhetoric, for example, it is crucial that the audience not suspect that the speaker is making gestures with ulterior motives. Above all, the soft advisor must deflect any suspicion on the reader's part that the writer is 'handling' him this way. In this, a highly personalized Footing of equality, solidarity, and informality is useful in casting the reader in the role of confidant and suggesting the guilelessness of an unplanned chat; the writer is not staging a calculated performance. But, in addition, the soft advisor must keep reminding readers that they will be winners despite his eschewing of dominating language.

The first section of this chapter will take up two treatises advocating soft rhetoric—Dale Carnegie's *How to Win Friends and Influence People* and Manuel Smith's *When I Say No, I Feel Guilty*—with a view toward studying their treatment of the reader as an example of their advice. To put it the other way, they conveniently provide us with an explicit account of the assumptions underlying their own writing. Then we shall take up two very confrontive and aggressive books—Robert Harper and Albert Ellis's *A New Guide to Rational Living* and William Coles's *The Plural I*—once again to see how what they say explains the way they say it.

I.

The two parts of Carnegie's title hark back to the very fundamentals of rhetoric: "winning friends" is an elaboration of the passage on friendliness just discussed from Aristotle, and "influencing people" might be taken as the object of rhetoric (as opposed, say, to ordering or compelling them). But Carnegie's enthusiasm for his methods carries them well beyond the confines of traditional rhetoric, for he believes he has the key not just to winning political debates and legal cases, or indeed of winning anything specific, but to creative power and mastery in personal relationships. In order to achieve this mastery, one must give up being *masterful*.

Carnegie grounds his account of what will win and influence others on a somewhat harsh view of the gains and limitations of social interaction. For readers familiar with only his reputation as the man who tells you to smile, it comes as a great surprise that the axioms defining Carnegie's world of human possibility and motivations are quite similar to La Rochefoucauld's, whom he quotes. Here is a sampling of Carnegie's maxims:

> There you are; human nature in action, the wrong-doer blaming everybody but himself. We are all like that. (p. 23)
>
> [The craving to be important] is a gnawing and unfaltering human hunger, and the rare individual who honestly satisfies this heart hunger

will hold men in the palm of his hand and "even the undertaker will be sorry when he dies." (p. 30)

A boil on one's neck interests one more than forty earthquakes in Africa. (p. 88)

The truth is that even our friends would far rather talk to us about their achievements than listen to us boast about ours. (p. 143)

People are not interested in you. They are not interested in me. They are interested in themselves—morning, noon, and after dinner. (p. 58)

Some of Carnegie's maxims are even harsher rebukes to our general pride and self-esteem:

If you think people are interested in you, answer this question: If you died tonight, how many people would come to your funeral? (1936, p. 58)

[citing the German proverb "Die reinste Freude ist die Schadenfreude"] Yes, some of your friends probably get more satisfaction out of your troubles than out of your triumphs. (1936, p. 144)

This last passage continues by reminding you that if a nickel's worth of iodine were removed from your thyroid gland, you would become an idiot. In another passage, Carnegie concludes that the insane, generally speaking, are happier than we. The *you* and the *we* in these maxims are crucially generic: the maxims refer to "our" plight as humans with no limitation of social and historical circumstance, relative social class, or the like. Thus they may challenge the pride of the reader, but they do not threaten it. In fact, these rebukes are great levelers: we are all in the same boat. This is a technique common in religious teachings and sermons. Carnegie is not stripping our illusions to leave us desolate, however. In both his advice and his language he offers us what he calls, in vaguely religious language, a new way of life.

Even as these maxims pose the problems of getting friends and getting your way, they suggest solutions. Carnegie's solution has two parts: meeting the other's need to feel important and restraining one's own aggressiveness. You meet that hunger for importance by showing a regard for the feelings and viewpoint of the other, even to the point of agreeing with him that you (or your company) have treated him badly (if such is the case). You restrain aggressiveness by never criticizing, arguing, nagging, giving orders or a piece of your mind—"Old Harry" is Carnegie's folksy term. He also advises self-deprecation and, as he says, "Let the Other Man Save His Face." The leading ideas here are very much the same as the goals of politeness that Brown and Levinson analyze, but in Carnegie's application, they are the keys not to social cooperation but to the enhancement of the reader's individual prestige and power. We should emulate the dog, Carnegie says, who leaps and wags and pants his way into our affections, but we should do so in order to make ourselves the masters of others.

Because he advocates showing more concern and less anger and contempt for others than one may feel, Carnegie has been roundly assailed for advocating insincere or phony behavior. Carnegie is certainly aware of this criticism as a possible basis of resistance to his advice. In fact, he brings it up himself—though in a slightly oblique way—by imagining readers talking back (fig.: *anthypophora*): "Some readers are saying right now as they read these lines: 'Old stuff! Soft soap! Bear oil! Flattery! I've tried that stuff. It doesn't work—not with intelligent people'" (p. 36). In responding, Carnegie exemplifies his own advice by not arguing with his (imagined) heckler (fig.: *epitrope*): "Of course, flattery seldom works with discerning people. It is shallow, selfish, and insincere. It ought to fail and it usually does. True, some people are so hungry, so thirsty, for appreciation that they will swallow anything, just as a starving man will eat grass and fish worms" (p. 36). He first of all agrees with the heckler, recasting the objection in loftier terms (the heckler having noted only the ineffectiveness of flattery), and then concedes (to somebody else?) that this position is a little too strong ("True, some people are so hungry . . ."). In short, even if his method *were* mere flattery, it might well work. But it is not flattery, Carnegie explains, for one should in fact *be* sincere in one's expressions of interest, concern, and appreciation. One should try to develop one's actual interest in others, which amounts to a "new way of life." Carnegie does not address the potential vicious regress in adding sincerity to one's bag of tricks—one must feel like feeling concerned, and so on. Indeed, according to the evangelical tradition he is faintly echoing at this point, the only solution would come from outside the world as an act of grace.[6] Carnegie's theory offers no escape from the sincerity regress, but his affirmations of high ideals and allusions to spiritual regeneration suggest some means of escape from the consciousness of bad faith—without, however, requiring any religious commitment.[7]

Instead of instructions on how to become interested in and concerned for others, Carnegie offers us a way of forgetting the problem through his language. A sustained note of enthusiasm that at times verges on the lyrical (and the sentimental) runs alongside the harsher rebukes to pride. Having as it were stripped the reader of illusions, Carnegie resupplies him with ways to think well of himself if he follows the new path. Carnegie repeatedly reminds us that in making others happy, we add to the fund of happiness in the world. In one example, he describes encountering a bored postal worker and deciding to make the clerk like him by praising his head of hair. This, he maintains, was a pure act unmotivated by desire to get anything out of the clerk. Then Carnegie qualifies that disclaimer: "Oh yes, I did want something out of that chap. I wanted something priceless. And I got it. I got the feeling that I had done something for him without his being able to do anything whatever in return for me. That is a feeling that flows and sings in your memory long after the incident is past" (p. 93). There are numerous other references to leaving sparks of warmth behind one and adding to the fund of human happiness. Similarly, Carnegie occasionally speaks of the loftiness of surmounting one's anger or admitting one's errors. One may suspect, however, that he is illustrating in these passages one of his principles, which is to give the reason that sounds good, not the real one: "The person himself will think of the real reason. You don't need to emphasize that. But all of us, being idealists at heart, like to think of motives that sound good. So, in order to change people, appeal to the nobler motives" (p. 160).

Indeed, Carnegie's altruism with the postal clerk is ripe for the Nietzschean critique: pleasing the postal clerk is an exercise of pure power, manipulation that is sweet to remember because it is for its own sake, an act of absolute freedom. Carnegie is not Nietzsche or Sartre, however, and prefers to turn manipulation into creativity: "Talk about changing people. If you and I will inspire the people with whom we come in contact to a realization of the hidden treasures they possess, we can do far more than change people. we can literally transform them" (p. 188). Again, that is the nobler motive, and Carnegie seems to be illustrating his own advice, offering readers the means of thinking well of themselves, even though they are not being masterful. Carnegie in fact provides many illustrations of his method in his handling of the reader. He rarely criticizes (either the reader or third parties), preferring positive examples, often making an example of himself as the worst of offenders, and the follies and vanities he reproves are treated as universal. He handles the question of his qualifications and source of his expertise with considerable deftness—and this is a ticklish point, since Carnegie is not a top executive and at best a self-made expert on success. He has asked great men the secret of their success and reports what they told him, but he is careful not to claim to be an intimate of the great. The great men whose personal lives and doings he does claim to know are Abraham Lincoln, Benjamin Franklin, and Theodore Roosevelt—no privileged access here.

In the preface to the recent revised edition, Dorothy Carnegie, his widow, speaks of his "brash, breezy style" and assures us that "Dale Carnegie wrote as he spoke, in an intensively exuberant, colloquial, conversational style."[8] The style is not remarkably brash or breezy by modern standards—standards Carnegie may have had a hand in shaping—but it moves rapidly from formal and 'written' to colloquial and oral language, the latter engaging the reader as a conversational partner to whom Carnegie is accountable. Here is the very beginning of the book:

> During the first thirty-five years of the twentieth century, the publishing houses of America printed more than a fifth of a million different books. Most of them were deadly dull, and many were financial failures. "Many," did I say? The president of one of the largest publishing houses in the world confessed to me that his company, after seventy-five years of publishing experience, still lost money on seven out of every eight books it published.
>   *Why, then, did I have the temerity to write another book? And, after I had written it, why should you bother to read it?*
>   *Fair questions, both; and I'll try to answer them.* (p. 12)

Just as Carnegie can modulate from clichés (*deadly dull*) to fairly learned diction (*temerity*), he can play both the confidant of the great and the writer accountable to his reader. He is on equal terms with all men and ready to negotiate his meaning with all comers. In fact, he likes to introduce into writing the give-and-take of conversation (fig.: *sermocinatio*), using it as a model of how one should handle conflicts and potential arguments. The reader is always free to object and make his own judgments, as in the following response to the advice to give the good reason, not the real one: "Right here the skeptic may say: 'Oh, that stuff is all right for Northcliffe and Rockefeller or a sentimental novelist. But, boy! I'd like to see you make it work with the tough babies I have to collect bills from!'" To this he replies (*epitrope* again), "You may be right. Nothing will work in all cases—and nothing will work with all men. If you are satisfied with the results you are getting, why change? If you are not satisfied, why not experiment?" (p. 162).

This leaves the reader the maximum amount of room: he may or may not be a skeptic, he may or may not voice that objection, and he may or may not be satisfied with the results he is getting. Carnegie is after all entitled to say, "See here, my friend, if you're so smart, how come you're reading my book?"—but that would be an aggressive act, which his own method rules out. He is showing us how a Carnegie-man stands up to a direct challenge. If we find his way persuasive, it is because we find *him* agreeable and yet still powerful; we experience him as we would like to be experienced by others. These debates with readers introduce an element of competitiveness into the writer/reader relation, but just enough to make the game interesting, on the order of that between a couple of children shooting baskets in somebody's driveway, or like puppies tussling over an old sock.

Carnegie offers a method of dealing with people—the words are carefully chosen and appropriate for relatively structured relations between nonintimates when everybody should know what the game is about, where each party can easily surmise what the other stands to gain. His preface promises "training in the fine art of getting along with people in everyday business and social contacts"—again, the word *contacts* is well chosen. And such a model is not inappropriate for the relation of writer and reader. He gets into deeper water, however, in the last section of the book, entitled "Seven Rules for Making Your Home Life Happier," where his principles are applied to the handling of spouses. What seems very clear here is that "home life" does not necessarily involve a relation of equals or a high degree of self-disclosure; a basic hierarchical relation is assumed in a way that is not only sexist but dated, as for example in its numerous legends of bad wives.

The new, revised edition of the book has recently appeared with Dorothy Carnegie as a consultant, and it is instructive to note some of the changes that the revisers felt were needed to suit the book to an altered milieu. Some of the harsher maxims, such as those dealing with the unattended funeral, the delight of one's friends in one's failures, the happiness of the insane, and the humiliation of the nickel's worth of iodine, have been dropped. The sexist language and examples have also been edited away and replaced with more modern stories of successful maneuvers by women in business. The entire last section on spouse-management has been omitted. However, the revisers have extended Carnegie's methods into family life in new ways by adding to the ends of many chapters examples of how to handle teenagers and other 'problems,' all following the standard Carnegie formula of nar-rating the experience of real people. We learn how Dale O. Ferrier of Fort Wayne, Indiana, encouraged one of his young children to do his chores, how Clarence Zerhusen of Timonium, Maryland, got his fifteen-year-old off cigarettes, and how various others succeeded in getting children to put toys away, cut long nails to play the piano, and go happily to kindergarten, as well as how one teacher handled a troublesome new pupil in the fourth grade. The prose in these additions breaks with Carnegie's idiom in the direction of the psychological language of problem solving:

> Seeing things through another person's eyes may ease tensions when personal problems become overwhelming. (1982, p. 173)

> John Ringelspaugh of Rocky Mountain, North Carolina, used this in dealing with his children. It seemed that, as in so many families, mother and dad's chief form of communication with the children was yelling at them. And, as in so many cases, the children became a little worse rather than better after each such session—and so did the parents. There seemed to be no end in sight for this problem.
> Mr. Ringelspaugh determined to use some of the principles he was learning to solve this situation. (1982, pp. 229–230)

Finally, the revisers even modify Carnegie's text. *This*:

> So if you want to influence the conduct of a man without arousing resentment, or giving offense, remember Rule 7. (p. 192)

is replaced by *this*:

> If you want to excel in that difficult leadership role of changing the attitude or behavior of others, use. . . . (1982, p. 237)

Something has gone out of the prose in these revisions and additions. Partly I think it is a loss of candor ("if you want to influence" changing to "if you want to excel in that difficult leadership role," etc.), and partly a loss of the earlier mild competitiveness with the reader. In the new sections, the reader never queries the text or its implications— there is no sparring or tussling between reader and writer. This new prose avoids the tension Carnegie maintains between agreeableness and mastery, but it does so by recasting the roles of reader and writer into the rather bland general category of 'problem solver.' This is nothing less than a fundamental change in the view of personal interaction: Carnegie never proposed reducing tension and avoiding strife for their own sake, but as a means of reducing resentment and giving the impression of voluntary choice. It appears that the so-called feminine goals of harmony and camaraderie have been substituted for enhanced mastery. Both the top and the bottom of Carnegie's vision have been clipped—both the disillusioning and the re-illusioning. Carnegie's letter-day followers may cope effectively with the many tensions of living, but they will lack the nobler view of themselves as the architects of human happiness.

People in Carnegie's world do not care very much about others; the only social glue that binds individuals together is the desire to see one's importance acknowledged and enhanced by others. In the world of Manuel Smith's *When I Say No, I Feel Guilty*, people are more social, and other people are the source of most of our problems. Other people sometimes treat us rottenly, Smith says, manipulating us to avoid a loss of control that they fear—and we let them. We must become less dependent on others for our sense of worth; we must become the only final judges of ourselves. The strategies Smith proposes are essentially defensive, aiming at stymieing the manipulative other (and later to make the other less manipulative); Carnegie's expansive note of magic and godlike power over men is not struck. Smith's is a book not about power or felicity but about coping, though coping is at times a thinly veiled euphemism for getting one's own way. Smith observes that verbal assertion may not always resolve conflicts as we desire, but we will at least come out of them feeling better about ourselves.

The solution, for Smith, lies in verbal assertiveness, which he contrasts with flight, fight, or passive aggression. Ridicule, sarcasm, arguing—all are aggressive moves, not assertive. The book progresses from easier to harder situations, beginning by desensitizing the victim to criticism and guilt—a judicious loosening of the moral and social bonds by which he is manipulated. He then is taught moves, by means of scripts of schematic dialogues, to handle highly preformulated interactions with doctors, salespeople, and managers (demanding a refund and so on). These and other transactions, Smith says, are essentially commercial, ultimately contractual, inasmuch as one has a reasonably good idea of what one's rights are and how one should be treated. He then moves on to treat relations with employers and other authorities (where roles, obligations, and expectations are somewhat less preformulated) and finally takes up "equal" and "really close equal" relations, the last being the hardest to manage, he notes, because everything is negotiable.

The heart of Smith's technique is to make certain verbal gestures that are conventionally interpreted as implying flexibility ('You may be right'), self-questioning ('What else do you think is wrong with me?'), and admission of fault ('That certainly was stupid of me'), but that are uttered as formulas only, with no commitment to the attitudes they conventionaly imply. That is, when one offers no resistance where resistance is expected, the manipulator is caught off balance. Similarly, one is to respond just to the words that others say, not to their implications.

These techniques obviously pose a problem of insincerity in the simple sense of deception or lying. Smith considers such objections, which are "invariably" voiced by novices, and dismisses them with jokes, anecdotes, and the general observation that in most cases we do not know that what we say is *false*, hence we are not lying.

The deeper problem of sincerity, namely, the self-monitoring and loss of spontaneity involved in following a script, arises indirectly as Smith takes up "really close equal" relations, such as those between spouses. Smith repeatedly tries to inject personal coloration and mood into the dialogues to assure us that assertive speaking need not be impersonal or "machine-like" (pp. 283, 305, 316). Here, I think, Smith bumps against the limits of his own method, or at least his skill as a writer of illustrative dialogue, for any particular interest in "Jack" or "Jill" as individuals would distract from the points being illustrated. The dialogues are in fact fictional (though, Smith assures us, based on many real and reported incidents), but extremely abstracted, like a grammarian's sentences—or, as Smith says, stereotyped—and cannot, in their nature, offer more than rudimentary dramatic identification with the learner-victim trying to cope. Worse, the last dialogue lacks a plot, which generally in the dialogues is a problem that the assertive learner is trying to solve, or what in fact amounts to a verbal duel in which the learner tries to defeat the manipulator. Earlier dialogues bear such titles as "Bobbie uses NEGATIVE INQUIRY to Cope with a Neighbor's Manipulation" and "Carl Copes with a Manipulative Movie Producer." These are always success stories, by the way, in the usual Carnegie fashion. "Coping" in these cases is clearly "having the best of it"—the psychological euphemism is virtually transparent. But the final dialogue is entitled "A previously manipulative wife (or husband) assertively prompts her (or his) mate to say what is wrong with their marriage so that both of them can work on it." It is much the longest and lacks the closure of a duel or a problem solved. It may be unfair to expect it to serve as a model of personal intimacy, however, since the marriage in question is clearly a troubled one. But how does one know when a relationship is finally beyond manipulation? When can one allow oneself to stop monitoring one's application of strategies? Smith does not say. This is a crucial omission, for the use of strategies implies that the other person is being manipulative; it is insulting to those that are in on the game and self-defeating if inappropriate.

As long as manipulation is going on, however, to be assertive is consciously to play a role, and it is crucial to Smith's purpose that role playing seem a mode of freedom rather than self-division and suppression. Smith again and again 'discloses' himself as a player of such roles as teacher and therapist, student, colleague, and target of manipulation, in order simultaneously to claim the role of expert in human relations and to debunk himself as an authority. He narrates his own performance and then comments on it, suggesting the freedom of a self that stands apart from its performances. He also quotes the responses of others to his "style," as in this comment by one of his supervising professors: "You don't get defensive about learning and how you can improve your down-home, folksy, low-key, cornball, seductive style of therapy" (p. 131). Though the professor is referring to Smith's personal style, he might well be speaking of the book. Implicitly, Smith acknowledges that he is an object of observation to the reader, but he shows at the same time that his style is his free and conscious choice, and he never seems dissatisfied or at odds with his role, even when he describes himself acting a bit excessively or botching up a piece of therapy.

Smith also varies his roles toward the Reader, and hence casts the Reader in different roles as well. Sometimes the Reader is a 'learner' and sometimes a member of the general public addressed by the hypothetical or impersonal *you* and often included in the writer's *we*, as in this typical application of an anecdote: "If you are like him, like most of the rest of us, in order to cope more realistically with your errors in life, you must learn to change your verbal behavior when confronted with your error and modify your trained belief that *guilt* automatically is associated with making a mistake" (p. 115). Smith obliquely invites the Reader into the role of 'manipulated' via the dialogues. Only at the very end of the book does he touch on the reader as manipulator, easing into it via *we*:

> The major stumbling block for coping well with our conflicts in living with each other is set up when we interfere with another person's decision-making process, when we routinely manipulate our fellow man's wants by making him feel anxiously threatened, guilty, or ignorant. If you find yourself coping poorly in conflict, particularly with someone you care for, you might try asserting your wants in place of being manipulative, asserting your wants without taking away the dignity and self-respect of your equal and then see what happens. (p. 319)

Even here the Reader is hardly confronted or ordered about—Smith would not have us feel "anxiously threatened, guilty, or ignorant." His is not a book requiring much self-examination on the part of its reader.

The reader, in this instance, need only decide that he is "coping poorly in conflict," not that he is being a manipulative bastard/bitch. The book is, as Smith's professor suggested, more in the nature of a seduction. Assertiveness is playful; it's fun; it's something to try out to see what happens.

Given the axioms of Carnegie and Smith that confrontation and aggression do not 'work' to bring about more favorable dispositions of others towards us, it is understandable that the writers adopt a soft approach to the reader. If we are to give up arguing, criticizing, sarcasm, and other forms of verbal aggression, we certainly will not tolerate them on the part of the writer. Carnegie and Smith are indeed extremely oblique and self-deprecating (hence equalizing), and make maximum use of humor and solidary *we*. The Reader's negative face wants ("freedom of action and freedom from imposition") are repeatedly acknowledged and honored; his positive face wants ("to be ratified, understood, approved of, liked, or admired") are equally respected. Brown and Levinson's theory of face preservation, however, is only a metaphor in the present connection, since 'face' is not directly in question and since it is hard to see the advice as exceptionally threatening to either sort of want. That is, there is no obvious way to explain the function of Carnegie's and Smith's styles as *redressive*.

Their style does have a function in relation to their advice, but it must be formulated on a deeper level: their soft approaches are means of overcoming a resistance on the Reader's part, a sense that some aspect of self is being denied in the editing, a suspicion that following these writers' principles, some feelings and impulses will never be disclosed. These feelings are the least social that we have, so editing becomes censorship; aggression, competition, hostility, contempt, and malice must be ruthlessly edited out of our acts, but never uprooted or transformed. The Reader's suspicion is likeliest to arise when the methods are extended into the domain of personal intimacy—'close' relationships—and it is here that our soft advisors exhibit the greatest inventiveness in demonstrating that their methods constitute a mode of creativity, experimentation, and play. The brashness, slang, and cornball humor function not to redress but to authenticate the Writer's discourse—to suggest a spontaneous, unmonitored flow of talk with nothing systematically held back: we are all fundamentally good-natured (i.e., not malicious), buoyant creatures needing the approval of each other and willing to make 'workable compromises' to obtain it.

Although this account of soft advice makes it sound rather like Burke's notion of style as ingratiation—"the attempt," as Lanham has it, "to make oneself over in the form most agreeable to the other"⁹—there seems to be a crucial difference, since for Burke this conception of style is offered as an alternative to competitive success; it is a higher harmony through which one enacts and celebrates one's membership in a culture. But with Carnegie's axiom of primary, unalterable narcissicism and Smith's assumption that people exploit our desires to live in friendly harmony with them, no vision of higher cooperation, no merging into a congregation, is possible. The function of language—of rhetoric—with others is to project the appearance of cooperation. Its function with respect to the reader is to allow her to think well of herself, and think herself powerful, while she pursues entirely selfish ends in ways that some would consider devious. More flies are caught with honey than with gall, Carnegie reminds us, but after all it is business as usual: one is still catching flies.

II.

Certain axioms of aggression—that we are each out for number one and that we wish to destroy those who hinder us and to compel those weaker than us to do our will—are not exactly denied by the soft advisors; rather, direct expressions of these impulses are dismissed as inefficient. They advise the reader to speak as if these darker impulses do not exist and offer the reader ways of not acknowledging them. In short, to be effectively social, man must mask his aggressiveness.

In another view of matters, however, social existence requires the disciplining and channeling of aggression; personal and social gains are to be had from anger, confrontation, and the especially social modes of disdain and contempt. Against 'feeling better about yourself' this harder view would set the code of 'self-respect'—which is born of challenge and forged in conflict. This has an old-fashioned sound to it, but the books to be examined in this section suggest that this view still has some currency.

Like Manuel Smith, Albert Ellis and Robert Harper assume that it is futile to expect other people to treat one well; like him, they advise a change in the individual's attitude toward what forces itself upon him; and, like him, they want to disconnect feelings of guilt from the events that occasion them. The disconnection, however, does not come between the subject's private thoughts and verbal gestures. Rather, it comes via alteration in the 'Belief System' of the individual that ascribes personal significance (or emotional consequence) to what happens. Because they are behaviorists, Ellis and Harper describe belief systems as sentences we say to ourselves. By changing these sentences, we can change our responses to events: we can avoid becoming terribly unhappy by refusing to draw that emotional consequence. Their method is to employ argument and debate to displace our less reasoned 'sentences' with more reasoned ones. They question, dispute, and argue with patients to teach them how to question, dispute, and argue with their own 'sentences.' They frequently refer to therapy as struggle, contest, and battle, and describe their own moves as hammering away, counterattacks, seizing the advantage, and the like. The text is made up largely of dialogues with patients punctuated with comments like this:

> [Harper] "Seeing a good opening, I rushed in where less directive therapists often fear to tread." (p. 34)
> [Ellis] "And the battle of therapeutic de-indoctrination continues merrily apace, until (usually) I win or (sometimes, alas) the client flees from me and the work he or she has to undertake to eliminate his exaggerated view of pernicious past influences." (p. 169).

Despite all this gleeful commentary on their skillful aggressions, Harper and Ellis maintain that their method is nonauthoritarian, aiming at direct internal change in the patient without requiring dependence on an external figure (the therapist). It offers no distractions or 'feel-better' maneuvers. They certainly do not encourage patients to depend on them for acceptance or support; they show themselves contradicting and rebuking patients and twisting their words to ridicule them. Here is a typical exchange, beginning with the patient:

> "Well, in a sense, yes, But not in the sense I mean."
> "No, not in the *non*sense you mean. But what 'sense' *do* you mean?"
> Of course, she couldn't tell me. She reverted to saying again, in a vague and evasive manner, that she just didn't think it *right* and *natural* to make herself look good, but that somehow she found it right and natural for her to use knives, forks, and spoons. I saw she kept getting nowhere, so I interrupted. (p. 84)

Harper and Ellis also dissociate themselves from 'mind cure' and 'positive thinking' therapies, mainly because Harper and Ellis don't offer the patient happiness, just relief from feelings that things are perfectly awful. Their therapy has much in common with Stoicism, which they note, citing Epictetus on numerous occasions.

There is nonetheless a great deal of 'will power' and positive exhortation to the reader assuring him that he can achieve the more limited objectives of the book. It is full of testimonials and positive examples in the classic Carnegie fashion, a practice that even occasions this comment: "Naturally, in books like this one, we tend to present as models those cases where the counselees quickly saw the A-B-Cs of RET and worked hard at changing themselves. Don't feel amazed in your own case, however, if you have trouble zeroing in on and changing your irrational Belief System" (p. 121). Harper and Ellis assure the reader that it will be hard, but become easier as you go along, and in general repeat in a cooler and more deliberate fashion the sort of bracing challenge they hit patients with, as in this exchange (patient again first):

> "Goddammit, I *hope* I will."
>
> "Hope sounds like a very nice sentiment; but not firm enough. You'd better get *determined* to overcome your childish rebelliousness and fear of failure. *Actively* determined. Which means actively ferreting out and vigorously disputing the antidisciplinary nonsense that you've fed yourself for all these many years." (p. 166)

As Harper and Ellis say, they *are* directive, but the directiveness here and in many other places comes down to a version of 'you can do it if you really try.' In keeping with the boosting of will power are the vigorously verbal chapter titles, such as "Thinking Yourself out of Emotional Disturbance," "Recognizing and Attacking Neurotic Behavior," "Controlling Your Own Destiny," "Controlling Anxiety," and "Overcoming Inertia and Getting Creatively Absorbed."

As the previous paragraph suggests, Harper and Ellis do not draw a sharp distinction between readers and patients. Chapter 1, "How Far Can You Go with Self-Analysis?" begins by positing and then erasing this distinction in the course of discussing whether disturbed people can be helped by reading a book—whether, that is, reading this book is a substitute for intensive psychotherapy. By page five it is exhorting us: "So you *can* do it. With or without prior psychological knowhow, you can read or hear about a new idea, forcefully set about applying it in your own thought and action, and carve amazing changes in your own life. Not everyone, of course, can or will do this. But some can; and some will. Will you?" (p. 5). The *you* here seems clearly 'addressee,' not impersonal—though the authors employ that heavily also throughout. The reader, however, is not yet entangled as a patient, for he is not engaged in an argument with the writers. Harper and Ellis do draw the reader into arguments, however, mainly by expanding the convention of question and answer, with the questions sometimes posed by 'others,' sometimes by the writers, sometimes by the (implied) Reader. Chapter 3, for example, begins with an argument with others who habitually object:

> "What do you mean by a person's intelligently organizing and disciplin-
> ing his thinking?" our clients, friends, and professional associates often
> ask.
> *Answer*: "Exactly that. Just what we say." (p. 13)

This response to a general query gradually changes from paraphrase
and summary to literal, immediate debate with increasing emotional
heat:

> "Then you've practically admitted our charge," our questioners often
> interject at this point. "You've just said that rational thinking and
> intense emotion cannot coexist and that the former drives away the
> latter."
> Nothing of the sort! You've illegitimately substituted the word 'in-
> tense'—which we did *not* use—for our words 'inappropriate, self-
> defeating, and disorganizing.'" (p. 14)

(Note the omitted opening quotation marks in the authors' reply.) This
is a very odd use of the past tense ("which we did *not* use") along with
habitual aspect ("often interject"). This hovering between summarizing past arguments and dramatizing a present one is sustained on the
next page, as this dialogue continues:

> "Very interesting. But this remains your hypothesis. And, as you so
> cleverly noted before, the onus now rests on *you* to prove your view
> valid."
> "Right. And prove it we shall, in the remaining pages of this book, by
> presenting a mass of clinical, experimental, personal, and other data.
> But the most important and unique proof remains the one you'd better
> try for yourself."
> "Who—*us*?" (p. 15)

Who could know what the phrase *this book* refers to except the reader?
So the reader is drawn in as one of the objectors: to be a reader of
Harper and Ellis is to be the target of their attacks and counterattacks.
The reader is an adversary in debate, not a detached observer (as in
Smith), and, as noted above, this is the role Harper and Ellis cast their
patients in. Having maneuvered the reader into his role, they sketch
some of their basic principles using indefinite *you* and *we* (humans) and
then *we* (straight thinkers). There arises a Question:

> *Question*: Since we have four basic life processes and cannot truly
> separate thinking from perceiving, moving and feeling, why do we give
> it top billing in rational—emotive therapy?
> *Answer*: For reasons we shall shortly make clear. (p. 16)

The *we* of the question suggests that the Reader has joined with Harper and Ellis, but is still distinct enough to pose questions—either that, or Harper and Ellis are repeating a question posed to them, changing the pronouns appropriately. They argue with their critics, and when no other adversary offers, they question and debate with themselves, as at the beginning of chapter 9:

> Anyone who tries to give you a rule by which you can always feel happy speaks foolishy or knavishly. And yet we brashly declare: We can teach you the art of (virtually) never feeling desperately unhappy.
>   Do we contradict ourselves? Seemingly so; actually not. (p. 75)

The effect of these Questions and Answers, dialogues with general others, the reader, and patients, is to establish an incessant debate between the authors and others—a debate, moreover, that the authors report, control, and virtually always win.

Clearly Harper and Ellis break most of Carnegie's rules, with both patients and the reader. They are neither self-deprecating nor indirect, and they certainly think they can win an argument. What strategic sense can one make of this apparently egotistical self-display? One possible line of explanation takes its start from the indubitable sincerity of Harper and Ellis. We will never suspect them of contrivance, calculation, or concealment of their aggressiveness and high opinion of themselves. And if they are blunt, tough-minded straight shooters who lose no occasion to flush out fools and shirking, then their reassurances that 'you can do it' are something more than the soothing of well-wishers. Similarly, their advice is based on changing yourself through willpower, and one can perhaps believe in one's willpower by observing the power of the writer's wills. That is, through identification with their confidence and dominance, one can gain such a feeling for oneself: we internalize not just the writers' method of questioning, disputing, and arguing but their mode of mastering others as a mode of mastering ourselves.

Like Harper and Ellis, William Coles shows himself treating his clients—in this case, students—very roughly, arguing, mocking, and scolding them for their behavior. Unlike Harper and Ellis, however, he never engages the reader as a student, so that his dramatized interaction with students and his implicit relation with the reader remain distinct. In the classroom he is extremely superior and confrontive, but toward the reader he remains decorously cool, never addressing him as 'you,' never questioning him or anticipating his reactions—never, in short, engaging him as interlocutor. Officially, then, the reader is treated as something like a professional colleague. The effect of the book, however, is quite a bit more complex than this sharp distinction would suggest, for Coles often places the reader in a position where he can identify with the students.

The title of *The Plural I* is calculatedly ambiguous, William Coles says, "for my concern is with both writing and the teaching of writing" (p. 1), the latter involving a great deal of personal response to the writing of others. This response concentrates on the voice of the student writer, but Coles is equally concerned to enact a vivid public image of himself as the reader his students must answer to. For Coles, the problem in student writing as a mode of relating to others is that students tend to write phony essays ('Themes'), to posture, and to avoid serious commitment to the act, the teacher, and each other. If the teacher is to enact what is for him involved in writing, he must express his indignation and contempt for the fakery and vacuity and make the student personally responsible to him and to his classmates to learn and use his own voice. On Coles's analysis, student writers start out excessively—one might say supinely—social, seeking without much investment to please the teacher, and to please him in ways that do not please William Coles.

The Plural I is an account, or dramatization and account, of a particular course that Coles taught in the late 1960s. He employs dialogues heavily for dramatization and adds commentary and analysis along with citing his assignments and representative student writing. The mode of the book is unusual; Richard Larson notes in the preface that the commentary has much of the "fictional omniscient author" about it, by which I assume he means Coles is narrating from the advantage of hindsight while maintaining suspense about the outcome of his experiment in teaching and giving both 'inner' and 'outer' views of himself—outer as he appeared to the students in class and inner in regard to his intentions and critical self-evaluations. The two modes cast the reader alternately in the role of observer (or class member) and in that of professional colleague. Both Larson and Coles observe that the dialogue is not a transcript and that the book reenacts an experience more as a work of literature. Larson likens it to good drama or fiction—it is to be taken as an image of what good teaching *might be* and should not be taken as an historical document, based though it is on the actual events of one section in one semester. At the same time, however, Coles must demonstrate that his method does work, that students do improve under it; for that reason the students' papers *are* offered as historical documents. The accounts of class exchanges are not schematized and idealized after the fashion of Harper and Ellis, Smith, and Carnegie, and Coles records some of his botches and questionable successes. Coles's own evaluations are sometimes enigmatic. As a result, the reader is put to considerable extra effort evaluating the whole experience.

Coles's confrontive classroom style is at times eerily reminiscent of Harper and Ellis. Their techniques for forcing patients out of their 'crooked thinking' are very similar to Coles's confrontive, aggressive style with students. Consider for example the following section of a grilling he gave one student on the use of 'highfalutin' diction:

> "Come on, man. Come clean. Did you ever speak of 'delving' into a subject?"
>
> "I guess so."
>
> "Where did you say that? Where did you use the word 'delve' that way? Would you use it to talk to Carl over there? 'Carl, I want to delve into a subject with you'?"
>
> "No, I probably wouldn't use it that way with anyone I knew."
>
> "Would you write it?"
>
> "Sure. I have."
>
> "To whom? Someone you knew? Or to some nit-wit of an English teacher."
>
> He laughed.
>
> "OK. So why do you think the writer here uses 'moil' in his paper?"
>
> "OK. He wants to sound good." (p. 31)

In such dialogues, Coles uses a rich array of intimidating devices such as the series of rapid-fire questions, interrupting the students in mid-sentence and sometimes finishing it for them, and picking up their words to mimic them. The voice of the narrator/interpreter is even more savage and contemptuous when describing the students' early efforts than it is in the dialogues. Coles is taking great risks at the outset, both with the students and with the reader. The patients of Harper and Ellis have only themselves to blame if they put up with insulting treatment, but Coles's students are subject to his tirades under more compulsion. Is this the way to get students to write more honestly, to find their own voices? Coles's consciousness of what he is doing does not make any of this more genial or agreeable. He refers in a dialogue at one point to his "authoritarian fascist pig methodology" (p. 82) with an irony not self-deprecating, but rather deprecating the limited categories of the students.

This highly antagonistic, superior, and confrontive stance is not maintained throughout, however, for Coles wants to show change and growth in the students and the class. As the semester moves into its last

assignments, it becomes harder to identify Coles's voice in the dialogues (lines are unattributed throughout) and one has more the sense
of a response being negotiated by the group. Coles's authorial commentary is more restricted and qualified, more appreciative and, at
times, respectful. The final student paper, which has nearly the last
word in the book, deals with the student's leaving the nest—going
beyond Coles's leading and that of the class as well on a path of his own
determining. It is with this gesture—"one in which rejection and
acceptance become adjuncts of each other"—that the book ends. It is,
Coles says, "the most meaningful paradox of teaching and learning"
(p. 270).

Viewed as a whole, *The Plural I* is an extremely ambitious book that
tries to capture and enact this paradox, moving from predominant
rejection (on both sides, one assumes) to a respectful acceptance (again
apparently mutual). Aggression is the prelude to peace and mutual
esteem. It is significant that these displays of hard, confrontive rhetoric
take place in an all-male class at a technological institute, for in that
context they evoke a code of ritual challenge and combat. They call up
the stereotype of recruits and tough drill sergeant, athletes and coach.
In our culture, these roles are distinctively male, as is the exercise of
verbal aggressiveness generally, but it is interesting to note that there
are cultures in which overt verbal aggression is the province of women,
obliqueness and impersonality the norm for men.[10] I do not know
whether girls in those cultures are taught to channel their aggression
through identification with an aggressive woman teacher.

Coles is confrontive because his students are evasive; they must
learn, like him, to take the risk of speaking their minds. By telling them
what he thinks of their early, phony writing, Coles avoids what he calls
the besetting sin of a teacher—unacknowledged self-contempt. There
is another besetting sin of teachers, however, which is contempt for the
students, usually acknowledged, though not to the students. Coles not
only acknowledges it, he threatens them with it in class. His acceptance
of them is not posited by the teacher-student relation: it must be
merited. Clearly, this is a man who is not afraid of his aggressiveness,
and in that regard he may help the student to view writing as an act by
which he extends and develops himself, not merely a ceaseless series of
accommodations to what the other wants or is willing to put up with.
Thus ultimately Coles's hard rhetoric evokes the codes of 'manly'
plain-spokenness and the courage of one's convictions.

The last pages of the book, with the discussion of acceptance and
rejection, also explain the book's title as involving the students' former
selves, new selves, and the collective negotiations of selves in the writ-

ing class. Coles clearly is not worried that his students will simply turn into his younger clones: his difficult and at times obnoxious classroom personality should generate enough rejection. And too, Coles may be touching on the reader's response as a mixture of acceptance and rejection of Coles's plural selves of classroom and study. Coles has not courted the reader's approval any more than he has that of his students, and he insists on a number of strongly negative opinions (e.g., of *The Catcher in the Rye* and C. P. Snow's *The Two Cultures*) without regard for whose toes he may step on. He is sometimes superior and enigmatic, as in his obiter dictum on "the most meaningful paradox." Coles forces the reader, like his students, to draw her own conclusions about his style and methods. We are here at the pole exactly opposite Carnegie, and if we are uneasy about what Carnegie and Smith leave out, we may find ourselves in a complex mixture of acceptance and rejection of what Coles leaves in. The complexity of this response is due in part to what one might call a spillover of aggressiveness directed at others onto the reader. It is as if the hard writer, having established a disposition to intimidate, is surrounded by a cloud of ozone. We have already encountered this effect with T. Berry Brazelton's denunciation of the Tuckers in the previous chapter, and we will encounter it again with John Simon in the next chapter. Hence, hard and soft rhetoric don't mix; they are not poles on a continuum.

It is striking that our hard writers, who play such 'heavy' parental roles with their clients, should maintain that their methods do not foster dependence on them, but instead set the clients on their own two feet, channeling their own aggressiveness into productive modes of self-mastery and self-creation. Of course, their relation to their clients is a special, circumscribed one, basically that of teacher to student, and they do not propose that the clients generalize their modes as methods of dealing with everyone in all circumstances. Their mode does generalize, however, inasmuch as they show themselves to the reader valuing their own opinion and beliefs more than the 'face' or good opinion of others. By risking rejection from clients and the reader, the hard writers give at least an impression of integrity that is beyond the reach of soft persuaders.

But there is more to the appeal of hard rhetoric than its appearance of candor. Considerations of face preservation, Brown and Levinson note, are commonly suspended when the act to be performed is overridingly urgent, or in circumstances of intimacy.[11] Indeed, one might almost take this suspension as a definition of intimacy, other criteria (e.g., nakedness) being neither necessary nor sufficient. The hard rhetoric of the dialogues certainly conveys the speaker's sense of urgency, and it may be of intimacy as well, insofar as the speaker assumes that the relationship will bear the strain. Brown and Levinson also note, however, that one may suspend politeness if one feels immune to retaliation from the other, in which case hard rhetoric appears as the supercilious enactment of raw power. Hard rhetoric is highly charged because it can suggest both trust and intimacy and overwhelming superiority. If it suggests both simultaneously, the addressee is carried back to childhood and stands, head raised, before his father, the big voice saying, "Come on, boy. Come clean." And how we feel about *that* situation will determine much of our response to hard rhetoric.

The 'scene of advising,' then, is susceptible of many different treatments; the writer/reader relation can be analogized to different models. About the only inherent conditions of advising are that the writer have a respectable amount of wisdom in the area (not necessarily exceeding the reader's own) and that he believe the advice is in the reader's best interests. Soft rhetorics manifest their concern for the reader's self-esteem by not criticizing or confronting him and by offering him ways of thinking well of himself while taking their advice. This is really the approach of someone who wants to be your friend, rather than someone who is. The harder rhetorics manifest their integrity by their very indifference to the reader's immediate response and offer the reader a similar independence if the advice is taken. Each rhetoric provides an image of socialized man, but the nature and strength of the social binding force is quite different.

Both hard and soft rhetorics echo and associate themselves with the colloquial, the voice speaking without heavy monitoring. With soft rhetoric, the colloquial functions in contrast to coldness and calculation. It authenticates by projecting vitality, buoyancy, and good nature. With hard rhetorics, the colloquial leads into a different network of codes: it says 'cut the crap' and contrasts with evasive, pretentious, irresponsible language. The spoken, Derrida has emphasized, is always the term of presence, immediacy, wholeness, and singleness, but here we see that there is no foundation, no rock-bottom core of what 'spokenness' or 'orality' *is*. It does not always connote investment or commitment by the utterer[12] because, via its ties with casualness, it connotes offhandedness, rough sketches and first approximations, vague feelings, a reluctance to be quoted, and also, in a somewhat different direction, exaggeration, freewheelingness, and play. Clearly it is not sufficient merely to note that a style is colloquial, since it can participate in framing a discourse as dead serious or as playful. Colloquial by itself does not signify; only in constellation with other code does it develop its particular function and value.

It appears neatly concise to say that soft rhetorics evoke the codes and engage the reader as benevolent Peer, hard rhetorics, as substitute Parent, but immediately we see another level of analysis looming: what constitutes a peer, and what a parent? These roles are themselves defined within a social structure or a theory of social structure (an ideology). Similarly, the formal/informal (colloquial) distinction has associations of hierarchy, which has a social as well as a personal meaning. Books on interpersonal relations remain resolutely apolitical by viewing motive and action purely in terms of individual self-aggrandizement. In the next chapter, we will examine books that characterize writer and reader as actors in social and political worlds—that define action not as the pursuit of personal desires but as the response to social forces.

III

THE RHETORIC OF
US AND THEM

THE CODES OF SOCIAL
RELATIONSHIPS

At one time early in the planning of this book, I used the phrases 'writing as personal interaction' and 'writing as social interaction' interchangeably, according, presumably, to what I had been reading last, but it now seems clear that there is a rather sharp distinction to be made, which is also the distinction between chapter 2 and this one. To view action and interaction in personal terms, as the works of the previous chapter do, is to limit the range of the discussion and the implications of the rhetoric in several ways. Accounts of interaction are overwhelmingly dyadic; the reader's 'best interests' are defined in terms of the individual's sense of well-being; life is conceived as a struggle, but it is a struggle between individuals, not classes, parties, factions, or ideologies. It is the rhetoric of 'I' and 'you,' and the 'we' of solidarity tends to mean "we humans": there is no differentiation by age, sex, class, or ethnic background, or by values and allegiances. In short, it is a 'we' without a 'they.'

Writing that conceives interaction, including the interaction with the reader, in social terms, however, contrasts with the personal view in at least four ways. First, it is generally 'harder,' more critical and aggressive with regard to the groups that are on the wrong side. Second, the *we* is narrower, since certain groups have been excluded; it is a 'we' defined by opposition to a 'them.' The writer's use of *we* is an attempt to recruit readers to his side. Third, the problem to which the advice is directed is external, and the solution is not just to be had by tinkering with one's beliefs or editing one's language, but by engaging in some form of social action. Fourth, the codes of interaction evoked are ideologically articulated; they are no longer those of parent/child,

68

husband/wife, colleague/colleague, but those of elitism/egalitarianism, patriarchy/equality, conformity/individualism, exploitation/resistance, along with their particular stereotyped figures—the Common Man/the Snob, the Male Chauvinist/Feminist, Corporation Man/Hippie Freak (now 'member of the counterculture').

To detect these codes and study their operation, we need to listen with an ear tuned in a slightly different way from the tuning exercised in the last chapter. This task is made easier when the codes are rather overtly named, as generally is the case with books on good usage, or when a previously apolitical writer revises his advice to make ideological implications more overt. Advice on child rearing is an interesting area in this regard, since we can view child rearing as a matter purely of the child's felicity (and the parents')—i.e., 'psychologically,' as the handbooks of twenty and thirty years ago did—or we can view it as fraught with ethical and political implications, the 'private' life of the individual and family as conditioned by social structure and forces.

In treating books on usage, we will survey several that could be spread out on an ideological spectrum, concentrating on two—John Simon's *Paradigms Lost* and Richard Mitchell's *Less Than Words Can Say*—that elaborate the most extensive social visions. I will adopt a different procedure when discussing child-rearing books, examining Dr. Spock's positions and his treatment of the reader in early and late versions of *Baby and Child Care*. As before, we will maintain a dual focus, partly on the writing of the social worlds in which relationships are embedded and partly on the relation with the reader as it is shaped by the writer's ideological vision and purpose.

I.

Currently, most books on good usage of American English are purist in approach, which is to say that they identify 'pure' or correct usage chiefly by negative examples ('faults' or 'solecisms'). Inherent in the purist stance is some judgment of inferiority, but the inferiority need not be pinned on individual or social groups. Hence a purist treatise need not be highly politicized—Jacques Barzun's *Simple and Direct*, for instance, is not, though he has a few words to say about verbal pollution and about language as a natural resource—but a number of recent books do engage the reader in a critique of trends in contemporary American culture: the struggle to defend good English escalates into a full scale *Kulturkampf*. To say that *language* is decaying or in crisis is to say that one does not like the way other people talk and write and that one likes it less and less. In books following the dictionary-of-usage format (e.g., those by Wilson Follett, Kenneth Hudson, Theodore Bernstein, and William Safire),[1] the explicit discussion of moral and social values is confined to the introductions, but such discussion becomes the dominant theme in Richard Mitchell's *Less Than Words Can Say* and John Simon's *Paradigms Lost*: the crisis of language becomes a springboard for extended polemic and fairly heated social satire. These works are trying to get readers to "care" or "wake up" or "resist" menacing forces and to ally themselves with the author and other right-thinking people. This appeal goes well beyond the traditional one of pride in one's craft and the pursuit of excellence for its own sake ("What is life for," Jacques Barzun concludes his book, "unless to do at least some things right?"). The feelings Mitchell and Simon appeal to are considerably less austere and lofty: feelings of powerlessness and loss of a uniform and secure world where virtue was valued and speaking well the key to power and esteem. William Safire touches these themes, though in a way that avoids bitterness or reproach, in explaining an upsurge of interest in 'the world of words':

> But most of the interest, I think, comes from a search for standards and values. We resent fogginess; we resist manipulation by spokesmen who use loaded words and catch phrases; we wonder if, in language, we can find a few of the old moorings. We are not groping for the bygone, we are reaching for a firm foothold in fundamentals. And we are pushing for the personally possible: Since we cannot get our hands on macroeconomics and defeat inflation, or single-handedly sweep back the Soviet tide, we seek some other area where personal action has effect—we can stand fast against the tide of solecisms that enshrines ignorance and fight the inflation of modifiers that demeans meaning. (p. xv)

The language is both abstract and figurative—the 'tide of solecisms' is on a par with historical and economic forces; we can stand fast against it without being against anybody in particular, and the tone is playfully erudite.

Purism, Safire continues, gives a sense of personal power and rootedness in the unchanging good and beautiful, a more than momentary stay against 'our' confusion:

> The sense of powerlessness that has been bothering so many intellectuals—anomie-tooism—should stop at the edge of language. There, in classroom and home, some personal muscle can be flexed: "Different from" is preferable to "different than," because "from" separates more strongly than "than." Oldsters may find it hard to discuss the old spine

of self-reliance, or to adapt to the tieless-in-Gaza dress codes, or to hear children call their teachers by their first names, but when it comes to the basic tool of human communication, some guidance bottomed on the unchanging values of clarity and grace can be provided. A start can be made by denouncing mushy meanings and high living in syntax.

The geniality here and the self-deprecating sense of perspective restrain Safire from the savage indignation of the Classical satirist. The language avoids confrontation and personal attack in several ways. What we denounce are again posed in abstract and figurative terms ("mushy meanings and high living in syntax"). The shift into the impersonal in this paragraph is adroit, as it allows Safire to suggest that we are intellectuals or better than intellectuals, depending on how we feel about the term. Changing dress codes and modes of address may dismay some people, but even the dismayed would not call them evils, or signs of evil, and the gains from purist muscle-flexing are on the order of jogging or gardening. Safire does call up feelings of displacement and powerlessness, but they do not seem to afflict him with the pain of a wound; instead, the alliteration and clichés frame the discourse as somewhat playful. Safire glories in the huge numbers of letters his columns have evoked and cites them frequently; they are evidence of his success in calling into being a community of those who "care about language"—"language lovers," he calls them. Purism is thus saved from its own aggressiveness and the distance and separation resulting from censoring others; it even moves beyond personal action to social action, insofar as writing in to Safire becomes an act of membership in the *we*—most of Safire's entries include citations of these letters from readers. In his picture on the back of the book, Safire strikes a kindly pose with a slightly bemused smile.

Mitchell and Simon are not smiling on the jackets of their books, nor are they smiling inside. Not for them the fellowship of the mailbag with its "constructive criticism and warmly apoplectic chastisement" (Safire, p. xiv). For them, The Problem is of an altogether different magnitude: current usage is symptom and cause of cultural disintegration, and this prospect calls forth extraordinary aggressive forces—lurid fantasies, fierce sarcasm, bitter ironies, and violent attacks on the moral character of enemies.

One advantage of Simon's and Mitchell's books is that their versions of our world are so highly colored that we can more easily see them as products of the imagination. Barzun's world and its roles are familiar: the language of culture is difficult to master, with hundreds of pitfalls, confusions, troubles, and temptations; pronouns are wild beasts;

words are rebellious; the essence of a writer's proper stance is courtesy; the only commendable tone is "plain, unaffected, unadorned." The social implications of 'courtesy' and 'plainness' are left largely implicit and unexplored. Safire's world is likewise familiar from the op-ed page in the daily newspaper, though it is enhanced with the journalist's flair for naming current types and fashions. Safire's and Barzun's worlds are, of course, no more nor less versions (writings) of the world than are Mitchell's or Simon's, but they are not elaborated with the zeal and fervor of Mitchell and Simon, and it will be easier to study the building of worlds and their shaping of rhetorical choices in Mitchell and Simon.

Before turning to Mitchell's and Simon's books, however, I want to introduce as a foil a work on writing and usage that at one time was very popular and influential and is currently in its thirteenth printing as a Collier paperback. Its main fault rhetorically is that its world is out of date, or out of phase, at least, for it is a world in which The Common Man (or ordinary citizen) plays a central role. The book dates from the presidency of Harry Truman and evokes a stage in American culture that, if it ever existed, is certainly implausible today. I refer to Dr. Rudolf Flesch's *The Art of Readable Writing*.

In Flesch's world, the adversaries of 'readable' (good, zestful, vivid, appealing) writing are Aristotle (who represents the dead hand of traditional school lore), the phony high culture of literary types that promulgate the prose style of Henry James and Thomas Hardy, and the tendency to conform to arbitrary and distorting conventions instead of harking to the source of natural force and dignity—one's own voice. This central opposition reappears in other usage worlds, of course, like Ken Macrorie's; what is special to Flesch's configuration is its combination with two other themes not usually found in more recent 'liberationist' works: the appeal to science and the unabashed celebration of material success. How does Flesch overthrow 'Aristotle'? By getting a more accurate description of how language actually works, specifically, "What you really need is a good working knowledge of informal, everyday, *practical* English" (emphasis in original; p. 24) available to us from scientific observation and experiment. Indeed, so high is the prestige of science that Flesch injects this little note meant, I think, to be reassuring: "No wonder psychologists have analyzed language as a key to personality; they have even tried to trace mental diseases in statistics of sentences and words. But don't let that scare you; these studies are still far from being practicable for everyday purposes" (p. 218).

And how do we know when we come across good writing? Because it *sells*, pays off. Flesch quotes with approval from Mr. Elmer Wheeler's *Tested Sentences That Sell* and eagerly cites good copy by "our modern wizards of advertising." He is full of praise for successful popular novels and magazine stories, popularizations, business magazines and books, and zippy feature articles. But these are good not just because they sell, but because they reach the people. The chapter called "Other People's Minds," which begins by sketching the massive ignorance (but not stupidity) of the people, concludes on this extraordinary note: "If a worthwhile idea or work of art is skillfully popularized, everybody stands to gain. After Iturbi had played Chopin's "Polonaise in A-Flat" in *A Song to Remember*, people bought two million copies of the record. Which was a good thing for Iturbi, for Chopin, and for two million American families" (p. 35). High culture must make itself accessible to the people if it hopes to have an impact on them. If the intellectual wants power, let him learn to popularize.

It should come as no surprise that Flesch embraces the 'usage is democratic' maxim. Here it is in unqualified form, taken from the beginning of the chapter called "It's Your Own Language":

> Language is the most democratic institution in the world. Its basis is majority rule; its final authority is the people. If the people decide that they don't want the subjunctive any more, out goes the subjunctive; if the people adopt *okay* as a word, in comes *okay*. In the realm of language everybody has the right to vote; and everybody does vote, every day of the year.
>
> The way you talk and write makes a difference in the English language that is being talked and written today. There is no fixed set of rules: *you* are making the rules. To be sure, there are limits to what you can do with your language; but they are wide limits, and there is lots of elbow room for everybody. (p. 218)

This is not a world torn by race and class and sex antagonisms; there is harmony in the diversity and room enough for all. The marketplace and ballot box efficiently and decisively reveal the popular will. In particular, there is nothing wrong with 'the language.'

Since the natural eloquence of the Common Man plays such a crucial role in most nonpurist worlds, a few notes on his history, remote and recent, are germane, if not in order. As an American figure, he can be traced back at least to Emerson and Whitman and is a close relative of 'Mr. Dooley,' a fictive commentator on the American scene from the turn of the century, and of Will Rogers. Sometime after 1950 the Common Man seems to have gotten lost, and the purists who do recall him, such as Barzun, do so only to lament that he too has lost his innocence and integrity, corrupted by the many falsely sophisticated voices of TV and our bureaucratized world. He has been most recently sketched by Arn and Charlene Tibbetts in their purist *What's Happening to American English?* The Tibbetts actually knew him: He was Arn Tibbetts' unlettered grandfather, whose speech "was as clear and natural as the spring water that was piped by gravity into a large barrel in the corner of his farm kitchen."[2] He is gone, replaced by taxidrivers and teamsters with upward social aspirations: his common language is slowly being crushed to death. But you can't keep a good man, or a necessary figure, down, and he has suddenly reappeared in Jim Quinn's *American Tongue and Cheek* (Random House, 1980), where his function is performed by both the antiwar freak M. J. Weed, who rebukes John Simon and tells it like it was about the Vietnam War, and, more abstractly, by a renewal of the German Romantic notion of the 'speech instinct' of the folk. Quinn is not about to bring back all of Flesch's world, however, for commercial success, according to Quinn, can be had by pandering to the prejudices and meanness of the public. How else, he asks, in 1980, can one account for the commercial success of so many purist diatribes? Quinn's Common Man is a somewhat marginal or fugitive figure, since he does not control the marketplace.

It is perhaps worth noting, before we leave Dr. Flesch's benign and optimistic (albeit small-town, small-business, and small-minded) world, that in his hands the democratic maxim is not the blunt instrument for leveling fine distinctions it is often made out to be. Here is one slight application of it: "*Presently* means *soon* (except in archaic English) and *to scan* means *to read carefully.* The dictionaries are beginning to yield to the universal mistake and to list *presently* (in current use) as *now*, and *to scan* as *to glance at*. Which is as it should be, of course" (p. 189). The *American Heritage Dictionary's* usage notes on these words, roughly twenty years later, shows that Flesch read the trends right: *scan* now means "glance at" and *presently* is doing well in the sense of "now"). The maxim is also employed with great subtlety in arguing against *which* in restrictive relative clauses. Citing Jespersen and his own historical researches, Flesch calls *which* in this use an imposition of "writers, the literati, the clerks" (p. 150) and thus advocates using *that* as preserving the natural idiom of the people against spurious, affected Latinism! Present day purists also advocate *that* instead of *which* in restrictive relative clauses, but not to preserve the idiom of the people!

It is hard to escape the conclusion that the usage game proceeds by identifying certain points of variation in contemporary language, choosing one variant over the other, and then justifying the choice within whatever scheme of values the writer has chosen to project.

Flesch's book is dated not because the points of usage he discusses are no longer at issue, but because the codes and stereotypes he invokes in discussing them are no longer current. The optimistic confidence in a broadly based consensus of values, in an open society developing by means of an inevitable twin dynamic of social and material progress, has not survived the decades of conflict since *The Art of Readable Writing* was published. The change in 'paradigm' in John Simon is breathtakingly complete.

Flesch's world is not among the paradigms whose loss John Simon regrets. Simon's general attitude toward the people and their advocates can be gathered from his account of the maxim of democracy in usage. It is, he says, "a benighted and despicable catering to mass ignorance under the supposed aegis of democracy, of being fair to underprivileged minorities" (p. 148); it is sprung from "populism, Marxism, bad social conscience, demagoguery, inverted snobbery, or even moral cowardice" (p. xiv). The Problem, for Simon, is external and social, since in his world the problem of correct usage has been solved and the rules guaranteeing unambiguous meaning and instantaneous, elegant communication have been codified and widely disseminated. There are numerous and powerful forces at work in his world, however, that threaten to bring chaos, barbarism, and total insanity. In addition to the aforesaid, these forces range from Simon's unholy trinity—structural linguists, permissive dictionaries, and demagogic educators—down to individuals such as Noam Chomsky, Wayne O'Neil, Rex Reed, Barbara Walters, Erica Jong, and a host of other less-well-known writers. As the later names on the list suggest, Simon finds The Problem everywhere in the cultural scene. He moves easily from verbal to 'spiritual' literacy (p. 94), and among the fine old forms and the distinctions threatened are the pure innocence of girlhood and the difference between the sexes. He even reaffirms the ideal role of the true woman.

But *problem* is too flat a word for Simon's perception; even *crisis* fails to capture the underlying image of beleaguered culture facing its own annihilation and threatened as well by the treacheries of its own appointed defenders. The pressure from outside is intense: "Let down the barrier in one place, and all language is promptly trodden into the dust by a stampede of uninventive illiterates and graceless disimprovers" (p. 41). But there is danger from plague and infection as well: citing David Guralnik's likening of a dictionary that records usage to a thermometer for culture, Simon adds, "But suppose that the thermometer has become infected by mouths diseased with ignorance;

should we stick it into every other mouth as well, including our own, and so have all of us sicken?" (p. xvii). His language at times is so sweeping as to suggest a collective paranoid psychosis: "What creates this confusion bordering on chaos is the loss of boundaries" (p. 53).

Though scarcely original, all of this is heady, fervid stuff. How with this rage can beauty hold a plea? In a world populated with violent, hate-filled adversaries, one's best defense is to fight—the combat imagery that runs through purist manuals here becomes serious business. The enemy is everywhere, and is armed with "heavy demagogic weaponry" (pp. 29–30). Wit—"aggressive, often destructive (though, one hopes, in a good cause), and almost always directed at others" (p. 72)—wit, alienating to the soft-hearted and insecure, "whose claws pierce dangerously through the glove of irony" (p. 74)—wit will defend culture and rout the enemy. But wit, in Simon's view, is not just a technique but a way of life and the epitome of high culture. It is personified in Gore Vidal, whose quick mind and wit

> is just what the American public needs, particularly when it is expressed in magisterially cutting, fastidiously cultivated language . . . . Frequent exposure to his manner, consisting in equal measure of a devastating irony, a lucidly applied and expressed culture, and a casual arrogance, might give those in TV land an idea of which way lies civilization, which is where Vidal lives. (p. 110).

One senses a certain amount of self-commentary in these descriptions. Simon's own displays of ironic wit are always sarcastic—i.e., assumed to be an affront to the victim; he does not practice the subtler mode, which, as Dryden says, separates the head from the body and leaves it standing in place. This higher mode, Dryden says, can criticize the other while getting him to laugh; it can soften (i.e., redress) the face-threatening act of criticism.[3]

Simon speaks of his own writing as prescriptive, aggressive, and optimistic, but the aggression has other outlets in addition to wit, including outright vituperation, impugning of motives, sneers at physical appearance, and playing on personal names. Simon takes most of the liberties of the Old Comedy: a good bit of his 'wit' is nasty, vicious, and jejune. I will cite just one example—the conclusion to his review of Edwin Newman's *A Civil Tongue*: "I wish only that there were more watchdogs like Newman in positions so visible and prestigious, and barking, like him, up the right tree. Most other newsmen, alas, are very ordinary dogs, and what they do to the tree of language relieves only themselves" (p. 61). Violence must be met with violence, and

Simon urges lashing with the ferule. If the world is that of extreme right-wing politics, the role of the writer is that of Juvenalian satirist. Simon's is the rhetoric of pure intimidation, about as hard as one can get, save that it does not confront the reader; its violence is justified by the pervasiveness of iniquity in a world far gone.

What, the reader may ask, rubbing his eyes, does all of this have to do with *which* and *that, who* and *whom, between* and *among*? There is a problem of disproportion between Simon's vehemence and the nature of the faults: it is simply hard on the face of it to see such faults as sinful, damnable, staggering, or chilling. Is *between you and I* "a grammatical error of *unsurpassable* grossness" (emphasis in original)? Well, the general current of hyperbole may carry us by some of these. The real problem arises when Simon tries to gather himself up to a grand vision of the collapse of our culture—the final triumph of Dullness—while picking nits. At the end of his first chapter, he attempts such a plunge. After a little disease imagery, he zeroes in on *between you and I* and says, "You should see, then, that to avoid adding to the already raging chaos in English usage and communication, we must urgently stop *between you and I*. Otherwise, it will led us to every kind of deleterious misunderstanding" (p. 21). After citing a sentence that would be ambiguous if the objective case were not used ("Would you rather that I take you or she?"), he continues: "Multiply this kind of obscurity, as committed by future millions, by an infinity, and you have a fairly accurate vision of hell: sentences and paragraphs will have to be resaid and personal and business letters rewritten and resent through the mail at who knows what cost in time, money, energy, and serious blunders." We should get off so lightly! More effective is his later vision of the apotheosis of the intellectually inferior in a world run by stupid and cowardly liberals, where not one point of usage is debated.

Paradigms Lost is not a usage book in the way that term is ordinarily understood; it is rather an argument for the puristic *stance*. The details are secondary (and indeed are already codified), and there is more glory and fun in arguing for the stance than in arguing for or against *which*. The experience of reading the book will therefore yield little in the way of pointers, novel or otherwise. Nor does Simon attempt to forge a community of concern—a party, as it were—for his criticisms cut rather deeply into Barzun's and Newman's books, which are certainly on Simon's side of the angels. His mailbag provides further opportunities for contempt and derision. In his final, slightly more temperate chapter (originally an address to college students) he does name his party—Old Fogeys. Despite his call for an Academy of Anglo-American Language and a new prescriptive dictionary, there is no basis in Simon's world for consensual agreement—no common good or right reason. He even complains about the qualifications of some of the *American Heritage* usage panelists. There doesn't seem even to be a basis for a cease-fire. In the battle with evil, one must give no quarter and no benefit of the doubt:

> Whenever, wherever we hear someone say "between you and I" or one of the related horrors, and whoever the offender may be, we go into action. To strangers in the street, we have to be polite; to superiors (in position, evidently, not in knowledge), we may even have to be somewhat humble. But correct them we must. To all others we may be as sharp, forceful, tonitruous as the circumstances permit or demand: let family, friends, and neighbors hear us correct them loudly and clearly—let *between you and me* resound across the land. (p. 21)

Three points about this call to action are worth our noting. First, it can be carried out without the cooperation of others. *We* are Simon's newly recruited party, but we act as individuals, not in concert. Second, what is advocated is the puristic act of criticism itself, not self-criticism or self-improvement. Third, the action is antisocial in its aggressive boorishness: it does not attempt to teach or to persuade, except by intimidation. But of course throughout the book, Simon has been demonstrating how much glee is to be had from violating norms of social behavior.

Throughout *Paradigms Lost*, Simon makes little or no attempt to cultivate solidarity with the reader, though he occasionally presupposes it, as in the passage just cited. For the most part, he ignores us, and enacts a fantasy of autonomy and unmitigated superiority that engages the reader only as spectator. We can at least respect his integrity, for he will not cater to a mass audience. Of course, while refusing to acknowledge the *official* values of readers, he may be voicing many of the mean, petty, and splenetic feelings that many readers actually do harbor, though they might prefer not to be caught holding them. This is approximately what we understand the function of the Old Comedy to have been in Greek society. And, of course, the reader is not caught holding them. Almost as if we were reading pornography, we can shake our heads in disbelief and rejection even as we scan forward for the next burst of invective and arch disdain.

Simon's world is basically a very simple one: society is an arena in which competing groups attempt to impose their tastes and practices on others; the elite must ceaselessly assert its own values (a formulated body of usage rules, in the case at hand) and attack others who uphold different norms and observe different practices. The function of 'wit'

or irony is rendered with all the subtlety of a Punch-and-Judy show. All
of this amounts to a simplification of adult life: for once we do not need
to remind ourselves of our own limitations, or rein in our aggressive
contempt for others with different values. In the end, the world is
monochromatic, and so is its rhetoric.

Although Richard Mitchell has in common with Simon an embattled
stance, the world of *Less Than Words Can Say* is an altogether more
complex one, and The Problem has more numerous and far-reaching
ramifications. Mitchell's target is not the prominent figures in the
'current scene.' Indeed, a good bit of the book is fantasy and myth:
Mitchell invents an entire Stone Age culture (I think) and numerous
narratives of the genesis of Deans, the rise of Educators, Projects for
teaching reading, minimum competency testing, and, above all, four
extended accounts of the descent of culture into torpor and unknow-
ing. The surface of many passages shimmers between fact and fiction
and the tone is often sly enough not to give the matter away. Mitchell
never refers to the butts of his criticism by name and has much fun with
the conventions of anonymity. Here is one example (brackets in original): "Consider P. [That's not his real name, of course, his real name is
Legion.] He is a member of the most elaborate and successful
bureaucracy since the days of the Austro-Hungarian Empire. Is there a
Kafka hidden away in one of its back offices? Maybe, but he surely isn't
P" (p. 166). No, P is not the Kafka of the American educational
bureaucracy; perhaps this is a role Mitchell would cast himself in. In
general, this preservation of anonymity has two functions: first, it
decorously avoids personal attack, but second and more important, it
merges the imagined figures with those sketched from life, thus height-
ening the exemplariness of them all. Fact merges into parable.

Mitchell gives The Problem the literal name *inanity*—a term that
straddles social and moral realms. For him, The Problem is essentially
moral, for it debases the medium of thought itself; it numbs the mind.
Moreover, when people in responsible, public positions offer it, it is
perversion. In parable and metaphor The Problem takes on a quasi-
objective existence that is more insidious than violent. It is a worm in
the brain, chemical waste, sterilizing pill, narcotic drug, termites, cancer, and infection. These of course are not accepted as natural facts;
rather, The Problem is always traced back to human vanity, greed, and
self-deception in a progression from ineptitude, venality, and self-
importance to conspiracy and charlatanry of almost limitless scope.
Mitchell certainly does not expect these traits to be uprooted, but he
does attack the institution that seems to him most monstrously and

faithlessly given over to them: the educational establishment. This establishment, he concludes, must undergo massive change, perhaps "annihilation and total reconstruction" (p. 216). Mitchell's stance is, finally, that of the prophet or seer,[4] and his call is not just for personal awakening and renewal, but institutional change as well. Literacy, which he defines as discovering thought and making knowledge in writing (p. 171), can be taught and is the foundation of American democracy as envisioned by Jefferson and the other founding fathers. But American public education, it gradually emerges, has abandoned that objective for over-ambitious and naively idealistic attempts to solve personal and social problems. There is a very deep and pervasive tension in Mitchell's book that stems from his position as a professor at a state teachers' college.

Less Than Words Can Say could well be a casebook for the study of irony. Dan Sperber and Deirdre Wilson argue in a recent article that irony springs from mimicry,[5] and Mitchell has a great fondness for mimicry, introducing voices at times, it seems, for the sheer pleasure of invention. One such figure is a "waspish psychiatrist" who speaks a Teutonic patois. The effect is oddly self-deprecatory, since he turns out to be a mouthpiece for Mitchell, not the butt of satire he conventionally is. 'Waspish' is not a bad term for the predominant voice in the book, Mitchell's own characteristic mixture of literary and liturgical allusion, colloquial bluntness, and desecration of selected sacred cows.

Somewhat more problematic is a voice he creates for 'us,' which is a voice of self-delusion:

> We like to make jokes for instance, about the language of the tax forms. Heh heh, we chuckle, ain't them bureaucrats a caution? Just listen to this here, Madge. Them bureaucrats, however, don't chuckle at all, and if you'd like to see just what the term "stony silence" really means, try chuckling at their jargon when they haul you down to the tax office to ask how you managed to afford that cabin cruiser. Even your own lawyer will start looking around for some lint to pick off his trousers. (p. 51)

This bizarre combination of folksiness and fraud seems quite peripheral to Mitchell's main point—that sneering at the bureaucrats' language does not diminish its power over us—and raises entirely extraneous and distracting issues. We can be persuaded to repudiate this stance without the implication of dishonesty. The satiric imagination is proliferating its own targets.

Mitchell's favorite imitation, however, is the voice of the enemy, and here the intent is plainly satiric. Following is one fairly clear shift into and out of this voice:

> Public education is also an enterprise that regularly blames its clients for its failures. Education cannot, after all, be expected to deal with barbarous and sometimes even homicidal students who hate schools and everything in them, except, perhaps, for smaller kids with loose lunch money. If the students are dull and hostile, we mustn't blame the schools. We must blame the parents for their neglect and their bad examples. If the parents are ignorant and depraved, then we must blame "society." And so forth—but not *too* far. Those who lament thus seem not inclined to ask how "society" got to be that way, if it *is* that way, and whether or not public education may have made it so. (p. 80)

The shift into the enemy's voice in the second sentence is abrupt and probably requires some re-processing when we realize it is ironic. The transition back to the narrator's proper voice at "And so forth—but not *too* far" is more clearly marked. Mitchell repeats this pattern of educationist talk sandwiched between 'straight' authorial comment in the next paragraph. Later on in the book, however, the interweaving of perspectives is such that it could not be punctuated in terms of alternating speakers or voices, creating an effect like certain passages of Free Indirect Style in fiction, where the line between narrator's and figure's perspective seems to blur:

> These modern spell-casters must always be mindful of pesky and impertinent outsiders who nowadays presume to poke their noses into all sorts of things too deep for them. The very taxpayers and parents of school children have come to think that they have some right to understand—and even to question—the intentions of the rulers and the clergy, the professionals, as they call themselves. It's exasperating, but lacking a general return to the social beliefs and standards of an earlier and easier time, there isn't a hell of a lot to be done about it. Nevertheless, although they can't send an uppity laity back into the Dark Ages, they can at least find a way to keep it in the dark. Their language must serve the double purpose of showing the hidden powers that they deserve the dough and making the ordinary layman believe that what they think about is terribly complicated and important, too complicated for him to understand and too important for him to meddle with. (p. 128)

The two perspectives occur in the same sentences—as in the "Nevertheless" sentence, where "Dark Ages" is author's term for "an earlier and easier time" (and perhaps a needful contrast), but "uppity laity" continues the perspective of the educationists. Mitchell's mimicking of the enemy's voice is not without its dangers, especially when the enemy is endowed with vitality and sardonic humor. The enemy may become too appealing, too close. Mitchell does not identify particular spokesmen or statements of the enemy, or cite historical facts or trends (as the Tibbetts do, for instance, preserving the objectivity of the evil). Mitchell's enemy is like the Devil, always ready at his shoulder to obtrude himself into our thoughts. And Mitchell does not cite any of the host of like-minded critics of American public education—a decision that heightens his (and 'our') isolation as we explore the Horror.

One of the purists' cardinal principles is that one's language reveals one's personality and thought processes. Irony provides a vivid 'proof' of that principle, since in comprehending it we construct the sort of person who would say the sentence literally; when we reject the literal sense, we can easily be induced to reject the perspective and values of its imagined speaker. This is the heart of irony's polemical power. Irony presupposes a polarized world with recognizable, antagonistic perspectives—black hats and white hats, "us" and "them"—though, as Wayne Booth points out, it is an easy way to create solidarity in that very little may hold "us" together beyond our dislike of "them."[6] Irony is simplest to interpret when all sympathy for the victim is blocked out; if for any reason we begin to feel that the victim is being treated unfairly or reductively, we may become uneasy, disoriented, and uncertain as to whether we want to be a party to an unqualified sneer. If he wants to preserve solidarity, the writer at this point must guide us very clearly, indicating that a blanket rejection is not intended. Simple irony is reductionist and simplistic; Mitchell's instinct for complexity leads him into the more difficult area of partial repudiation, but he leaves at least this reader in some uncertainty. In the following passage, I am not sure how much to scorn:

> There was a young lady in Pennsylvania who was incensed when she found two typographical errors and even an error in grammar in her local newspaper. Fortunately for the course of Western culture, she knew the right thing to do, and she did it. She fired off a stiff note of protest to the editor. And who better to do it? She was, after all, a school teacher, and rightly mindful of the baleful influence of the popular media on her impressionable charges. (pp. 61–62)

This is especially ironic, because the writer commits several errors of spelling and grammar in her letter. Her folly is clear enough—she exposes herself as more ignorant than those she accuses when she should be entirely free of these errors—but are we meant to reject the purist attitudes she represents as foolish? Should she not have taken exception to the errors? Is she "rightly mindful" (there certainly is someone "better to do it")? Considering Mitchell's general point of view, I *think* he means for us to see her as complacent in writing the letter—she notes the mote in the newspaper's eye and ignores the beam in her own—but still not to reject her concern as misplaced. Mitchell's indignation devastates a wider area than he probably intended, suggesting that the teacher was foolish in writing the letter of protest in the first place.

This tendency of the ironic rejection to overflow its banks and threaten a flood of undiscriminating destruction is most pronounced in the opening of the final chapter ("Sentimental Education"). It begins in a slightly self-mocking vein: "We Americans are wondrously religious, or at least apocalyptic. We believe that the meaning of things is to be seen not in the way things are but in the way they will be someday" (p. 202). The paragraph continues by developing the notion that belief in improvement through education keeps us from judging the way people actually are. Mitchell then continues:

> Education will wipe out stupidity and ignorance. Informed and intelligent people will know better than to stick up gas stations for a lousy thirty bucks. They will have the skills to make good honest livings, mostly as chairmen of the boards of General Motors or IBM. As we learn more about each other, black, white, brown, whatever, we'll find new respect for each other and new values in the mingling of our variously rich cultures, and the black and the brown faces will be seen not only in the halls of Congress and the faculties of our venerable universities and colleges but even on hockey teams. Now that's the real America, look, right over there, you have to squint a little, see, there just above that fruited plain? (pp. 202–203)

If irony is a means of enacting solidarity, where are "we" at the end of this paragraph? If this is a naively Utopian vision, is it an illusion that undermines and corrupts? Are we being taunted with our sentimental idealism? It is perhaps an example of what Wayne Booth calls unstable, romantic irony: we feel drawn to the ideal even as we are being derided for desiring it. And indeed, from this ironic Pisgah sight, the chapter leads directly downhill, through a recapitulation of themes and a final, almost frantic pursuit of the source of disorder into an infinite regress, a recital of reasons why there is little basis for hope, and our final descent into sleep: the purveyors of unclear, foolish, and mendacious language have the victory. Our ideals may not, finally, be wrong, but they are utterly unrelated to what is going on. There is no call for action in Mitchell's book (except for radical change in the educational system), and in all our imagined confrontations with educators and administrators, we listen passively as they do their numbers on us. We do not argue, we never make our point, and we go away wiser but sadder. Essentially there is no way to cooperate with the system without losing your integrity and becoming an Acting Assistant Dean or something higher. There is a closed, paranoid quality to such encapsulated virtue. The 'we' that Mitchell has gathered in solidarity through the book does not apparently constitute a saving remnant but a group whose chief bases for association are moral superiority and indignation at its own powerlessness. It is a group that may well, like Candide's, end up cultivating its garden.

Although it follows from the definition of purism that its practitioners are committed to censoring the faults of other people's writing, it is not inevitable that they sketch a social vision. One may suppose that Simon and Mitchell do this to mobilize a more passionate and deeply grounded resolve on the reader's part to eschew faults and to join in the active suppression of the faults of others. We have seen how nicely simple irony is adapted to this end: it calls into being a solidarity of hostility or contempt toward the party mimicked, and it serves the generalizing purpose by suggesting the dismissal of the entire perspective or the target. The irony also sidesteps the matter of the writer's superiority by including the reader as an accomplice. Readers may otherwise become uncomfortable in the presence of so much superiority and aggressive fault-finding; though it is directed at third parties, it might also be turned on us. By engaging the reader in completing the sneer, irony avoids the spillover effect.

If Simon and Mitchell use their worlds to establish the importance of avoiding bad writing, their books should be no more or less convincing than their worlds. Matters are a bit more complicated than this, however, since we are used to polemical accounts that employ exaggeration, caricature, and even parable. We manage to assess these accounts by some complicated process lying midway between the interpretive processes of fact and those of fiction. It is not even clear that we make decisions about the accuracy of all the claims. Is the educational system radically perverted? Are the ignoramuses and vulgarians out to drag us down? Clearly, the appeal or persuasive force of these books does not rest on evidence and argument, though we should perhaps allow for several different sorts of readings, some of them accepting much of the writer's world as an accurate portrayal of our own, others rejecting most or all of its truth claims and experiencing the work more as satire or fantasy, with appropriate fictionalizing of the Reader's role. As readers and writers move in this latter direction, however, they move away from advice and practical action; the books are no longer urging the reader to change his action or equipping him with skills to act. The advice ends up being a point of departure for the sketching of worlds, using 'faults' to trigger the portrayal of the disease.

II.

Child-rearing guides are another body of writing that inherently involves detailed construction of moral and social worlds—the kind of world you bring children into should have a lot to do with the way you bring them up. To examine the relation of the world to rhetoric, I will contrast two versions that for convenience I will call A and B, focusing on the handling of three sensitive issues: setting standards and limits, aggression, and the father's role as parent. The comparison is a peculiar one, because, though separated by thirty years, both versions are by the same author, Dr. Benjamin Spock, and both are published under the title *Baby and Child Care*. A is the Cardinal Paperback edition of *The Pocket Book of Baby and Child Care* (1946); B is the "revised, updated, and enlarged edition for today's parents" of 1976. All passages cited from A have been cut or heavily revised in B. I will in addition make occasional reference to an intermediate version, the "new, revised edition" of 1957.

In the world of A, children are naturally social and eager to please. They know what they need in many basic ways. Parents too are endowed with a sense of the natural, decent, and sensible. (The book begins, "Trust yourself. You know more than you think you do.") There are occasional suggestions that society is not quite so sane and benign as it might be on certain points, but there is not very much the individual can do about this, and society is after all the arena where adults work out their destinies as contributing members. The advice aims at allaying parents' anxieties about the difficulties of their job and encouraging them to see that much apparent disorder and badness are simply stages children naturally pass through on the road to maturation. Here is A, for example, on limiting a child's reading of comic books: "But when children show a universal craving for something, whether it's comics or candy or jazz, we've got to assume that it has positive, constructive value for them. It may be wise to try to give them what they want in a better form, but it does no good for us to cluck like nervous hens" (p. 304). Setting standards and limits is thus always a matter of compromise and the channeling of basically sound impulses.

It is a little hard to see the constructive payoff of candy, but interfering risks making the child a social freak: "A mother hates to make her own child an exception or a sissy. If he only has the desire once in a while it's probably best to let him be one of the boys. But if he craves sweets, and especially if he has teeth that decay easily, it's better for the parents to limit him strictly" (p. 231.). The middle-of-the-road position here apparently is willing to sacrifice the child's physical well-being to norms set by peers.

The child's instinct for his own development will guide him through successively more controlled expressions of aggression culminating in adult life:

> And when a person goes out into the world and takes a job, he still needs his aggressive instincts, but they are still further refined and civilized. He competes for a better position in the organization. He works to make his business concern the most successful. On a farm he fights the elements and the insects, and competes with other farmers at the county fair.
>
> In other words, when your child at 2 bangs another over the head, or at 4 plays at shooting, or at 9 enjoys blood-and-thunder comic books, he is just passing through the necessary stages in the taming of his aggressive instincts that will make him a worth-while citizen. Let him be his age all along the way. (p. 241)

Here passive voice and nominalization conspire to avoid mentioning who does the refining, civilizing, and taming. Apparently it is not the parent or other authority figures. In fact, what seems to be contemplated is an autonomous process of growth and adjustment. As Spock says earlier,

> The same thing goes, later on, for discipline, good behavior, and pleasant manners. You can't drill these into a child from the outside in a hundred years. The desire to get along with other people happily and considerately develops within him as part of the unfolding of his nature, provided he grows up with loving, self-respecting parents. (p. 19).

These passages make it quite clear that their advice is to be understood as countering a certain strongly 'interventionist' style of child rearing; taken without that implicit context, they seem uncritically approving of apparently antisocial behavior. It is true that in the revision of 1957, these lines were added to the summary of development in aggression:

> I don't mean by all this that you should let your young child be

unusually mean to others or that you should think nothing of it if your older child is preoccupied with violence much more than other boys his age. Extra aggressiveness needs curbing, and if it can't be easily controlled it needs looking into. ("new, revised edition" of 1957, p. 311)

Clearly, however, there is plenty of latitude in the notion that only *unusual* meanness or aggressiveness in excess of other boys' needs looking into. This is a writer who advises fathers not to "jump on him too hard when he cries" (p. 315). A's is the rhetoric of moderation, the one hand and the other. But then again, there are no very serious and refractory problems to be dealt with. The function of the language is to enact calm, balance, and 'sensibleness.'

Perhaps the most difficult problem A poses is how to involve fathers in the care of their children, and here the rhetoric that defuses conflicts and avoids confrontations is quite strained. Some fathers, Spock says, think child care is entirely woman's work. How can one persuade somebody like that? After explaining the basic desirability of a man being a real and warm father, A adopts the man's point of view, or at least employs categories and values thought to be men's:

> Of course, I don't mean that the father has to give just as many bottles or change just as many diapers as the mother. But it's fine for him to do these things occasionally. He might make the formula on Sunday. If the baby is on a 2 a.m. bottle in the early weeks, when the mother is still pretty tired, this is a good feeding for the father to take over. It's nice for him, if he can, to go along to the doctor's office for the baby's regular visits. It gives him a chance to bring up those questions that are bothering him and of which he doesn't think his wife understands the importance. It pleases the doctor, too. Of course, there are some fathers who get goose flesh at the very idea of helping to take care of a baby, and there's no good to be gained by trying to force them. Most of them come around to enjoying their children later "when they're more like real people." But many fathers are only a little bashful. They just need encouragement. (p. 15).

Except for the convoluted "of which he doesn't think his wife understands the importance," which is the formal way of avoiding stranding the preposition (changed in 1957 to the stranded form "that he doesn't think his wife understands the importance of"), the language is especially colloquial ("It's nice," "it's fine," "still pretty tired") and good-natured in its invoking of male attitudes ("those questions," "'when they're more like real people'"). Male negative face wants ("freedom of action and freedom from imposition") are not to be questioned, and male balkiness cannot profitably be confronted or challenged ("forced").

So eager is A to avoid conflict that the writing becomes unusually diffuse. What exactly does "It's fine if" mean? Does it mean 'He's a fine person if' or 'It's okay if' or 'It's good enough if'? Is it the same as "It's nice"? And are they both substitutes for "It's good if"? The word *good* is misplaced in "a good feeding"—only a baby would think a 2 a.m. feeding is good. Version A habitually avoids judging actions as good or bad ('It is good for the father to take the 2 a.m. feeding'), perhaps because such judgments produce division. Behind this passage we can glimpse real horrors—selfishness and condescension and fathers who are repelled by their progeny—but they are prettified and made light of. Perhaps the last word says it best: this is the rhetoric of encouragement.

B's treatment of each of these topics is quite different—virtually opposite—and can be traced directly to a contrasting version of the world. Some of B's assumptions about individual good sense are not much different from A's, but there is real evil, perversion, corruption, and radical injustice in B's society and culture. It is a society that oppresses and exploits women and warps the emotional life of men; it serves unwholesome and adulterated food and provides unsafe 'safety devices.' Much in the popular culture is brutalizing and degrading. Aggressiveness is out of control, not a force that makes worthwhile citizens. It is our obligation "to show our disapproval of lawlessness and violence in television programs and in children's gun play" (p. 351). The battle lines must be clearly drawn, for children are not so infallibly able to turn fantasies to constructive account: "The sight of a real human face being apparently smashed by a fist has a lot more impact on children than what they imagine when they are making up their own stories. I believe that parents should flatly forbid programs that go in for violence. I don't think they are good for adults either" (p. 355). Spock goes on to explain why and how to forbid such viewing, and concludes, "Even if children cheat and watch such a program in secret, they'll know very well that their parents disapprove, and this will protect them to a degree from the coarsening effect of the scenes." A little guilt may be serviceable to the child! Though the recommendations are couched as personal opinion, they are not hedged or left to the parents' own good judgment. Even on the question of candy, he sees no reason for compromise: "I would encourage parents to explain the bad effects of sweets on the teeth and make a flat rule against them" (p. 338).

The tone of righteous indignation at its most intense becomes witheringly ironic:

> When we let people grow up feeling that cruelty is all right provided they know it is make-believe, or provided they sufficiently disapprove of certain individuals or groups, or provided the cruelty is in the service of their country (whether the country is right or wrong), we make it easier for them to go beserk when the provocation comes.
>
> But can we imagine depriving American children of their guns or of watching their favorite Western or crime programs? I think we should consider it—to at least a partial degree. (p. 352)

This is not advice at all, although the practical and necessarily qualified advice soon comes. In B's world, there is no consensus on values; indeed, there is a tendency to replace values with "psychological concepts" that B feels are entirely too value-free. For B, it is necessary to articulate basic human ideals and to inspire parents to hold and inculcate them.

B's discussion of "a father's capability and responsibility" is similarly unqualified, uncompromising, and ready to proclaim the values that cannot be taken for granted. I will cite only part of it, for it is long and advocates many basic changes in men's traditional priorities:

> I think that a father with a full-time job—even where a mother is staying at home—will do best by his children, his wife, and himself if he takes on half or more of the management of the children (and also participates in the housework) when he gets home from work and on weekends. The mother's leadership and patience will probably have worn thin by the end of the day. (The father's would, too, if he alone had had the children all day.) The children will profit from experiencing a variety of styles of leadership and control.
>
> When a father does his share as a matter of course when at home, it does much more than simply lighten his wife's work load and give her companionship in the work that she has had to do along all day. It shows that he believes this work is crucial for the welfare of the family, that it calls for judgment and skill and that it's his responsibility as much as it is hers when he is at home. This is what sons and daughters need to see in action if they are to grow up without sexist attitudes.
>
> In child care, fathers can give bottle and solid foods, change diapers and clothes, wipe tears and noses, bathe and put to bed, read stories, fix toys, break up quarrels, help with questions about homework, explain rules and assign duties and see that they are carried out, correct and reprove. (p. 47)

The last paragraph is just a list, but how artfully ordered in progression and concluded in severe simplicity! There are some qualifiers—the passage begins, "I think," and the list is only that of things fathers *can* do, but in the context *can* means "perfectly well able to." There is no 'other hand' or middle road. B sees the problem with fathers as far more deeply rooted and pervasive than A, requiring resistance to pressures at work as well as commitment at home, but this vision inspires an outpouring of eloquence far beyond anything A ever attempted.

Dr. Spock, it is commonly said, has gotten less permissive (toward fathers and mothers as well as children, one might add), as if he himself had concluded from the campus disorders of the late 1960s that more discipline and order are needed. This saying is at the very least highly misleading. We can give a better account of the changes in Spock's advice and attitudes by saying that he has become more ideological in tracing the political and social implications of child rearing and that his version of society has taken on qualities of an arena in which strong forces threaten to warp the values and attitudes of individuals. The world of B, with its menacing forces, is structurally similar to Simon's, although the values are sharply different and in most ways antithetical. The 'system' is no longer benign and magically integrative: it no longer gathers up, refines, and disciplines the aggressive forces of individuals into a productive and harmonious whole. Like Simon, Spock advocates resistance and counterpressure for his values; unlike Simon, however, he understands this counterpressure as a collective undertaking. The *we* he employs is that of a political activist, and the actions he urges are anchored in our responsibilities to and for society. The world of B is a harder place than that of A, and Spock's rhetoric alters to meet the challenges head-on.

The function of rhetoric, of writing, in the politicized worlds surveyed in this chapter is not only to persuade the reader, but in so doing to change the world as well. In the next chapter, we will examine writers who also decided that they wanted to change the world, but who wished to stand clear of traditional modes of authority. In the course of becoming successful authors, however, they become new authorities, and hence have interesting problems to work out when they come before the public with revised editions and sequels.

IV

WHO WRITES?
THE CODES OF AUTHORITY

> As institution, the author is dead: his civil
> status, his biographical person have
> disappeared . . . but in the text, in a way, *I
> desire* the author: I need his figure (which
> is neither his representation nor his
> projection), as he needs mine.
>
> Roland Barthes[1]

In his essay "What Is an Author?" Michel Foucault suggests that we
interrogate a wide range of discourses with the question "What difference does it make who is speaking?" not as a gesture of indifference,
but as a way of developing a typology of discourses according to the
way the notion of author functions in them—according, that is, to the
way they authorize themselves.[2] It is not possible to carry out the whole
of Foucault's project, but it does yield some interesting similarities and
differences when applied to advice writing. In particular, one can see a
traditional mode of authorizing still alive and flourishing, but also a
more recent mode that questions and disrupts the traditional one,
pushing the writing of advice into more complex interactions of
reader, writer, and author.

The general need for authority in advising seems fairly evident, but
it is worth articulating nonetheless, especially since it might be alleged
that no authority is intrinsically exercised when one gives advice. It is
often said that in speech acts such as ordering and permitting, which
involve the exercise of authority, the Speaker takes responsibility for
the consequences of Hearer doing 'p.' One might suppose that advice is
categorically different, that the adviser takes no responsibility for
Hearer's doing 'p.' Doing p is his own voluntary choice. Such a conclusion, I think, is legalistic and naive. It ignores why people seek advice to
begin with, why they seek the counsel of an authority or leader. We

must often act without being able to foresee the consequences, and the possible consequences of many actions matter a great deal to us, whether these are the behavior and character of our children, our financial security, our health, our sanity, our happiness, or our satisfaction in relationships. Advisors define our choices for us and assure us of outcomes. Recognition and management of the implied responsibility is a recurrent theme in advice books and an important dimension of the interaction between writer and reader. Its most extreme manifestation is the disclaimer of legal liability that now prefaces most investment advice: "The Author and Publisher specifically disclaim any liability, loss, or risk, personal or otherwise, which is incurred as a consequence, directly or indirectly, of the use and application of any of the contents of this book".[3] Apparently somebody thinks that the advice giver has some responsibility for wielding in public whatever persuasive power she has managed to accumulate.

What we may call the traditional mode of authorizing advice follows the broad outlines of Weber's dominance by authority, which he contrasts to dominance by leadership.[4] When exercising authority, one exerts sway as a representative of an institutionalized body of norms and beliefs that is of recognized legitimacy; one's personal attributes are basically irrelevant, except for qualifications as a spokesman. In the case of leadership, one exerts sway by force of personal attractiveness, conviction, and 'charisma'; the leader does not necessarily come into conflict with institutionalized, received wisdom, but there is a tendency for this to happen, as prophets have at best an uneasy relation to priests. One can advise as an authority or a spokesman for authority, or as a leader, out of one's own experience and discovery; characteristically, one does not do both.

The prototype of advising from authority is the medical doctor writing on health care or diet. The 'M.D.' is a very useful rhetorical credential, for it activates the conventional relation of doctor to patient, which is that of disinterested concern for the patient's physical wellbeing, and ties in to a body of technical knowledge and expertise and full-time experience in the role of adviser. There is a certain amount of fuzziness about the limits of the authorizing expertise, and sometimes one wonders whether all of a doctor's advice is grounded in medical science. Especially in child-rearing guides, some doctors pass from medically grounded advice to advice about toilet training, discipline, or playing with other children with little or no shift in the implicit claim to authority. In this connection, we can see that what appears to be almost a mannerism of Dr. Spock's style—his heavy use of "I think it is reasonable/sensible . . . "—is his way of noting that there is no more basis for the particular advice than reason or common sense.

Medicine is atypical as a body of authorizing expertise, however, in that doctors very successfully conceal from the public their differences of opinion and changes in received views. Advisers with Ph.D.s in psychology have some of the advantages of M.D.s, but the public is more aware of the arguability of most psychological theories. In general, any 'scientifically based' body of norms and values may require some defense when it comes into conflict with traditional wisdom and common practice—as it does, for example, in some sex-advice books and child-rearing guides. In practice, it does not often happen that a writer can simply refer to a body of norms and beliefs of unquestionable legitimacy and relevance. The spokesman is almost always to some degree a salesman. When Dr. Thomas Gordon writes in 1970 that modern psychological research has developed a stable consensus about human behavior that nobody before him has tried to apply, we note the *topos* while reaching for the salt. Such straightforward invocations of the traditional author-function give a simple answer to the question "who writes?" In general, then, the author-function is shaped by what it supplements or displaces, where the supplementation can be no more than popularization, though even that involves some act of interpretation of authoritative sources.

Writers who eschew the role of authority in favor of one of leadership are in a sense the entrepreneurs of authority; their persuasiveness is not based on association with existing external institutions but is fashioned out of their own experience, often out of an admittedly impassioned quest. The quest may include a search of existing scholarship, but they read as laymen, not experts, and they characteristically see a significance in their reading that others have not. The subjective roots of their wisdom are stressed rather than concealed. A writer who tries to exert leadership has two problems the spokesman for authority does not: she must establish that her counsel is sufficiently well grounded and stable to provide a basis for other people's decisions— i.e., though an outsider, she is not a 'flake' or crackpot—and she must be able to explain why traditional or established wisdom is less adequate than her own vision. This latter problem varies in acuteness with the weight of traditional authority one pits himself against. In advice on composition, for example, the weight can be relatively slight; in other areas, relations with existing authorities can be considerably more complex and troubled, ranging from appeals to the authorities to take the eccentric view seriously (as in Dr. David Reuben's *Save Your*

Life Diet[5]) to outright rejection of "the experts—those credential-laden officials and academics who have the answers *for* us."[6] As we consider this more overtly political end of the scale, it becomes clear that terms such as *authority* and *leadership* are not metaphorical when applied to advice writing; to read and be persuaded is to follow.

The issue of power and responsibility is a particularly troublesome one for writers with antiauthoritarian leanings. Even 'leadership' is suspect—it sounds like the *Führerprinzip*—if your guiding objective is free people freely determining their lives. If you believe that change is necessary to realize that objective, however, then there must be some means of effecting it that does not reduce the reader to the status of follower. During the 1970s, a number of writers achieved considerable prominence as advocates of change and began to develop a new rhetoric and a new basis of persuasion. A recurrent word in these writings is *experience*: this is what is set against the institutionally authorized experts with their certified learning and science. (This invokes an old theme in American culture.)

In certain respects, this rejection of established abstractions in favor of articulating one's own experience resembles the inward turning of Romanticism, particularly in its emphasis on individual liberation and renewal. The writers I am concerned with have not chosen to write lyric poems, novels, or autobiography, however, but books of advice—their experience must in some way become valid as a basis for the action of others. The aspect of the new rhetoric of experience that most sharply differentiates it from that of Ruskin or Carlyle, Emerson or Nietzsche is the axiom that the self is social from the first and can only define itself and act within the concepts and possibilities of its social and cultural milieu. A consequence of this axiom is that personal change involves social change (and vice versa); the bridging concept is that of a community of concern in which one shares and checks one's experience and through which one attempts to alter the social framework. The *I* tries to make itself into a *we* through writing, with the *we* extending beyond that achieved in the text to become a community for change. The extreme of such a development is to write under the name of a 'we,' as does one author we shall examine—The Boston Women's Health Book Collective.

Foucault suggests that we pay particular attention to the function of the author's name, and such attention yields not only a succinct image of the difference between (traditional) authority and leadership, but points to a third possibility as well. The names of the traditionally authorized authors come with initials and titles following them (M.D., Ph.D., Director of Such-and-such Institute for Child Development, etc.); the names of leadership, however, are at first of no authorizing power. They are the names of writers, not authors. But if the book should succeed, the name of the writer no longer indicates an obscure outsider, but the author of a 'classic' or 'best-selling' work. The writer is no longer who she was, and the writer who writes a sequel to a successful book, or a revision of it, has possiblities as well as responsibilities she did not have at first. The 'personal experience' now includes the experience of having affected other people's thoughts and lives; the writer has become an authority and must be concerned with power in a way she was not before. Because the rhetoric of experience and change became almost fashionable in the later 1970s, a number of its early practitioners found themselves in just this situation, coming before the public as figures in various ways transformed by their own success. It is thus possible to study the transformation of the author-function in writers committed to a nontraditional mode of exercising sway. This chapter will examine three such cases: the first is Peter Elbow, whose *Writing without Teachers* (1973) was succeeded by *Writing with Power* (1981) and whose struggle with his role as writer seems dominated by uneasiness about power and aggression; Frances Moore Lappé, whose *Diet for a Small Planet* appeared first in 1971 and underwent massive revision in 1975 and 1982, and whose role as leader has been dramatically revised; and the Boston Women's Health Book Collective, whose *Our Bodies, Ourselves* (1971, 1974) has been joined by a book on being a parent, *Ourselves and Our Children* (1978). The last pair of texts introduce a further complexity, since the writer's name does not indicate a person, but, as we shall see, the question of the continuity and identity of the writer-turned-author is not entirely different from that faced by individuals.

I.

In 1973 appeared a book by a relative unknown named Peter Elbow, a member of the faculty of Evergreen State College. In this book, *Writing without Teachers*, the author claims the authority solely of wisdom derived from personal experience and self-examination: "The authority I call upon in writing a book about writing is my own longstanding difficulty in writing" (p. viii). This is the most unimpeachable and uncontroversial basis for authority; Elbow does not claim originality ("much or all of this may be in other books, some of which I have probably read"—p. 16), only the ability to convey his experience and what he has learned from it. The reader is to "try on" his experience to see if it works for her. The relation to the reader is both close and intense, since no third parties (such as Elbow's anonymous possible sources or like thinkers) are introduced. Usually his experience is narrated in a generalized form, but he sometimes includes journal entries and free writings that he produced when struggling to work through a block or tangle of feelings. These entries attempt to convey his experiences in as unmediated, unreflected, and unedited a form as writing allows. One might suppose that Elbow's success would result from his openness and awareness of his own feelings and processes, but about these, of course, we know nothing except what we learn from the book. To make this experience accessible to the reader, it must be written; Elbow's project really hangs on his ability as a writer to evoke and articulate experiences in the reader. The danger of his approach lies in the trick of indefiniteness about the actual occasion and subject that gave him difficulties: we get the experience and process, but never the product, and we may wonder whether Elbow's experience is so very like our own or not. He is really attempting a stylistic coup or new mode of writing, one in which his own experiences are rendered as occasions or instances of general mechanisms; he does not dwell on the particularity of his experience, as autobiographical writing does, but always on the ways 'I' is like 'you.'

The 'you' of the book is a fairly direct projection of the 'I'—Elbow over and over shows that he knows how it feels to get stuck or bewildered or frightened; he deals out assurance and permission and support in large doses. He never scolds. The language is informal. Much of the advice is couched in fairly prosaic analogies and metaphors ('cooking an idea,' "let them reflect heat on each other like logs in a fireplace"), making it clear that it is suggestive rather than definitive or 'authoritative' in nature. Elbow thus cultivates a Footing of extreme solidarity, equality, and obliqueness with the Reader as fellow fumbler and struggler. Although somewhat more general than some passages, the following reflects the characteristic Footing:

> The developmental model, on the other hand, preaches, in a sense, *lack* of control: don't worry about knowing what you mean or what you intend ahead of time; you don't need a plan or an outline, let things get out of hand, let things wander and digress. Though this approach makes for initial panic, my overall experience with it is increased control. Not that I always know what I am doing, not that I don't feel lost, baffled, and frustrated. But the overall process is one that doesn't leave me so helpless. I can get something written when I want to. There isn't such a sense of mystery, or randomness. (pp. 32–33)

If this is preaching, it is fairly low-key, and done by the model, not the author at that. The language is informal to the point of inexactness. The model preaches lack of control *in a sense*; he isn't left *so* helpless (but still helpless, much less helpless?); there isn't *such* a sense of mystery (as what? as you thought there would be? as you felt about writing generally before trying the method?); *things* and *something* abound. It is a little unfair to judge this passage by the criteria of written text, for it seems intended to be heard as speech evoking attitudes, not making promises.

Because it is an extreme, this Footing is easy to parody, and in fact Elbow cites an anonymous take off of it in *Writing with Power* (hereafter *Power*): "I'm *really* sincere. You can really believe me. I know just how you feel. I'm a good guy. I wouldn't steer you wrong. Only, don't get mad at me if it doesn't work. I'm really trying as hard as I can. Besides, I'm having a hard time with my writing too" (*Power*, p. 262). As the parody suggests, Elbow's claims are modestly and earnestly couched; they would not *offend* anybody. Feelings of vulnerability and weakness, frustration and self-disgust are 'known' and accepted; other feelings such as hostility and contempt are not. They are simply not brought up.

This nonrecognition of aggressive and 'territorial' feelings is of a piece with the overall strategy of *Writing without Teachers*: institutionalized instruction in writing is brushed aside with the preposition *without*. Although it is clear that Elbow must regard standard classroom approaches to composition as valueless when not pernicious, he himself does not spell out these implications, providing only a personal narrative of how he became unable to do business in the usual way and so abandoned his role as 'teacher.' Even when he goes so far as to acknowledge that he is "fighting" an "old, wrong model," it is a *model*, not institutions or persons that he "fights," and the fight is quickly resolved by acknowledging that the old, wrong model is a partial truth after all. One way to respond to 'Peter Elbow' in this book is to take the lead of the parody and assess him as an extremely nice, sensitive, and well-intentioned man—the kind of person who probably, in the words of Casey Stengel, finishes last. Looking a little more deeply, we may ask what all this stylistic disarmament and demystification of authority is in flight *from*. What terrible power or act is this man trying to redress?

As it turned out, Peter Elbow did not finish last. The book established itself, in the words of the publisher's puff, as "a classic in the field," and in 1981 Elbow came again before the public with *Power*, a book well over twice as long as *Writing without Teachers* but in many respects a revision of it. Very much as in the case of Lappé, Elbow now appears as a public figure with a following: he has taken positions in *Writing without Teachers* that have been criticized and sometimes misunderstood, but this criticism has triggered rethinking and further development, and he even uses misunderstandings of the first book to show how feedback can help you (p. 60). In addition, we get more personal details about his young daughter, his activities as a conscientious objector and pacifist, his viola-playing, voice pitch, and occasional sexual preoccupation.

Consistent with Elbow's emergence as a public figure is the recasting of his one-sided, teacherless vision into a more comprehensive view of writing that includes writing for teachers. The "old, wrong model" has now become one method, albeit "The Dangerous Method"; responses to writing now should be objective (criterion-based) as well as subjective; and the narrative of how Elbow came to repudiate the role of 'teacher' is replaced by advice on how to derive benefit from your teacher. No longer the graduate school dropout and solitary outsider, Elbow has written articles, two of which he cites, though not without some uneasiness about having become one of 'them' (p. 348).

These changes are a natural outgrowth of Elbow's new resolve to make himself heard and taken seriously, which for him is to accept the act of writing as aggressive. This seems to be the terrible secret that *Teachers* went to such lengths to conceal. As he observes, the writer is really trying to play with your mind, which is as much an invasion as saying, "Why don't you take off your clothes and let me play with your body?" (p. 319). The story of his deciding to be more forceful and aggressive in writing and speaking is told several times from several angles in *Power* (pp. 22, 122, 182, 210–211). Here is the conclusion to one account: "I wanted lots of people to believe what I was saying, to change their minds, and, damn it, to change their behavior" (p. 122). *Power* is not a manual in verbal assertiveness, however. There is almost no militancy or scolding, even when discussing phoniness and evasion in language: Elbow advocates the Quaker style of quiet witnessing when arguing with one's opponents; and he observes that it is often much easier to criticize someone in writing than face to face. He even quotes an imagined (but, he says, correct) comment on his humble, self-effacing voice: "'Oh, Peter's fallen into his helpless, stuck gear again; that's not him, that's a tiresome habit. He's not daring to be as opinionated and stubborn and pushy as he really is'" (p. 293). I don't know how aggressive Elbow 'really' is, but he stops short of elaborating an account of writing and reading as an agonistic struggle. Perhaps this reflects in part his conclusion from his own experience that sensing the audience as an adversary chokes off his power and sends him into defensive maneuvers. Indeed, he urges the writer to feel his audience as a friend and helper (while acknowledging that we have plenty of reason to distrust and guard against the responses of others [pp. 144–145]; later, he speaks of using a 'loving audience' for support until we can internalize it and stand on our own two feet (pp. 189–190).

Elbow is thus still at pains to 'sanitize' the concept of power, which gives the book its title. Power comes from plugging in to your own unconscious energies. It is a personal rather than a political concept, and Elbow debates whether it is the consequence of harmony between the writer's self and his words or between the words and the reader's self. It is true that when we speak with power, we may frighten ourselves and others (pp. 294–295, 310), but he reassures us that it is not self-aggrandizing, for it is *meaning* that resonates, not the sound of an individual personality (p. 311). Similarly, he describes our experiencing real voice as an overpowering of our being by the writer, but assures us that it is we who consent to experience this power. "Besides," he adds in a curious lapse, "it's just reading, after all, not real life. We can afford to let someone snatch us completely into her power in books, even if we have learned to resist it in real life" (p. 321)—this from one whose declared purpose is to change your behavior! It is true that he is talking about fiction in this chapter, but he also suggests elsewhere that fiction can be a powerful means of changing others, and that great fiction can be didactic. Power in writing cannot so easily be kept separate from power in life.

Thus far, *Power* has been largely an expansion of *Writing without Teachers* and could have appeared as a 'revised, enlarged' edition. In one chapter, however, Elbow raises the issue of writing in an institutional setting, namely, "Writing for Teachers," and acknowledges the fact that students' feelings of powerlessness are not wholly a result of their relations to themselves or words, but of their actual relation to their teachers. In this chapter, too, he comes closest to his own social role as teacher and expert on writing. Suddenly the Footing changes dramatically. When discussing 'compulsory writing' he touches on passive-aggressive resistance to compulsion and becomes unusually argumentative and confrontive:

> If you have to do a piece of compulsory writing it helps to face the central issue squarely: are you going to consent or refuse? To consent is not necessarily to cave in. You don't have to like the task or the taskmaster, you don't have to grovel, but if you want the writing to go well, you have to invest yourself in the job wholeheartedly.

He goes on to explain that you have the choice to refuse:

> But you may not believe in your power to refuse unless you really use
> it—openly and with full responsibility (instead of fooling yourself into
> being sick or having an emergency or "trying as hard as you can" and
> somehow not succeeding). Perhaps refusing is not the ideal solution,
> but it's better than that familiar worst-of-both-worlds compromise: you
> don't get the fun of saying No or the satisfaction of doing the job quickly
> with investment. All you get is a ruined weekend and a sense of
> powerlessness. (p. 208).

For once Elbow is not trying to soothe the reader into letting down his
defenses and taking small risks with his own processes of writing;
resentment of compulsory writing is a problem that must be confronted. It is not to be solved by getting in touch with your feelings, but
by taking responsibility for your actions. The limits of sharing and
support have finally been reached.

Despite his inveterate tendency to view writing as a personal, private
activity, Elbow discusses in "Writing for Teachers" the specific institutional setting of the college composition class. Here he drops entirely
the oblique, equal stance of fellow fumbler that is carried over from
Teachers in favor of a more learned diction, periodic syntax, and sweeping generalizations. In part this reflects the inclusion of teachers in the
audience. One discovers how extreme Elbow's self-imposed constraints
have been when he simultaneously addresses the profession—in its
language of power—and also the student (see, e.g., the last *you*):

> It is also unhelpful to evaluate and give feedback to student writing
> about its quality *in general*. It is meaningless, really, to try to tell a
> student how successful his writing is in general without saying how
> successful it is at achieving a certain effect on a certain audience. The
> only way you can give feedback on "quality in general" is by doing what
> teachers have historically tended to do: concentrate mostly on the
> conventions of writing as a medium, namely, spelling, grammar, foot-
> notes, and paragraphing, and ignoring the question of how well it could
> work on what kinds of readers. It's not that the conventions of writing
> as a medium are unimportant or easy to learn. Quite the contrary. They
> are *too* hard and onerous to learn if you try to learn them by them-
> selves—as mere push-ups—without the incentive of actually trying to
> use them in real communciation to real readers. (p. 226)

This is a strong stand on a controversial issue; it hammers away until
the opposing position ("'quality in general'") seems ludicrous and
mechanical; there are few hedge words ("really") and many sweeping

quantifiers, negatives, and strong judgments. It strikes fire on the errors of others. Since *you* at the end seems to be the student, the passage invites students to criticize the pedagogy of their teachers.

Something about the reality of the roles of teacher and student, and the undeniably agonistic tension in their relation, allows Elbow to speak finally in the 'I' of the teacher. He advises students to treat their teachers as friends of whom they were asking a favor: "You would probably make your paper neat and easy to read. I get mad at students when their papers are messy. I begin to feel them as the enemy" (p. 233). He also advises students on how to take responsibility for their roles as composition students—pages of good suggestions, ranging from asking for variations from topics assigned to suggesting criteria for responses by the teacher—in short, to treat the power relations of the classroom as more negotiable than they are traditionally assumed to be. The voice of authority in this passage is grounded in long and shrewd observation of things outside the self and its processes, and its resonance springs from Elbow's allowing himself to be in public what success has made him in fact—one of 'them,' or rather, one of us. In acquiring visibility and a following, he has concrete proof that his experience has been shared. He has the means of enlarging the self of 'Peter Elbow,' and the at times almost claustrophobic 'I' and 'thou' of *Writing without Teachers* is now relieved by testimonials, acknowledgements of sources, and the comments of readers either of the first book or a draft of the new one. These all become part of the text and suggest a network of real historical people—allies—who share Elbow's concerns. He is now willing to risk offending some readers, but it remains to be seen how he will manage the responsibilities of his new public role as expert in writing, and whether he will ever dare to be as pushy, opinionated, and stubborn as he really is.

II.

> So while many books about food and hunger appeal to guilt and fear, this book does not. Instead, I want to offer you power. Power, you know, is not a dirty word!
>
> Frances Moore Lappé

Although *Power* is officially a different book from *Teachers*, and refers to changes that the writer experienced over the decade between them, the Writer remains basically the same in his address to the Reader and to the act of writing, the confrontive passages aside. The changes in the author, both in success and recognition and in acceptance of aggressive impulses, have not brought about a complete overhaul in the *I* writing. With the work of Frances Moore Lappé, we encounter a rather different outcome. Like Elbow, she has seen the success of her private testament transform her into an author and writes of this experience in her later editions; like Elbow, she has come to address the question of power directly in her most recent revision of *Diet for a Small Planet* (1982); but, though she has written only one book, the *I* writing in each successive edition differs much more significantly from its predecessor than does the *I* of Elbow's two books. To follow this pattern, I will first sketch the changes in content and point of view of the book and the changes Lappé narrates in her personal self, and then turn to the changes in the Writer as reflected in parallel passages from the three editions of her work.

From the first (1971) her extraordinarily successful cookbook was more than a list of recipes; each edition begins with an analysis of world food production and hunger—the ethics and politics of eating—and proposals for changing the systems allocating food resources around the world. The sections, which become longer and more inclusive in scope with each edition, are intended to motivate the reader to adopt the meat-free diet that is defended in theory and outlined in the recipes in the later part of the book. The driving impulses behind these first sections are a sense of moral obligation not to eat meat while others starve and a sense of moral outrage at the institutions and forces that govern the distribution and consumption of food. Although each edition is more political and global than the last, the attempt to mobilize the indignation of 'we common people' is a constant. This is vegetarianism not on its traditional bases of health or reverence for life ("Love animals, don't kill them") but as a step toward a more just and humane world order.

At the same time, however, the two revisions of this book (1975 and 1982) raise in the most pointed fashion the question of identity in the midst of change. The 1975 "Revised edition" was really a new book, Lappé says, and the same could be said of the most recent "Tenth Anniversary Edition"—which, by the way, the publisher notes as "First Edition, 1982." The analysis of The Problem changes substantially in each revision, as do the proposals for change. In 1975, for example, Lappé advocates public-interest lobbying in Washington to change the policies shaping land use, but in 1982, this 'liberal' solution is dropped in favor of general references to planning, which, one gathers, is a good bit further off, after we the powerless gain power. The implicit view of the government as the extension and vehicle of our personal idealism also has been abandoned; Lappé now thinks in terms of alternative structures (food co-ops, networks of information, policy study, and support), and she has dropped the assumption that America has the understanding, the effective means, or the will to ameliorate world hunger. But she has also broadened her attack on the current American diet, now including excessive sugar and salt, low fiber, and processed food. Food remains the focus of her analysis of what is wrong, but many specifics of the analysis, and the cure, keep changing.

This flexibility is potentially a source of considerable embarrassment for a leader, and Lappé devotes considerable energy and originality in 1982 to describing the inner unity of her work. On some points she defends herself against charges of inconsistency, but much more strikingly, she embraces the process of change as the very objective! The 1982 edition begins with fifty-seven pages of autobiography, fifty of them entitled "My Journey," in which Lappé sketches the changes in her understanding, confidence, and values since her disillusionment with the government as a student in a small Quaker college during the Vietnam war, changes that parallel and interact with her emergence as a public figure. Much personal material is narrated—her struggle with depression and loss of direction, her dependence on her husband and later decision to terminate her marriage, her experiences as a single parent—but the intended function is not an apologia so much as an exemplum: the rubric is 'if I have changed and increased in power over my life, so can you.' Her experiences do not authorize her text; rather, they illustrate her personal learning of a new style of living, above all of risk taking, that is not merely incidental or instrumental to her ethical and political quest but the very essence of it.

Lappé moves from the shelter of a basement library in Berkeley, where she poured over agricultural reports as an isolated graduate-school dropout, into the glare of publicity as a talk-show personality and lecture-circuit speaker after the publication of the first edition and then, after the publication of the second edition, as co-founder of an international food policy foundation with numerous employees, projects, and publications. This is not just a rise in 'eminence,' but a development in her definition of herself as a member of a collaborative team and far-flung community of concern. When she travels to the Philippines or Africa to observe food policies and practices, she travels with a "buddy" or friend, and her accounts of what 'we' learned spring from a concrete 'we.' To underscore the typicality of her experience, Lappé weaves into the text the accounts of other journeyers as well as their responses to her writing. Her sense is now of participating in a movement larger than herself and the aroused reader. At times she breaks into full-blown myth of historical change: a "train" of resistance to injustice and oppression is already moving; the question for us is only how to board it and remove the obstacles that lie in its path (pp. 55–56).

Such then is Lappé's history of her 'external' self, the self extending beyond and behind the text. The common thread is an impulse to improve the world, but the relation of the self to the world, the kinds of action it contemplates, has broadened and shifted from a private witness of conscience toward public and collective endeavor. One special mode of action for Lappé at all stages, however, is writing, and we should examine the Writer in her several versions to see how it parallels and plays off against the 'growing' self of the author. We have seen how Lappé's address toward the world changes: what is the relation between that and her address toward the Reader and the act of writing? To answer that, I will compare the passages in each edition that most directly address the question of how your personal action can make a difference in the larger scheme of things.

The original edition (1971) does not propose a program of political action; rather, it emphasizes feeling better about yourself as a world citizen:

> Some will find little value in my thesis on the grounds that it doesn't offer a practical guide for solving the world's food problems. But reestablishing a sense of our direct impact on the earth through food may be the first step toward changing our cultural pattern of waste. However, I'll have to admit that the appeal to me has been more to my feelings than my rationality. First, it has to do with the tremendous personal satisfaction of being able to make real choices; indeed, how rare this is! Previously, when I went to a supermarket, I felt at the mercy of our advertising culture. My tastes were being manipulated. And food, instead of being my most direct link with the nurturing earth, had become mere merchandise by which I fulfilled my role as a "good" consumer. But as I gained the understanding that I have tried to communicate to you in this book, I found that I *was* making choices, choices based on real knowlege about food and about the effect on the earth of different types of food production. It was a gradual process in which there was no question of a sacrifice in giving up meat. Rather, as new types of food combinations became more attractive, shopping for food and cooking was no longer unconscious and boring, but a real adventure. The adventure was the discovery of ways, the best, most delicious ways, of making the most of the earth's productivity. (1971, p. xiv)

This is low-key and modest, with its *mays* and limitation of persuasiveness to "feelings." The sentences move reflectively, often opening with a word and interrupting with a subordinate clause. The writing does not strike one as artful, learned, or literary (not with three *reals* in one paragraph and a *first* with no apparent *second*), and there is an upbeat, Madison-Avenue quality to the last sentences (*real adventure, best, most delicious ways*).

In the section of the 1982 edition entitled "My Journey," Lappé describes the exhausting period of travel and public appearance that followed publication of this first edition. She chose to become a 'personality' and promoter of her diet and, at the end of this period, she wrote the 1975 edition and collapsed. In the course of her lecturing, she evidently became aware of some of the political implications of her views and grew more practiced in the art of moving audiences. Here is the comparable section from the 1975 version, which comes at the end of the chapter "Meatless, Guiltless?" (pp. 43–55). She is defending her position against the charge that the diet is worse than ineffectual, since for some people it may substitute for real action. After advocating organizing for political change in policies of land use, Lappé claims responsiblity as a world citizen:

> But I am responsible for the future—the direction that the human community now takes. I am responsible now for the policies of my government that directly affect the world's food supply and the world's maldistribution of wealth.
>
> A change in diet is not an *answer*. A change in diet is a way of experiencing more of the *real* world, instead of living in the illusory world created by our current economic system, where our food resources are actively reduced and where food is treated as just another commodity on which to make a profit—a profit on life itself. A change in diet is a way of saying simply: I have a choice. That is the first step. For how can we take responsibility for the future unless we can make choices now that take us, personally, off the destructive path that has been set for us by our forebears? (1975, p. 55)

The *I* here is clearly a representative self, not a personal one, and the statements are to be taken as dramatizing an attitude each of us should take. The language is oral and stagy, depending heavily on *anaphora* (in its rhetorical sense: "I am responsible . . . ," "A change of diet . . .") and *anadiplosis* ("make a profit—a profit on life itself") and concluding with a sweeping rhetorical question. It doesn't invite analytical or critical scrutiny (Is food "life itself"? What is this "*real*" world like?), and it doesn't hang together unless you accept the notion that only by per-

sonal example can you change the world. This last is at times a gratifying notion and can be used to justify various activities, such as riding a
bicycle, turning out lights when you leave a room, and writing on the
backs of envelopes. It is a familiar appeal and an essentially sentimental
one that does not come to grips with the question of how a personal
decision can affect the distribution of wealth in society. The use of
language in this passage is strenuous, as if it is attempting to sweep us
into action on a lava flow of indignation. It is on the one hand vehe-
mently superior and controlling, with the reader's intended response
extreme and very narrowly specified. On the other hand, it can suggest
a grim desperation about argument and language; if the reader is not
swept away, then all is lost. This is a larger and more ambitious *I* than
the one in the original edition, but one that does not look much beyond
the impassioned present.

The parallel passage in the 1982 edition comes at the end of the
chapter called "Democracy at Stake":

> What we eat is only one of those everyday life choices. Making
> conscious choices about what we eat, based on what the earth can
> sustain and what our bodies need, can remind us daily that our whole
> society must do the same—begin to link sustainable production with
> human need. And choosing this diet can help us to keep in mind the
> questions that we ourselves must be asking in order to be part of that
> new society—quesions such as, how can we work to ensure the right to
> food for all those unable to meet their own needs, and a decent liveli-
> hood for all those who can work? How do we counter false messages
> from the government and media blaming the poor and hungry for
> their own predicament? (1982, p. 107)

The new diet, which Lappé generally refers to as 'whole foods,' takes
on a quality of almost ritual observance—no longer is it privileged as
simply the initial step of self-determination and escape from illusion.
The pitch of vehemence has been turned back down, with *can*s, like the
*may*s of the first version, qualifying the claims. There are, to be sure,
two *must*s—"our whole society must do the same" and "questions that
we must ourselves be asking"—these points are now beyond dispute.
Indeed, there is no dispute with either the reader or the authorities,
only "questions" to guide 'us' as we begin to change in the direction of
"the new society," here treated as inevitable with or without the participation of the reader. This is the language of faith. I am inclined to
conclude that the Writer/writer has found a good bit of what she was
looking for on her journey, if only because she doesn't need me so
much as an admiring spectator and assenter. The presupposed *we* are

both already convinced and seekers, saving remnant and journeyers toward the new society.

III.

Although both Elbow's and Lappé's later rhetorical selves are enlarged in the direction of collaboration with others, their accounts of their experience are still those of individual psyches, and the authority they claim is anchored in a personal name. They do not even share it in coauthorship.[7] The Boston Women's Health Book Collective moves beyond 'individualism.' The significance of its pooled experience is collectively negotiated and the name of the author of its books is "The Boston Women's Health Book Collective."

Some change in membership in the Collective occurred between 1969, when *Our Bodies, Ourselves* (hereafter *Bodies*) was begun, and 1978, when *Ourselves and Our Children (Children)* appeared, but most of the writers of the latter book also worked on the earlier project. Such changes in rhetorical stance as have occurred are thus a reflection of a collective that is ten years older, that wrote an extraordinarily successful and important book, and that comes before the public with the enhanced confidence that success confers. It is thus possible to compare the two books in much the same way that we have the books of Elbow and Lappé, though in this case we have to do so with a collective identity, not a personal one.

The prefatory materials in the two books are virtually programmatic accounts of the rhetoric of experience and change. The themes we have been tracing are laid out almost axiomatically: the self is socially constituted and personal change entails social change through collective support and action; the experience of individuals is the source of their authority; all people are or should be changing, and their current understanding is only provisional. These declarations are somewhat more overt in *Children* because they are not opposing a male-dominated medical establishment; there is no body of knowledge and expertise on being a parent of comparable weight to deal with. Also, it may be that the Collective is more confident and reflective about its by now well-known stance.

The Collective is still radically egalitarian and collectivist but has introduced one element of hierarchy in appointing Wendy Coppedge Sanford "overall editor and coordinator." In her introduction, she discusses changes in the outlook of the collective members resulting from their experience as parents, principally an increase in tolerance that makes them want to modify the "late sixties' rhetoric of feminism" to make it less "programmatic": "While it is true that we meant to encourage new possibilities in parenting—sharing roles, openness to nontraditional family forms, a certain kind of reflectiveness about what we are doing, a balance between home work and outside work—we do not intend to set these up as a new norm for parents to compare themselves to" (p. 14). This passage points to a mellowing and softening of doctrinaire stances, and there are indeed some traces of those stances in *Bodies*, particularly in the chapters on abortion (coauthored by Wendy Sanford!) and "Women and Health Care." There are also in *Bodies* miscellaneous swipes at men, as in this self-congratulatory comment on the collective's experience of writing: "But throughout this process we have in no way sacrificed the quality of our relationships with each other, as men often do when they work with each other" (p. 9). And too there are indignant citations of male treatises and myths about women's sexuality and health. In these places, *Bodies* is often superior and even confrontive, as in the summary of its section on doctors: "If you find all this disillusioning, then we are glad if we have helped you to lose some illusions. We want you to be more alert to your responsibility in the relationship, just as you would in any other adult relationship where you are purchasing services" (p. 253).

As Sanford's introduction suggests, this fierce militancy is absent from *Children*, though it addresses topics that could be and have been treated militantly by others. It is clear why. *Bodies* was struggling to gain a hearing and a public for accounts of women's experience that were not shaped by male stereotypes and expectations. And, as many have noted, that effort has been successful. There is now a large body of feminist literature on women's experience and roles, a good bit of which is cited in *Children*, and a considerable body of criticism of social institutions, such as schools, families, and work, which allows the 1978 Collective to say 'how shall we deal with this complexity?' rather than 'make room for alternatives.' Thus far the pattern follows that of Lappé's 1982 revision.

However, a problem surfaces with the Collective's rhetoric that was present even, I think, in *Bodies*, but concealed there by the vast amount of medical information on the one hand and by the feminist fervor on the other. Both books cite writings, 'interviews,' and transcripts of group sessions that broaden the base of the experience. Thus, instead of the self narrating its journey, as in Lappé or Elbow, we have brief sketches of moments in the journeys of many women, all of them presented anonymously, some of them gathered not from Collective members but cited from other feminist works. The effect is of a host of witnessing voices, but the cost is a rather high degree of abstractness: we learn nothing of the individuals who report their experiences and little or nothing of the contexts or consequences of them. The Collective chose to use the accounts to exemplify recurrent themes in the lives of middle-class white women living in the Boston area and to overcome thereby the isolation of child-bound housewives that is itself a theme in their lives. Thus the books function as a record and extension of a women's group, and the writing of the books, the Collective says, was itself a group experience that modified and enlarged its sense of power and purpose.

There is an obvious gain in enlarging the authority of one person to that of many, but something must replace the single author as the consciousness responsible for selecting and evaluating the experience. This role was filled in *Bodies* by the feminist intention to counter sexist myths and expectations; this is what endows the particular accounts with significance, in some cases even perhaps beyond the significance the individual was aware of. But a substantial number of the accounts in both books make pretty dreary reading—they have a flat, earnest, spoken quality that does not tend to heighten awareness or illuminate one's experience in the way good writing does. What are we to make of such passages as the following, which swell the pages of *Children*?

> You know, I didn't think about it the first time, but I think I would even plan the time of year that I had another child. It really makes a big difference. (p. 31)

> All the time, after I knew Ellie was going to have a baby, I would be in the middle of something else and stop and say, "Hey, man, you made a baby." (p. 37)

Or even this account of how the writing of the book affected one writer:

> One day after writing a section on the resources people can turn to as newly single parents, I found myself quite unexpectedly exhausted, feeling curiously vulnerable and shaky. My topic for the morning had been no mere academic one but a highly charged chapter of my own history. The writing put me in touch with all those feelings I'd had when I first separated from my husband. No wonder I felt exhausted and vulnerable! (p. 12)

The lack of obvious significance or direction in these accounts is much more problematic in *Children* than in comparable spots in *Bodies* because the whole book is about the experience of being a parent and the issues that raises. The treatment of these larger social issues is not polemical but rather done in a kind of droning welfare-ese that seems to accompany being taken seriously in our country. Here is an example of how it combines with personal testimony:

> A persistent question that arises around the issue of on-site day care is that of corporate control. Many of us feel that there is already too much in this country that is controlled by corporate interests and corporate values (witness the socializing influence of commercial TV, for example). Alice, a management trainee in an insurance firm, told us:
> Several companies in the insurance field in this city are talking about getting together to start a day care center for all the parents who work for these companies. But I don't think I would use it. I don't want my child in a center run by the company I work for. It seems like there would be a danger of too much control vested in one place. (p. 207)

Do we need Alice to make the point? Is Alice changing? Who cares about Alice? The book seems to be working from the same formula that worked in *Bodies*, but without the "programmatic" edge that defined the larger significance of the individual testimony.

If *Children* does have authority, it is not based on the experience of Alice and her even more anonymous companions, or on the experience of the Collective, but on the fact that it was written by the Boston Women's Health Book Collective, the author of *Bodies* (as the cover reminds us). But *Children* may not need much authority, because it does not give much advice; it describes problems and options that people have tried, but alas, there are rarely simple solutions. In a characteristic moment, it gives a single mother's account of how she would spend most of the night at her lover's house (with a sleep-in baby-sitter at home) but get back home about 5 a.m. to protect her privacy. The Collective praises this as a possible best of a bad lot of options. It is not clear what this account adds to common sense, except a collective seal of approval.

In a curious and unsettling way, the effect of many of these anonymous accounts is rather like that of excerpts from case histories in an institutionally authoritative book: the personal meaning and context is sacrificed so that the experience will illustrate the general point under discussion. It really doesn't matter whether the writer "combined situations into composites, with fictitious names, ages, and occupations," as Dr. Morton Glenn says he did;[8] changed just the names; made up the characters along with names, as Dr. Flesch recommends; or avoided the problem of names by using first person. The personal experience has been cut off from its roots in the individual personality and pasted into a scrapbook of 'experiences as a new woman.' To put the matter slightly differently, the experiencing self remains virtually anonymous. It is split from the self we encounter as Writer and who stands behind the experience, shaping, selecting, and evaluating it for us—in short, writing it. In this way, the book pursues to the extreme one impulse in nonauthoritarian rhetoric. We could say that the book is not completely *written*; it is, as it were, the first of the 'writerly' advice books—a development Roland Barthes could not have foreseen when he introduced this term in *S/Z*. Perhaps a reader's expectation and desire for an authoritative author to do her work for her is regressive and passive and returns her to a dependent status, entangling her in the old agon of identification or resistance. In any case, the author and writer suffer death by splitting and dispersion, though it is something less than a bacchanalian orgy.

Advice writing, then, insofar as it is written, posits an author as source of its wisdom, orderer of its arguments, and guarantor of its effects. The writer must credential himself as an authority, and becoming an author is in one sense an outer reflection of his success. Despite its antiauthoritarian leanings, the nontraditional rhetoric of experience and change does not in all respects displace this figure, but rather depends more heavily upon it to the extent that the experience pioneered by the writer is the source of his or her authority; the personal identity and credibility of the Writer are more crucial to the acceptance of his advice. And it seems that success turns even the lowliest of writers into authors.

When the writers we have been analyzing say that they want their experience and perspective to be taken seriously, they are acknowledging a desire for power and authority, however distasteful those words might have been to them at one time. Their strategy is to side-step the traditional figure of authority by stressing the subjective roots and provisionality of their wisdom and advice. At first they write as outsiders and private, essentially anonymous persons, postulating a kind of solidarity with the equally anonymous reader, a solidarity based on feelings of exclusion and powerlessness in a world where authorized counsel has little or no regard for their particular experiences and perceptions. The writer's solitariness is matched by the solitariness of the reader, and each finds in the other a validation not otherwise present in her life. But the process of being published, and well received, is an authorization both in the sense that it establishes the text as of interest and importance to some people who matter and because it makes the writer into an author. A new element thus enters into the relation with the reader; authors have publics, and what the reader responds to is not just a private, individual vision but an approach, a position, or, in some cases, a movement or cult. If an author continues to write of and from her own experience, that experience will include things that separate her from her anonymous readers; a certain cooling and distancing seem inevitable.

All of the writers analyzed exhibit some mitigation of their initial stances. The care Peter Elbow takes not to frighten or criticize the reader (or just about anybody else) in *Writing without Teachers* is complemented in *Writing with Power* by taking on institutions on their own terms (and not on the personal and somewhat private terms of "the doubting game and the believing game"). If it is really power that is at issue, institutional contexts must be addressed. Lappé has relaxed the hyperbolic urgency of the 'we must do something now' appeal as she prepares herself and her reader for the long haul.

As these writers move into public roles, their writing becomes more reflective and less one-sided, more like written Text and less like spoken Utterance, whether of the one-to-one variety, as in Elbow, or in the political rally model of Lappé. Comparable generalizations about the Boston Women's Health Book Collective are hard to come by because of the stylistic diversity of both books. One generalization that does hold for all of these nontraditional writers, however, is that the use of language to recruit followers is lightened in the later works. The later voices are less dependent on getting exactly the response they want from the reader; almost paradoxically, they are less controlling of the reader. The particular changes may go in opposite directions: Elbow has begun to see some uses of hard rhetoric, but 'militancy' is just what the Collective has thrown out.

Nonetheless, our writers do avoid complete acceptance of the role of author as father of the work. The 'father' metaphor, which one finds for example in Roland Barthes, should be taken seriously and does capture several aspects of the traditional advice book based on institutional authority. The traditional *I* bases its authority on its training, certification, and practical experience with clients or patients. It is a cumulative self, integrating all of these authorizing facts into its present perspective, and it is a naively untroubled self that does not experience writing as self-alienation and objectification: 'going public' does not seem unwarrantedly aggressive on the one hand or limiting and parodic on the other. The personal self of the author seems at one with its paper manifestation or paper self (the Writer).

The revisions we have examined, however, dramatize discrepancies between the old and the new personal selves and the old and new paper selves. Personal *I*s change their views and change also by becoming authors. The old paper and personal *I* becomes the object of commentary and criticism in the new text. The new paper *I* is composed of the initial opposition of real and paper selves along with the discrepancies that subsequently emerged and the resolution in the current text's presentation of the whole process for examination. By building in the principle of revision, the current *I* eschews finality or origin; this personal self does cumulate its previous experience, but not by simple incrementation. It must write and rewrite itself through transformations; it is the principle of the thoroughly revised edition.

V

GESTURE AND FIGURATION

The Self-Help Books

Why be backward, shy and futile?
  Here are ways to seize control,
To be forceful, even brutal
  As you elbow toward your goal!

Help yourself to new horizons,
  Read these guide-books, every one—
Full of self-assertive know-how
  They'll remake you! When you're done
With the final book, you'll thank it
  For the ego-trip; and then
Clutching your security blanket
  You can hide in bed again.[1]

This little poem from a collection of literary parodies points to one of the paradoxes of rhetoric. It uses the term ego-trip a little loosely to refer, I assume, to a general effect of preliminary pleasure to be had just by reading an advice book. The reader is often explicitly urged to imagine how powerful he will feel when he takes the advice and succeeds—and, the poem suggests, that pleasure may be sufficient to remove the impulse to change. So advice writing may be shadowed by a tendency to undercut its own ostensible purpose. This seems plausible and not wildly interesting. Rather more interesting is the idea, only suggested by the poem, that the reading of advice becomes itself the security blanket: not only does it allow the reader to indulge fantasies of power and success, but it manages to banish fears and anxieties.

    This line of thought leads directly to one of the most fruitful notions about writing promulgated, among others, by Jacques Derrida and Paul de Man—namely, that writing is the result of the interplay of forces that themselves escape formulation and are only manifest as oppositions, discrepancies, inconsistencies, and contradictions within texts. The opposition we have touched on, which could be called action/inaction, seems to arise from the very process of representation itself: to give name and shape to anxieties and uncertainties is already to counter the fear that they cannot be mastered. That process of naming may be essential to taking practical action, but the very manipulation of fears and names may provide a satisfactory substitute for action. Moreover, the fears are called up and mobilized by the text; the reader chooses both their provocation and allayment, much as one chooses to enter the House of Horrors in an amusement park.

Two other oppositions at play in writing are quite near the surface of advice: that which splits any utterance along the line meaning/gesture and that of figuration. The first force generates a specifically rhetorical doubleness for any statement, request, command, etc.: it can be taken either as a doing or a saying, an earnest 'doing' (Speech Act) or a (rhetorical) gesture, a move whose sincerity cannot be taken for granted. As a rather dramatic example, one may think of the previously mentioned disclaimer of responsibility that prefaces some investment advice: it both disavows the contents and suggests that they are quite potently present. Texts may be aware of themselves as making various gestures—advice books characteristically are—but commenting on the gesture is itself a gesture, and so on, without escape. This is the force that underlies the oppositions of sincere/posing (manipulating) and serious/playful that we have touched on in earlier chapters, and it also is at work in the opposition of personal experience/institutional authority that was the theme of chapter 4. Though it is a force capable of disrupting and disconcerting any discourse, it is often held in abeyance by conventions that allow it not to become an issue. One such convention, for example, would be that restricting parenthetical self-commentary (the one Safire enjoyed breaking). Any dramatizing of the act of writing, or reading, tends to rouse this force from its conventional slumber, and it will be seen at once that it stalks the landscape of advice writing. Above all, this force is kept down by the orthodoxy of 'seriousness' and 'commitment to what one is saying': in return for the reader's one-sided attentiveness and the price of the book, a writer is obliged to offer his best, most complete understanding and insight and to stand behind what he says. According to this principle, we tend to attribute inconsistencies and glaring omissions to the writer's lack of intelligence or information, not his 'unseriousness.' We do not accuse writers of bad faith, only publishers, readers, editors, and others involved in certifying the book as worthy of public dissemination. This tenet of orthodoxy is also reflected in the popular indignation at writers who 'tease' their readers. But as all writers instinctively know or speedily learn, there is a counterpart to serious commitment to the discourse, which is the art of not being caught off balance, of not saying many things, of coming down (if not squarely) on all attractive sides of the issue. Writing, like magic, is done with gestures and with an element of legerdemain. So the tenet of commitment means that writers should never use their powers and privileges to distract or conceal.

The other force very much on the loose in advice writing is that of figuration, which in its most obvious form is manifested in figurative language, cliché, analogy, and fable. Our earlier discussion of figurative language as a means of solidarity was based on the conventional, academic convention that figurative language is clearly distinguishable from the literal and that it is secondary or subordinate or ornamental— that it does not significantly counter or disrupt the 'ideational' plane of (literal) analysis and recommendation. But, it has been argued, all language is a displacement, and literal terms equivocate in the fashion of metaphors, depending for their value and interpretation on contrasts and affiliations within language, not on secure and established stipulations of reference. This is certainly the case for key terms examined so far, such as *aggression, power*, and *intimacy*. Connotations and figurative properties send one off in directions not explicitly recognized on the plane of logical argument. In this view, figuration is an unruly and potentially independent force that is kept in bounds only (if at all) by rigorous conventions isolating certain language as figurative and restricting its play in serious texts. Notice that the conventional alignment pairs serious with literal, play with figuration. But, as Derrida and de Man have demonstrated, it is not kept entirely in bounds even in great works of our cultural tradition: a number of philosophical and literary texts have been shown to be prey to incongruence and contradiction, 'illegitimate' transfers of properties between the figurative and the literal.[2] Again, there is no resolution or escape possible from the opposition. Reading/writing is movement, often between incompatible positions, sometimes patched over and concealed by figurative language, and figurative language is a force in the text not always subordinated to the general argument or nominal aesthetic intent. This potentially subversive, alogical force of figuration has been illustrated principally in relation to canonical texts of high culture, but the claim is that all writing is subject to the play of these forces. As with other prohibitions, these two orthodoxies committing the writer to seriousness and to subordinating figuration to logical argument bear implicit witness to the forces they aim to repress, and indeed a suspicion of these forces lies at the heart of the wariness of language and 'rhetoric' that runs from Plato through the Royal Society and into modern times.

It does not take much logical rigor or subtlety to discern incongruencies of imagery and counsel, inconsistencies, and contradictions in much advice writing, which from its very outset is less committed to the canons of evidence and logical argument than is philosophical and literary discourse, more akin to the sermon and the political speech than the products of high, academic culture. Nonetheless, the sentiment is widely and frequently expressed these days that good, solid, practical writing is not subject to the problematics and duplicities found, say, in Rousseau, Nietzsche, or Proust. Rhetoric has to do with identifying the reader at point A and finding the means to move him to point B, and that is that. Why is it then that the reader crawls back into bed?

These theses are about writing as such. If they are right, no writing escapes the play of representation, figuration, and gesture. Certainly if we think back over the previous chapters we can recall instances of troubled grasps at sincerity, or imagery of aggression at work in texts advocating stoical self-containment, but are these not perhaps isolated, occasional cases?

In this chapter, I will argue that they are not. Advice writing has its own special mode in which the doubleness of writing characteristically manifests itself, and the best way to explore that is in relation to texts in which the contradictions and discrepancies are most obvious, where the paradox of action/inaction is most extreme, and the levels of logical and alogical (figurative) argument peel apart, rather than being integrated into the appearance of seamless harmony. Advice premised on crisis, whether economic, social, or personal, is especially prone to become unglued and show its parts in this way, and it is to such works that we shall direct our attention in this chapter. Crisis writing epitomizes advice rhetoric insofar as the general movement from powerlessness is writ large: The Problem is a crisis, a total threat to the reader, and action is advised for survival, not just personal enhancement.

The characteristic discrepancies of advice writing are noticeable when the discursive line is weak (suggesting that the writer is engaged in alogical business with the reader) or when the figurative language obtrudes itself by its violence and contradiction. In regard to the first criterion, I have in mind analyses of the problem and recommendations for action that are either inconsistent, infeasible, or inconsequential (or all at once). Unorthodox or extreme premises are not of themselves particularly noteworthy; we are inclined to grant them provisionally. But a radical premise, such as that shared by crisis investment books (that collapse of the financial markets and currency is imminent), becomes striking when it is combined with infeasible or improbable recommendations—such as making oneself self-sufficient in a small town in the West with a year's supply of food, guns, water, and ammunition, or moving to the Bahamas—especially when these writers combine such 'ideal' solutions with relatively conventional advice about investments. And when the analysis of the problem is vague and contradictory, one may begin to suspect that some sort of displacement is going on. When there is little exact, rigorous, and detailed analysis of economic and social circumstances, then the writing is slipping its referential moorings and heading in the direction of myths of loss and decline. We have already touched on some of these discrepancies and inconsequentialities in the books by John Simon and Richard Mitchell, where the situation is deemed critical and the actions urged are scarcely a solution to the problem as they define it, but rather than take them up again, we will examine two crisis investing books, both of which were best sellers in the last few years: Howard Ruff's *How to Prosper during the Coming Bad Years* and Douglas Casey's *Crisis Investing*.

The second trait that highlights rhetorical discrepancies is violent and contradictory figurative language. The violence in itself might not reflect anything more than the polemical zeal appropriate to pressing a radical premise, but when the language is also contradictory and 'mixed,' and when the logical or argumentative plane is weak, then it is reasonable to begin to listen to the figurative language as a language of fantasy, and to read the books as a fantastic journey whose termination is not action but a resolution of feelings of powerlessness and inadequacy through symbolic action or dream work. Rather than simply underlining and concretizing the abstract line of argument, the figurative language can ramify and exfoliate into a subtext.

To trace some of the workings of figurative language, we need not have a theory of the psyche (Freudian or otherwise), a code book of symbols, or a structuralist systematics of myth. However figures work psychologically, they work rhetorically as a special type of *loci communes*: they are figurative commonplaces, collective, even stereotyped equivalences and analogies (e.g., self = body, crisis = storm at sea, destruction = fire), the sorts of things George Lakoff and Mark Johnson discuss in *Metaphors We Live By*. To grasp their elaboration, we need only follow lines of association available to us as members of a common culture. To be sure, this involves accepting the text into our own minds and elaborating it in a somewhat alogical fashion; for the text to work itself out, it must be allowed to work in us rather uncritically. Experiencing the text in this way may at times be somewhat distasteful, but this process is really no different from that of 'logical' connection and inference, though we may think we are supposed to do the latter, while the former seems by the convention of high culture secondary, gratuitous, less worthy of serious attention and study. The academic neglect of figurative language as a mode of working in nonliterary texts is always to some degree myopic; with texts that do not rely greatly on evidence and logical argument, it is blind.

Although one of the general concerns of this chapter is with figuration as subtext and dream work, I do not mean to claim that it always undercuts the recommended actions by rendering them superfluous, or covertly undoes what the book says, or plunges one immediately into a realm where contradictions are no impediments or objections ('primary process thinking'). The figurative thread may intersect the thread of rational discourse at various points and make now the same point, now a different one. And the thread of discourse may have its own doubleness, sometimes emphasizing acting to feel better, and sometimes feeling better to act more effectively. Such cases are more complex than those typical of the crisis investing books and draw more richly and variously on the common storehouse of tropes and figures. The last book we shall examine is one such more complicated case, a perennial best seller, veritable advice book of advice books, and model of contrived sincerity—Richard Bolles's *What Color Is Your Parachute?*

I.

At the end of the 1970s, there appeared a spate of investment advice books premised on an imminent hyperinflationary crisis: inflation would continue to accelerate, leading to the futile imposition of wage and price controls, financial and monetary collapse, and a period of barter and disorder. The Problem these books address is thus entirely external to the reader, and, it quickly appears, is not just economic, but rather includes social and moral degeneracy and crisis. The mode of thinking in these works tends toward the apocalyptic: the next depression will be worse than that of 1929, the social and personal suffering much greater. These writers address feelings of dependence on forces beyond our control—'things are in the saddle and ride mankind'—but, crucially, these forces do not exceed our comprehension. The writers analyze the forces in terms of personal morality and hold that we can respond by actions affirming and enhancing our independence of those forces. The solutions offered are not political, however, despite the heavily political attacks on the government, perhaps partly because political action conflicts with the affirmation of radical individual independence: the reader can by his own individual action step outside of the collapsing economic and social fabric, survive, and profit while others experience impoverishment and chaos, even hunger.

This much is common to these books, two of which became best sellers. Common too, and especially marked both in Howard Ruff's *How to Prosper during the Coming Bad Years* and Douglas Casey's *Crisis Investing*, is a violently hyperbolic and figurative mode of expression running to images of destruction, disease, and parasitism. Imagery of the body is especially pervasive and provides the image for both the initial frightening dependency (we are members of a diseased body politic) and the emerging solutions, which involve the separation and removal of our bodies from the corrupt, collapsing whole. This general formula leaves considerable room for individual variation, however, as we can see by comparing Ruff's and Casey's versions of the coming bad years. I will begin with Ruff, partly because he employs some of the rhetoric of experience discussed in the previous chapter and partly because he is considerably less subtle than Casey.

Ruff establishes the initial premise of a 'crisis' investing book—namely, that traditional wisdom and institutions cannot deal with the present reality, which is therefore 'out of control'—by assuming that the reader already shares it:

> You are reading this book because you are perceptive enough to sense that something is terribly wrong out there and you are one of millions of Americans with a growing sense of unease about the future. The institutions you always trusted are now giving you a queasy feeling, you are making more money but you seem to have less, and you know all is not well. I congratulate you for your insight. I share your feelings. (p. 16)

This passage illustrates the way imagery of the body ties the individual to the bad things going on 'out there'—they give us a queasy feeling—and it suggests also that the book will help to justify those feelings and allay their negative effects. In fact, Ruff tells us he is going to "scare the wits" out of us (p. 30), and later that he thinks he has done so (p. 96), but that this fear is part of the treatment. And what will happen in the future is really no worse than what is happening to us now: we are being raped by the government, inflation is chewing away at our savings, government money is a cancer that has spread through society ("The odds are, it's got you, too"—p. 47). Inflation, finally, is the Grim Reaper himself (p. 40). No wonder we have a queasy feeling! But if the stirring up of these feelings is to some degree a contrivance and performance, as Ruff says it is, then we are no longer at their mercy. The very representation and figuration of these terrors tames them.

Since traditional wisdom is not reassuring, Ruff can offer himself as a nontraditional authority. Like Elbow and Lappé, he has experienced crisis and change in his life, though, unlike them, he does not embrace it as a way of life. *How to Prosper during the Coming Bad Years* begins with an account of the author's business failure and personal bankruptcy in 1968. This is the event that changed Howard Ruff's outlook, an almost Providential humbling, on his account, that gave him "the perspective, the drive and, hopefully, the character to bring me to this point where I can speak with authority from a pretty good track record as a fore-caster and advisor" (p. 14). In short, he offers himself as a guide through the "hell" that lies ahead because he has already been through it; his own survival guarantees our own.

Ruff's account of the coming crisis and its causes is not original. There is the usual sequence of hyperinflation, controls, currency col-lapse, barter, and chaos in the marketplace. The causes are equally the usual ones: deficit financing and the welfare state, though Ruff gives an unusual amount of prominence to the distortions of urban life and 'the sexual revolution.' His answer is to reaffirm one's loyalty to one's family; to move to a small town; and to acquire bags of silver coins, a year's supply of food, and guns. Put in these terms, his "Plan" amounts to a primitive withdrawal from the complexities of modern living, the web of dependencies that knit modern American society together. To be sure, Ruff does not believe it likely that American society will ravel itself into an anarchic heap, but he does believe that a "time of testing," a Hell, lies ahead, and we will not feel secure unless we are prepared for the worst. The book in fact has a misleadingly upbeat title; its subtitle is much more indicative of its content: *A Crash Course in Personal and Financial Survival.* Over and over Ruff stresses personal as well as financial survival, and his advice is not aimed at making money but at sleeping well at night in a world on the verge of collapse: "Each of you who takes my advice will create a little pocket of stability which will stand you in good stead in hard times and will 'panic-proof' your life" (p. 16). "Panic-proofing" is almost a pun linking inner panic with financial events, and it is used repeatedly throughout the book. In general, then, Ruff's personal crisis foreshadows and exemplifies the crisis we are all about to pass through, and he advises us as one who has come through with his integrity and self-confidence intact. The self in which he has confidence is that of a Mormon *paterfamilias* (father of nine), a man who manages to sound firmly in control even when discussing his uncertainties (e.g., whether homosexuals ought to be legally discriminated against).

Above all, Ruff is not speechless; he is never troubled by inner doubts or the complexity of his subject. Indeed, he has very little use for the analytic resources of written prose. Ruff carries writing very far in the direction of colloquial monologue, such as one occasionally hears from a garrulous dentist, taxi driver, or barber. His style is notably imprecise (pronouns often don't have obvious antecedents, *thing* and *problem* abound) and peppered with the special hick expressions *heck* and *darndest*—the 'strong words' of the pious family man. "Sure, I wish we had lower rates," he says in a passage discussing interest rates. "Everybody does. But I still consider it worthwhile to use leverage to get a higher rate of return on my money. It cuts into the profit somewhat, but not a heck of a lot, really" (p. 229). (Ruff is often folksiest, by the way, when recommending something risky or dubious, as here, where the advice is to invest borrowed money.)

The writing is so imprecise, in fact, that one must more or less constantly rewrite it to get it into the intended meaning. The first chapter begins with the sentence, "Much of the American wealth is an illusion which is being secretly gnawed away and much of it will be completely wiped out in the near future." One might rewrite this to 'Much of the American wealth is illusory and is being secretly gnawed away,' since one might in fact welcome the gnawing away of an illusion (unless Ruff means this—i.e., 'you don't want to be a fat cat after all'). Similarly, he assures us that there are ways to profit from the dire crisis to come, so that we won't "slit our wrists prematurely" (p. 96). Again, this is probably just a slip, but one that might not go unremarked in even casual conversation. Ruff's use of language is so indecorously loose that it seems to be denying it is writing at all. Orthodox writing involves certain commitments to precision, consistency, and factual support; it must stand up under scrutiny, and it can be cited against you. Casual speech is not held to such standards; it enjoys a latitude to speak approximately, provocatively, and with some exaggeration, and it is to this mode that Ruff's writing constantly alludes. 'Colloquial' seems to connote 'provisional and negotiable' rather than 'plain-spoken' or 'earnest.'

Above all, Ruff cultivates the art of the cliché and the mixed metaphor. Some of these are just funny (e.g., the creeping bonds of tyranny, "Wild fluctuations indicated our security blanket was having a nervous breakdown"—p. 190), and some result from a collision of two figurative trains of association, as when 'inflation is fire' and 'inflation is whirlpool' combine to give us an "international monetary holocaust which will sweep all paper currencies down the drain and turn the world upside down" (p. 27). All of these may suggest a guileless sincerity, or a framing signal not to read in too academic a fashion, but some of them do heavier work in the book by establishing implicit control over threatening forces. Here is a rich example about responding to the sexual revolution:

> All we can really do to insulate ourselves is to create oases of sexual stability and fidelity in our homes and churches. If we don't, the next unstable generation will bleed us dry in welfare costs, crime, drug addiction, alcoholism, violence, police costs, fire costs, legal fees and gigantic government efforts to deal with these problems. If we sow the wind, we will reap the whirlwind. (p. 167)

It is hard to make much literal sense of this. How will loyalty to spouse and church insulate us from the costs of others' misbehavior? Unless, that is, 'the next generation' means 'our very own children.' The figurative bases are also blurry. How can the oasis be bled dry by costs, since the water of life is presumably not monetary? The real message of this passage, I think, is implicit: we can control our own behavior and that of our children, and in so doing, we can alter the course of history. Dedication to family life becomes the most effective form of social action after all, and not merely a retreat into a private fortress, a little pocket of stability.

Many of Ruff's metaphors of uncontrollable, malign forces convey this implicit assumption of control. For example, this is his answer to the question of why he has not tried to change the direction of society:

> The answer is that I do try, even though I have concluded that the trends are irreversibly beyond the point of no return, and by the time you've finished, you'll understand why. The juggernaut is headed for the precipice, and it doesn't matter whether we go soaring over the cliff with our foot on the accelerator (inflation), or skidding with our foot on the brake (deflation). (pp. 35–36)

Apparently a juggernaut is some sort of big car—but note the implication that we are in the driver's seat, potentially powerful even in our powerlessness.[3] In this book, there really is no need to control the juggernaut, since Ruff's advice basically is to get off, but if control seemed within reach—as it now does to him—then he might try to redirect the vehicle.[4]

Ruff is quite superior—vehement and free-swinging—when attacking current inflationary policies:

> Remember, deflation means an increase in the value of money. You can
> only increase its value by having less of it. You can only have less of it if
> politicians and money managers suddenly get the guts to reverse the
> process and kick us into a deflationary depression as a deliberate act.
> That just ain't agonna happen, although they may try cautiously for a
> while until unemployment rises, business falls off, and the resulting
> political and economic pain triggers Uncle Feelgood into cranking up
> the money machine again. (p. 57)

This seems more a well-rehearsed bit than an argument or thesis for
discussion and is, indeed, about as banal an observation, apart from the
expression, as one could come up with. But the language is playful and
almost self-parodying, not bitter, and the excesses signify that it is not
being forced down the reader's throat. Ruff tells us he was for twenty-
five years a professional actor and singer; he reports platform successes, and he occasionally shifts into question and answer. He is like a
big dog knocking things around a bit in the vigor of his play but
carrying it off by his good nature. Throughout the book, the process of
figuration is unclassically exuberant, lush, and 'uncontrolled,' but
Ruff's sense of it all as performance is almost a wink at the reader. The
figuration of doom yields a jolly vitality.

When he comes to actual advice, however, Ruff is usually quite
cagey, qualifying the more complex parts with many *ifs* and *buts*, as
when he manages to straddle the fence on whether to own your house
outright or mortgage it:

> If you can pay off the property completely, once you have decided
> you are in the proper area and that's where you want to live, then that's
> what you should do, because then you can never lose it. I learned the
> hard way that you have to be in debt to go broke, and if I can eliminate
> personal debt from my life, I feel better. In an inflationary spiral, the
> long-term borrower usually makes windfall profits, but ideally, I would
> rather not encumber my home, if I know I want to live there, all other
> things being equal. This decision—pay it off or have a big loan—is a
> matter of financial reality, temperament, and personal discretion.
> Either approach is O.K. (p. 204)

This is vintage Ruff—personal experience, emotional security, an instinct not to break too radically from conventional wisdom, and a
careful regard for the autonomy of the reader, all rolling along in a
conversational flow that is as reassuring as it is vacuous. Ruff has
experienced the worst, and if he says it's O.K. to mortgage our 'home,'
then it is, and we can even think of it as a deliberate, strategic decision.
Since many readers probably carry larger mortgages than they are

comfortable with, it's nice to be able to view this financial reality as an 'approach' to survival.

Why should anyone listen to Ruff's monologue? What qualities might account, in whatever way, for this being the best-selling financial advice book ever published?[5] The dentist, the taxi driver, and the barber, after all, have us as captive audiences seeking their services. Ruff must provide some service. On the face of it, one would expect Ruff's prophecy to be extremely depressing, since the forces that shape the reader's possibilities are beyond his control and the only security to be had is to wall oneself up in the economic equivalent of a bomb shelter. But the figurative language tells another story. The reader is back in the driver's seat, restraining his own dangerously anarchic (sexual) impulses, and 'approaching' the situation according to "financial reality, temperament, and personal discretion." Ruff's reader is not merely a survivor—he is the very epitome of the nineteenth-century rational, conscious, deliberate self.

Perhaps the most striking difference between Douglas Casey and Ruff is that where Ruff is aware of manipulating an audience, Casey is conscious of writing in a genre, specifically one that can be read for its value as fantasy—the thrills of "horror stories about events which inevitably accompany economic collapse"; his conclusions, he assures the reader, are as grim as any in the genre, though the basis and logic used in drawing them are different. When Casey turns to practical advice in his book's middle chapters, however, the figurative and hyperbolic strain is switched off in favor of much more hedging and qualification. Like Ruff, Casey offers us psychological as well as financial advantage over our neighbors "if you take the material to heart."

The problem for Casey is depression, and its cause is government. He bases his authority on both his grasp of free-market economics and his reading of history. The latter carries the discussion to a wholly different plane from Ruff's, but history, for Casey, illustrates a perpetual mythic fall. His position is the radical libertarian one that there is no such thing as good government. All governments are and have always been a drag on the energies of the governed; history is therefore the history of the depressing (stifling, lowering) of human energies by government (p. 35). Since all history is the history of depression, Casey's dating is very flexible: at times he dates the decline of the West from World War I, at other times from the Renaissance. Nor will he date the next depression: In an answer to a question of how long the next depression will last, he says, "At the risk of sounding glib, I answer, 'As long as you like.' Depressions come in all shapes and sizes"

(p. 59); he continues by describing the condition of life in the Sino-Soviet bloc as a persistent depression and the Dark Ages as the longest one.

Not only is history read through mythic lenses, it is read from a catastrophic or apocalyptic vantage point, and Casey does not articulate how it is possible to learn the lessons of history if we live in a time radically discontinuous with the past. The mythic mode of thought, however, can make this bridge readily, since the processes of decline and crisis are always at work, ever recurrent. The very words *depression* and *crisis*, like Ruff's *panic*, link the personal to collective, historical experience. Indeed, Casey's movement away from historical (referential) understanding culminates in a dystopian allegory that concludes the book. When key terms are undefined and equivocate between 'literal' and 'figurative' meanings, then it seems clear it is not 'logic' that will render us psychologically more prepared for what is upon us.

Government is the Adversary, armed with unrestricted force, driven by infinite desire, deceptive, and wholly parasitic. It is the very principle of degeneration itself (and degeneration spreads to all aspects of life, from business executives to workers, from the moral fiber to the fiber of civilization). Casey endows government with vitality even in surprising ways, as when he refers to government regulation as Pandora's box (most free-marketers speak of it as a stifling straitjacket). How can one beat this devil and all his lesser minions—greedy, dishonest, imprudent bankers; mercenary and ignorant insurance agents; self-interested stockbrokers; and the like? Officially, by buying certain stocks and Krugerrands, by transferring one's assets secretly ("privately," Casey slyly says) to a Swiss bank, by developing other sources of unreported income, and by moving to the Bahamas—in short, by a discreet form of outlawry and/or exile. Political action is not advised: "You may want to support political action that hopes to turn the situation around. But this book is dedicated to the proposition that, in the final analysis, *money* is the best way to insulate yourself from others' stupidity or malevolence" (p. 232).[6] This presumably means money of the type just described, which 'they' cannot monitor, regulate, tax, or confiscate. To acquire such money, most people will have to speculate—to gamble and win—and, rather surprisingly in a book that conjures up scenarios of bank failures, hyperinflation, collapse of real estate, and so on, Casey gives plenty of advice on speculating, as in commodities, options, gold mine stocks, and the like. As long as one knows he is doing it, he can be not only outlaw but gunslinger. Most of these techniques and attitudes are familiar to the very rich, and in relation to Casey's characterization of government they may provide the only means of individual autonomy, but what about depression? What has become of that?

Though Casey does deliver on his promise of horror stories of economic and social breakdown (several times, in fact), depression itself turns out to be a wholesome process in which the ailing body politic heals itself, a "painful period of adjustment" (p. 43), a self-cleansing (p. 49), like a drunk drying out or a heroin addict going cold turkey (p. 41). In addition, it will restore people's sense of the value of business, putting an end to the current hostile climate. Imaginatively, then, even if one does not succeed in insulating one's assets from the convulsive downward revaluation, one can at least enjoy a wholesome suffering and look forward to membership in a healthier polity to come. Imaginatively, all bets are hedged: one can run fugitive abroad or stay at home and take one's medicine—or, the nature of primary process thinking being what it is, do both.

There are nonetheless chains of imaginative consequence—'plots' of imagery—that can be traced through these books. As noted at the outset, the imagery associated with the body runs from problem to solution in both Ruff and Casey, though with differences that parallel other differences in their perspectives and values. Broadly, the problem is a hurt body. For Ruff, it is the individual body, the reader's body, that is under assault (chewed, gnawed, raped, etc.), and the solution lies in physical withdrawal from urban and suburban life, walling oneself and one's family up behind a year's supply of food and other things necessary for self-sufficiency. Finally, it is one's physical being and its means of sustenance that is preserved, not one's wealth. Indeed, Ruff, the survivor of personal bankruptcy, does not really believe in wealth; in that sense, the first sentence of the book, with its illusion of wealth being gnawed away, echoes the New Testament sense of the vulnerability and impermanence of earthly treasures.

For Casey, however, one's self and its security *are* its wealth, and wealth, he recognizes, is itself a function of complex social arrangements, such as rapid access to information, good tax advice, and the reputation for integrity of Swiss banks. Physical withdrawal into a family fortress will not protect wealth, but wealth, as the essential well-being of one's body, can be expatriated and in other ways secured and concealed. By severing one's attachments to states and nations, one's body can be set free to flourish where governments are weak. Though fastened to a dying animal, the self can sing as a golden bird, not in Byzantium, but in Tristan da Cunha.

Looking over the crisis investing books, one may be tempted to ask, Is this all a game, a form of attitudinizing and shadowboxing, a play of signifiers and stances with only the most tenuous and passing referential links to the world? Does it not all point inward, after the fashion of Hamlet's taking arms against a sea of troubles, but, in these cases, to anxieties about potency and instinctual forces? To the last question, I think we should say no, for it implies that there is a 'real' (though covert) meaning to be found in the inner, psychological realm. Such a psychological reduction yields a stability and determinacy of meaning where, arguably, there is no stability, no center, only movement, only 'approaches' to a constantly shifting target. Nor again should we regard this writing merely as covert promulgation of right-wing ideology—radical free-market evangelism—for the solutions it proposes do not require collective action. The only thing Ruff and Casey are overtly trying to sell is subscriptions to their rather expensive investment newsletters. That is, the experience their books provide is incomplete only in that it should arouse an appetite for continued mailings of more of the same.

Of course, to conclude that these works are play, even an endless play, is not to claim that they have no distinguishing features or that they are not in some way serious. They become entangled in diverse contradictions and *aporias*, but they do not come down squarely on all sides of the issues; they remain roughly within their ideological camps. And no one would accuse them of kidding, though they do consciously engage the reader in rhetorical set pieces. The game, one might say, is the rather serious one of the worst-case 'scenario' (one of Casey's favorite words), and just because it is a scenario, an exaggerated representation and figuration of nameless dreads, resentments, and desires, it is a mode in which free-swinging writing can enact feelings of mastery and control. And too, there is the special pleasure that one takes in the representation, or imitation, as Aristotle says, of 'serious' actions. These actions are not hedged round or framed by fictivity, as they are in a tragedy, but the relatively loose claims for timing and referential accuracy generally combine with the signals of conscious artifice to place the actions on a stage somewhere between the world of practical action and the theater.

II.

Although Richard Bolles's *What Color Is Your Parachute?* is a book about personal rather than collective economic crisis, its style resembles that of Ruff and Casey in its exuberant colloquialisms, vigorous figuration, and consciousness of gesture. It makes extreme and varied gestures and calls attention to them. In Bolles's case, though, self-presentation is an overt theme of the book, which is about finding a satisfying job, and hence does not separate as simply and as readily from the level of argument as it does in Ruff and Casey. Just as the self that emerges in writing is one read by others through the mediation of codes, so the self that is hired is the one that others see, one presented rather than simply revealed or disclosed. The reader must be reconciled to writing himself according to rather strictly limited codes, accepting the fact that he must make gestures and affirming that role playing as a mode of personal freedom and deliberate choice. Bolles runs himself and his reader through a dizzying gamut of roles, sometimes varying Footing within the same sentence, and through a course of fantasies both rosy and dark. What he is attempting is extremely ambitious—as he says in the preface, "If the mundane task of finding a job turns out for you to be a spiritual journey as well, I will hardly be surprised" (p. xii).

In the last sentences of this preface, Bolles launches his reader on the job hunt, promising help in finding not only a job, but "new increased self-esteem, adventure, and inner strength." From the first, then, the hunt is for inner as well as outer goods. Bolles's audience, too, is wider than one might suppose, since it includes not just the unemployed, but those never yet employed, the underemployed (which he estimates to be 80 percent of the work force), and those whose job is not yet threatened—in short, just about everybody. The jobs they aim for range from blue-collar and entry-level clerical positions to the upper reaches of management. What welds this diverse audience into a reader is the common experience of disorganization and apathy, isolation, paralysis, resentment, and low self-esteem. Bolles brings us to this point at the end of chapter 1, "A-Job-Hunting We Will Go," which reviews the first lunges at the job market and ends in abject despair. This chapter is printed with uneven lines that weave down the page suggesting the descent of a body without a parachute (along with marginal illustrations of balloonists, which run through the book). Bolles then begins to rebuild the reader's sense of himself as an agent shaping his own destiny through deliberate choice and plan.

His method is to move rapidly between the poles of basic oppositions, such as self-reliance/dependence on external aid: self-determination/meeting the expectations of others; expertise/common sense; predictability/randomness of the hiring process; and method and order/inner illumination. So although Bolles strongly advocates self-reliance and avoidance of professional services, he advises you to pay for help if you have not taken yourself in hand; to seek the aid of spouse, friends, and other job-seekers while maintaining control of your own search; and even to get therapy in some cases. On this last point, he touches the paradox of advising someone to be self-reliant. Realizing that his own book is built on just this paradox, Bolles becomes self-consciously chatty. One criterion for evaluating therapists, he says, is this: "Do they assiduously avoid giving you advice? Hope so. (You need someone living their life out through you like you need a hole in the head.) Beware of the therapist who gives lots and lots of advice. (Like this!) On the other hand, give them three stars if they come across as clarifiers, primarily" (p. 306). He insists on an orderly, structured process of job-hunting, with stages and exercises to be done along the way, and gives many lists and tables of facts and statistics, charts, reference works, inspirational self-help books on risk taking and dressing for success—all with the advice not to read any of them, unless the reader feels an immediate, urgent need. These displays of knowledge also occasion a little parenthetical by-play, as when Bolles cites a table on the effectiveness of various methods of job-hunting prepared by the U.S. Bureau of the Census with the comment, "(you do like tables, don't you?)" (p. 36). The answer seems to be that we do and we don't: the tables give a sense of mastery through knowledge even though they are inessential to the deeper changes of attitude Bolles is urging. The end of the main text seems to decisively subordinate order to attitude: "I repeat: beyond all mechanics of the job-hunt, all techniques, and all 'secrets': what you believe will happen, helps to determine what does happen" (p. 196), but then follow over one hundred pages of further exercises, lists, charts, and advice for special circumstances.

This doubleness, this alternating movement between inner and outer resources, structure and inspiration, knowledge and attitude, extends throughout the book on all levels. In the figurative language, for example, we are urged to identify our basic skills: "building blocks, which will form the backbone of your future job description" (p. 87), metaphors consistently in favor of order and structure, if mixed. But thirteen pages later we are warned against "getting locked in, in your thinking, to just one route to go in the future"—order must not lead to rigidity! The Footings with the reader, too, are extremely variable, ranging from solidary sympathy to confrontive prodding, from 'we' to 'you.'

It would be mistaken, I think, to evaluate all of this according to canons of consistency appropriate to a philosophical system or even a logical argument, for Bolles is not trying to persuade by evidence and proof, and in studying what he does rely on, I will ignore the outer, factual discussion to concentrate on the movements of fantasy, Footing, and gesture.

Overall, Bolles takes the reader from the nadir of despair at the end of chapter 1 through some baiting of experts and the system to the point at the end of the book where the reader has no valid excuses left for not finding a job. Bolles begins by assuring the reader that his plight is not his fault, and that he is not alone in it. After having read the book (and done the exercises), if the reader still does not have an acceptable job, it is his own fault: he is engaging in self-defeating behavior, and Bolles scolds him, mocking the foolish sentences he says to himself in a fashion reminiscent of Harper and Ellis. The figurative language follows this general progression, beginning with the self threatened by a "stormy sea of change" (p. 46) and subject to feelings that "surface" (p. 82), and then moving broadly toward hard images of concentrating one's energies like a rifle (p. 127), focusing down (repeatedly), and honing to a fine point (p. 187). But the movement along the way is a kind of tacking between repeated enactments of scenes of success and occasional reminders of failure. These 'you can do it' build-ups are the most obvious cases of wish-fulfilling fantasies, but there are somewhat more subtle ones in Bolles's accounts of what it all is like from the employer's point of view (e.g., pp. 13, 167–170) and in his descriptions of sitting down with high-level executives to explain to them how you can solve their problems for them. These are not fantasies that seriously undercut the impulse toward action, however, for, given Bolles's project of enhancing the reader's self-esteem, it becomes useful to think of oneself as the sort of person who might do such a thing—that such things are within one's power. This is all very nearly explicit in the section on dreams and visions of the future, where the reader is urged not to "foreclose your future prematurely" (p. 96) and is told that he can quite possibly be the president of a particular enterprise "*if your whole heart is in your dream.*" Extracted from its context for citation, this all sounds like the most elementary sort of 'positive thinking.' To see what makes it credible, or at least credible enough to be enjoyable, we must examine Bolles's play of Footings with the reader.

As noted earlier, Bolles is rhetorically and stylistically quite self-conscious, and indeed this note is struck in the preface, where he calls attention to his colloquial style (which made his English teachers "semi-suicidal"), his dislike of jargon, and his light-hearted tone. He is not, he says, the originator of these ideas, just a popularizer (though his endorsement of them is based on much interviewing and study of successful job-hunters). In short, Bolles will not lock himself in to any conventional stuffy poses, and this freedom is something he reenacts throughout the book, with parenthetical inserts, colloquialisms, and self-deprecating irony, as in this early passage:

> You will note that some of these statistics are not, ahem, *current*—to put it gently. That's because the most recent study about this-or-that part of the numbers game was done some yeas ago, and no-one has thought to repeat that study since that time. But, *hey*, we're lucky to be able to refer to *any* study—even one that was some years back. And besides—believe me—the numbers game hasn't changed that much, since the studies cited. So, on with our exciting story. (p. 17)

There is a rapid movement of the pronouns here: "you" makes a potentially critical observation (phrased by Bolles "gently" against himself) and then is called back to a sense of perspective with the *hey*, and the "we" of reader and writer are reunited to travel further down our exciting path. Bolles moves very rapidly and freely from addressing the reader to sharing his perspective in a solidary "we." Here is another characteristic passage:

> The secret of success for all job-hunters—employed or unemployed—is (to use my rich skills at overkill): keeping at it. Devoting every hour you can to the task. Having said that, however, we [!] can press on to our next truth about job-hunting or career-changing. Namely: it is very difficult to mount a sustained effort when you are job-hunting all by yourself. Motivation flags, energies get diluted, and frequently—to use a common expression—we run out of gas. (p. 57)

The 'common expression' remark highlights the relatively noncolloquial prose here: the effect is similar to Dale Carnegie's bringing the discussion back down to earth, here executed self-consciously. (Note, by the way, the crest-and-trough alternation of pressing on and running out of gas.)

As is evident from the passages cited so far, Bolles assiduously cultivates solidarity with the reader. In other places, he knows the reader's feelings (as, e.g., of shyness, p. 107, and of resistance to doing exercises, p. 82). He even scripts the reader's responses to his advice, in the fashion of the user-friendly printer manual cited in my chapter 1, as in this summarizing comment on the labor of studying the job market, printed with a box around it: "Phew! Lots of work, But the rewards: Wow" (p. 13). Bolles adopts a kind of eclectic pluralism of values ("If you are not religous, work on what belief system you do have: Karma, gratitude to the Universe, or whatever," p. 196; this is a characteristic use of *whatever*). The only common values he assumes are that you want to treat people as persons (p. 158) and that you want to be truly helpful to people (p. 189), though he does tease the reader a bit on the subject of remuneration (having exhorted him earlier): "Of course, if you don't need that extra money—or you couldn't care less that the person below you makes more than you do—great! But just in case you do, I thought I'd mention it" (p. 188).

The *of course* is one of a rich array of tags that Bolles uses heavily (also *granted, to be sure, admittedly, well*) to engage in conversational give-and-take, or sparring, with the reader, again very much in the Carnegie vein. He uses question and answer heavily, and the questions often voice resistance or objections to his generalizations. This easy sparring can modulate into somewhat stiffer finger-wagging ("I hate to tell you this, but . . . ," p. 70; "Well, yes, we're going to have to talk about money, at this point," p. 111), and sometimes into direct, superior confrontation:

> And realize that trying to get the job-hunt over with, just as fast as possible, taking short cuts wherever you can, giving the whole thing as little of your time and intelligence as you can get away with, is going to cost you money. Over the next decade or two, you can deprive yourself and your loved ones of many thousands of dollars, literally—due to your shoddy job-hunt. Not to mention your own misery, at ending up—as so many do—in a miserable excuse for a job, where you are undervalued, underused and ultimately burnt-out. (p. 65)

Directly offsetting this confrontive streak is the self-conscious, self-deprecatory humor, many examples of which we have already seen. Occasionally Bolles is even coy, as when he refers to another employment book he coauthored with John Crystal as written by Crystal and friend, and later by Crystal and 'a ghost' (p. 113). (There is reason to be coy—this book is cited at least a dozen times, and, though Bolles is eager for the reader to promote himself, he apparently is a little embarrassed by too much feathering of his own nest.) In his footings with the reader, Bolles runs the gamut from confrontive, superior straight shooting to playful indirect teasing, from sympathetic validation of the reader's bad feelings to mockery and scolding of the reader's stupid thoughts and behavior. The overall effect is of a restless, protean energy—role playing as freedom—that can deal with all resistance, discouragements, and follies and press on to success, that can make the jobhunt "our exciting story."

It would be particularly narrow-minded to conclude this discussion of *What Color Is Your Parachute?* and especially its 'imagery' without mention of the profuse etchings and engravings, generally of a turn-of-the-century cast, that illustrate the book. And indeed, these illustrations supply one further thread complexly related to the others in the text, providing sometimes a reinforcement, sometimes a boundary, and sometimes a displacement of other meanings. Here I will illustrate that complexity in relation to the central trope of the book—the metaphor of its process/method as parachute. There is only one textual mention of the parachute and its color (in addition to the title, that is): "I hate to tell you this, but the time to figure out where your parachute is, what color it is, and to strap it on, is *now*—and not when the vocational airplane that you are presently in is on fire and diving toward the ground" (p. 70). While on the balance, movement is affirmed in the book (and indeed, is a metaphor for the process of reading it—'on with our exciting story'), it is also not without its terrors, and this passage touches on some of them. Dangling from a parachute, one has at best very limited control of one's direction. It is true that the notion of picking a color for your parachute introduces an element of choice beyond that necessary for simple survival, but this image of the reader's plight is still a dire one. Nowhere in the book, however, is anyone depicted strapped into the harness of a parachute! There are some parachute-like things with baskets containing two or more people (some even wearing hats), and quite a number of baskets suspended from balloons, probably hot-air balloons. (The plunge in the first chapter follows an illustration of a blow-out in one such balloon.) The balloons, of course, are under the control of the riders (though one is depicted with its basket cum rider snared in a tree)—a much gentler and less strenuous mode of flying than a flaming plane. The illustrations undo what the text says, softening, diffusing, and displacing Bolles's image of the awful day to come into a multitude of less-frightening alternatives. These illustrations do not undercut or make light of the reader's feelings, or of Bolles's representations of them; rather, they add one more perspective, or set of perspectives, and hence constitute yet another level of self-commentary in the text. There is no simple irony of reversal, no true attitude toward the real situation. Bolles, and the reader, are everywhere and nowhere in this book, free of determinate specification, moving back and forth, but generally 'onward.'

At this point, the classical and purist-minded reader may feel that his allegiance to the orthodoxies of commitment and sober chasteness of figuration is well founded. Do we not simply have before us sloppily written, conceptually feeble hackwork full of easy, seductive claims to be the reader's buddy that are to be read only for their thrills, their laughs and winks, their righteous indignations, their dreams of wealth and executive success, and thrown away? *These* as windows into the very nature of writing, the play of representation, gesture, and figuration? If these, then anything—and all bases for evaluation are dissolved.

On the other hand, the advocates of practical writing may well feel that I have utterly lost sight of the occasion, the purpose, and the audience of these books, treating them as some odd sort of literary text-for-itself, discussing patterns of figurative language as if they were poems and complexities of self-referring gestures as if these books were display texts on the order of *Tristram Shandy*, when in fact all of these features can only be understood as means of persuasion, specifically means of establishing a familiar and effective *ethos*, which is historically the direct descendent of Dale Carnegie's "brash and breezy" style. Doesn't Bolles thumb his nose at his English teachers in an entirely conventional way? There is really nothing innovative or remarkable about this writing, and it is preposterous to claim that these writers are struggling with the very nature of writing itself and against its limits.

One source of these misunderstandings, I think, is an ambiguity in the way we use the term *work*. In discussing how figuration and gesture work in these texts, I mean simply how they manifest themselves, how various traits and features of the texts can be understood in terms of the forces said to be inherent in writing as such. And indeed, an indefinitely large set of texts could be interrogated in this fashion. In fact, one of the purposes of this analysis is to test the generality of such a characterization of writing. If it could not be applied to these books, then it would be covertly normative. But to speak of working in a text tends to suggest that the text "works"—i.e., that it functions effectively, triggers a valuable experience in the reader, and hence is good writing, worthy of rereading, study, or emulation. According to most canons of good writing, these texts do not work remarkably well, but it is not the task of this book to establish criteria for evaluating the interactions established in texts. I do not intend this analysis to argue that the books examined in this chapter should be upwardly evaluated as art.

Neither do I think they should be downwardly evaluated as non-art, however, in the way that the practical writers might intend, insofar as they regard some sorts of writing as not touched by the forces that so animate the writing of high culture, as being produced on some assembly-line of politico-psycho-babble. In the preface to his new book, Howard Ruff likens his experience of writing to "giving birth to a litter of hippos—before Lamaze," an analogy clearly intended to illuminate

his labor in writing, not its fruit. It is a typical Ruffian gesture—
exaggerated, self-deprecating, naive, possibly disingenuous—but it
does remind us that the appearance of fluency and ease, the untroubled, energetic monologue, may well be as much a work of shaping, a
struggle with and against the medium of words, as any other writing.

VI

WHO READS?

> I must seek out this reader (must "cruise"
> him) *without knowing where he is*. A site of
> bliss is then created. It is not the reader's
> 'person' that is necessary to me, it is this
> site: the possibility of a dialectics of desire,
> or an *unpredictability* of bliss: the bets are
> not placed, there can still be a game.

> Roland Barthes

In a much-cited passage in the *Phaedrus* (275e), Socrates puts the case
against writing as defective or orphaned in lacking the guiding presence of its author:

> And once a thing is put in writing, the composition, whatever it may be,
> drifts all over the place, getting into the hands not only of those who
> understand it, but equally of those who have no business with it; it
> doesn't know how to address the right people, and not address the
> wrong. And when it is ill-treated and unfairly abused it always needs its
> parent to come to its help, being unable to defend or help itself.

As Jacques Derrida suggests in his commentary in *Dissemination*,[1]
a great deal of intellectual energy has been expended over the years,
and recently, to constrain the drift and abuse of the orphan text.
Traditional rhetoric, with its advice to 'consider the audience,' offers
itself as the art of addressing the right people—of building in, that is,
the father's guidance. In some sense, also, doctrines of authorial intention attempt to subordinate the will of the reader to the will of the
father. Even more energy has been expended recently on 'the people,'
however, toward characterizing the kinds of readers, right and wrong,
a book might have, and the right ways that a good reader should read.

In order to clarify the concept of the Reader as a textual entity and
distinguish it from audience or readership, we introduced a difference
of textual Reader/real reader. In this, we have simply concurred with a

move made over and over in recent linguistic, semiotic, psycholinguistic, and literary theories of reading, a move I will call splitting the reader. It is, at least from one angle, an uneven division. The Reader, though abstract, is the party that receives most analysis—he is the public party, in or implied by the text, but the reader is of course the one who makes everything happen—his experience is what matters, and the Reader is only of interest as shaping or conditioning the real reader's experience. Thus on the one side something public, discussible, abstract; on the other, something variable, inaccessible, real. The gulf is wide and suggests a pathos of incomprehensibility, yet we will not let the obscure fellow go his mysterious way, for we believe the game of writing is finally being played out with him. All the Readers in the world are only the means of reaching and engaging him. But is he there, or what is the he that is there? How many different ways of reading are there? Is there any privileged reader of an advice book, any way of reading that is the best? And—a more difficult point—can it be *said* what that way, that reading, is? We will have to begin by examining the reader's double—the one that is described and theorized about, the Reader.

Most contemporary theorists of reading have introduced one or more abstract entities called variously the ideal, implied, model, or intended reader (hereafter, Reader) who is in some way presupposed or embedded in the text and in relation to whom the relative success or failure of a reading of a text can be measured. A fairly simple version of this model has been developed and employed by Charles J. Fillmore in an extended reading project at the University of California at Berkeley.[2] Fillmore defines the ideal reader of a text as one who possesses the necessary background information and interpretive skills to get the intended meaning of the text without difficulty, but who does not, by the way, have so much knowledge as not to be informed by a text attempting to inform him. A particular reading experience is successful when the reader matches the Reader in these respects; the experience can fail either because the text has an impossible or very unlikely Reader (it is not written, Fillmore says, "for anybody") or because the reader does not possess the right background knowledge (has too little or too much) or is not equipped with the requisite integrative and interpretive skills. Fillmore clearly recognizes most of the major limitations of this approach: it is concerned with meaning and comprehension of the kind measured by multiple-choice reading-comprehension tests (hence the interpretation the reader is to construct is not to be novel, interesting, or arguable), and the construction of the Reader depends on there being a single, determinable, correct interpretation. That is, the Reader is 'ideal' relative to an interpretation. One limitation Fillmore does not mention is that reader (and Reader) are regarded as 'language processors' with no particular attributes of human subjectivity.

The attributes of subjectivity are more in evidence in the tradition of literary theorizing extending from Wayne Booth and Walker Gibson through Walter J. Ong, Wolfgang Iser, Walter Slatoff, and Umberto Eco to the recent work of Peter Rabinowitz, all of whom speak of the reader playing a role, roughly the role of the Reader, and regard the attempt to do this as an ethical obligation of the 'good' reader. Thus the split reader is reunited by an effort of the actual reader, one which, moreover, he may choose not to make. This ethical obligation also binds the writer, it should be noted: since the Reader is based on a determinable interpretation, the writer is obliged to intend such an interpretation, so that a variety of bad faith is possible on either end. Not all texts may yield such an interpretation, of course, but the reader is obliged, in this analysis, to read as if each text does.[3] Plainly, what is being described here is an orthodoxy binding the reader exactly parallel to the orthodoxy of commitment binding the writer discussed in the previous chapter. These theorists agree that readers become Readers not by a simple process of matching but by a deliberate endeavor. About the nature of this endeavor and the obligation of the reader, however, they differ in significant ways.

This difference turns on the ambiguity involved in the phrase 'play a role.' Ong takes the extreme position in "The Writer's Audience Is Always a Fiction" that this role playing constitutes a fictionalizing of the reader—a pretending to be someone who knows one is not. Rabinowitz, however, says that the reader tries to *become* the Reader as much as possible. This may, for example, require going to the library to get the background information one in fact lacks (e.g., information about Hemingway's political beliefs); it also requires sharing the assumptions operative in the work. 'Becoming the Reader' is not merely Ong's notion of fictionalizing cast in phenomenological garb, however, for Rabinowitz goes on to discuss cases of pretense, as when one does not remedy one's lack of background knowledge or is unable to adopt the assumptions of the work because they "fundamentally contradict our normal way of thinking" (p. 132). To read on, in such a case, is to pretend to "join the authorial audience" (i.e., be the Reader), and, to the extent that one is pretending, "we are that much less likely to receive the work's intended effect." That is indeed a severe standard of the morality of reading—one against which, I suspect, we must all be judged fallen. I am sure I myself sin daily against the background information criterion, and my case is worse because of my relative indifference toward it. Am I really risking much of the intended effect if I don't look up a piece of background knowledge, waiting patiently instead for some contextual clues as to its probable import? When John Trimble tells me to try writing a "salty denunciation after the model of Mark Twain or H. L. Mencken,"—how much exactly do I have to know to receive the intended effect? More importantly, as Eco notes, texts *create* the competence of the Reader; insofar as a Reader knowing such things, holding such attitudes, and forming such expectations is represented, it is an idealization and projection of an ideal other.

The latter criterion is even less obvious, for I am less clear about what contradicts my "normal way of thinking." Does this refer to ideology, inference from 'common-sense' knowledge and expectations, or the Law of the Excluded Middle? Lurking in the shadows is the notorious problem of belief, which always seems to be posed in relation to reading *Paradise Lost*: do I have to hold all the tenets of Milton's theology to receive the intended effect of the work? I think I can *perceive* it without holding those beliefs, and is that not in some sense to *receive* it? So also Roland Barthes on the effect of unpalatable ideologies in a text:

> I pass lightly through the reactionary darkness. For example, in Zola's *Fécondité*, the ideology is flagrant, especially sticky: naturism, family- ism, colonialism; *nonetheless* I continue reading the book. Is such distor- tion commonplace? Rather, one might be astounded by the housewifely skill with which the subject is meted out, dividing its reading, resisting the contagion of judgment, the metonymy of contentment: can it be that pleasure makes us *objective*?[4]

And similarly, if we shift the question from special knowledge, atti- tudes, and values to that of *interest*: I can perceive the effect of a weight-reduction book without being fat (though I am unlikely to adopt its advice), or read *Our Bodies, Ourselves* responsibly without being a woman. I can't imagine how anyone could prove otherwise. Indeed, it is just through such reading that books may be said to enlarge our experience. To be sure, I suppose the effect on me will differ from the effect on some women—the shock and pleasure of recognition, for example, might be less—but if I have read other books or otherwise attended to women's experience, perhaps the difference is not too great.

Although it is not much discussed in literary theory, interest is a factor not only in the reading of advice (and other persuasive writing). The one exception in literary theory is the work of Harold Bloom, who has waged a sustained, virtually single-handed campaign against the notion that the reader of literature is disinterested, 'good,' submissive to the text.[5] One might also mention in this connection Judith Fetterley's *The Resisting Reader*, where it is argued that women readers can and should read classic works of American fiction without assenting to the role of the Reader—resisting it, rather.[6] For me to read Fetterley's book is to learn to read as woman, and not just any woman, but one who is suspicious of the role intended for her by the writer. We touch here on the question of the innocent reader. It is not clear to me that there are no innocent readers, but it does seem questionable whether one should privilege the experience of an innocent, assuming he could be sure he had found one.

A rather different handling of the split reader is advocated by Walter Slatoff in his early work on reader response, *With Respect to Readers* (1970). In fact, Slatoff objects to this absolute dichotomy between a Reader and a real, particular reading self, which implies that the individual reader should contribute nothing of his personal identity when he reads, that the meaning he makes is not meaning-for-him. Slatoff describes a reading self that is somewhere between his "fully defined personal self" and the universal, impersonal reader. Most readers, "except for the most naive," he says, "learn, that is, to set aside many of the particular conditions, concerns, and idiosyncrasies which help to define them in everyday affairs, but they still retain the intellectual and emotional experience and structures, and the temperaments and values, of particular individuals and respond largely in accord with that make-up."[7] Slatoff illustrates from his own case, which involves his Jewishness causing resentment at Hemingway's treatment of a Jewish character, and concludes, "This reading self tends to overreact to certain kinds of moral and psychological situations—to authority questions and pain, for example—much as I do in life, but also recognises this tendency and resists and watches it, but only up to a point" (p. 55). This is all sanity and moderation, and seems to derive those qualities by shifting from a normative to a descriptive account of how one engages a text. But if it's moderate, it's also normative, or at least a norm can be inferred: reading in this mixed way is not only what all but the most naive readers do but what they should do—mixing, consciously, their own assumptions and biases with those of the text and not, finally, trying to bracket them away or judge themselves guilty of pretense or abuse of the text. But it is not clear, on the other hand, why this mode of consciously monitored mixing should be more valued than another mode, or whether it is more than an uneasy compromise between total reception and total repudiation, a kind of net result of responses. Also, the term "fully defined personal self" invites some attention. Slatoff describes himself as a forty-eight-year-old, married, Jewish, American professor of English with two sons, and, while such people may have what they hold to be fully defined personal selves, it is not clear that all readers do, or want to, much less experience it as a steady pressure on their reading. If we want to think of successful, harmonious reading as the congruence of Reader and reader, then we should at least recognize that it is not congruence between a construct (a scripted role) and a given of experience, but between one construct and another. What is distressing about the normative bias is the implication that other real readers aren't really reading. What is clear is that Slatoff has moved the discussion from the purely cognitive concerns of generating the right inferences from a text to responses of attitude and evaluation, liking and discomfort—responses closer to the interpersonal dimension of writing.

With Walker Gibson, we come to a theorist who directly discusses interaction in writing and who is considerably less burdened by conscience and obligation than Slatoff, partly, perhaps, because he discusses responses to popular writing as well as great works of literature. The failure that Gibson focuses on in *Tough, Sweet, and Stuffy* (1966) results not from discrepant beliefs and attitudes but from dislike of the way the Writer treats the Reader. Beliefs and attitudes are not a problem for him first because Gibson says he effectively shares them with the writers he objects to and second, because he can adopt the orientation of a Hindu or a Hottentot if the writer is sufficiently engaging. He forsakes his role of the cooperative Reader and turns hostile, Gibson says, when an unsupportable gap opens between the Reader he is called upon to enact and his Own True Self (or Real-Life Self). His capitalization suggests an uneasy awareness of having had recourse to a most problematic concept. Suppose one does find the role of the Reader annoying or distasteful. Might not the reason for this range over many kinds of sources—a perception of indecorum, for example, as well as a sense of inner violation? We are, after all, explicitly taught that there are rules about how to behave in prose. In any case, Gibson's examples of dislikable styles, which he terms Tough (pushes the reader around—superior and solidary), Sweet (intrusively chummy), and Stuffy (ignores the reader), are really violations of how we would like to be treated by others, not violations of who we are.

Gibson's description of failure is one entirely in the interpersonal dimension, not in the domain of content and comprehension. In fact, Gibson does not fail to realize the Reader's role, and his discussion makes it clear that a kind of dialectical doubleness is involved in repudiating it. Discussing one such failed paragraph, he says, "I was aware, on the one hand, of the person I was supposed to be (one who knows what 'true meanings' are, for instance). But I was also aware, much too aware, that I was *not* that person, and more important, didn't want to pretend to be" (p. 17). He explicates his sense of discrepancy by responding to the passage (an article from the *Saturday Review* called "Unrequired Reading") in square brackets:

> The title of this essay may strike you as a typographical error. [Why, no, as a matter of fact that never occurred to me.] You may be saying to yourself that the writer really means required reading. [Don't be silly. I would be more surprised to see a title so trite. In fact your title embodies just the sort of cute phrase I have learned to expect from this middle-brow magazine.] (p. 22)

Such a 'dialogue' seems to me a great exaggeration of the sort of response, including discomfort, that we may have as we read. Gibson's annotations are written from a perspective of rigorous, reflective hostility, but a great number of our responses to the way we are treated are less determinate, and indeed, Gibson's method of annotation fails to capture the experience of being written on by a text—of having scraps of selves evoked that we didn't realize were alive in us, which we may on reflection sort out as views we may not hold, have serious reservations about, or try very hard to dissociate ourselves from. Or perhaps we may just ignore them and read on. Bridling at the Reader's role is only one possible point, and an extreme one, on a scale from relative assent and immersion to dissent and withdrawal. We may often be more provisional and wishy-washy in our assents and dissents than Gibson seems to think. More than that, one of the pleasures of reading is to play roles (e.g., of passive sheep led around by a strong shepherd, or lonely, hurt selves aching for the balm of understanding and approval) that we might be hesitant to play in a face-to-face interaction. The One True Self seems to be a limiting concept—'that way I will not go'—and ignores the possibility of plural and alternative selves intersecting in particular readers. Iser quotes Husserl on the self as plurality and potentiality: "We might say that the ego as ego continually develops itself through its original decisions, and at any given time is a pole of multifarious and actual determinations, and a pole of an habitual, radiating system of realizable potentials for positive and negative attitudes."[8] For example, I can perceive Dr. Spock as making equalizing and solidary gestures toward me, and also perceive them as gestures, the good manners of the Back-Bay mandarin who is utterly and unshakably sure of himself and his counsel, and I can be annoyed at that or gratified by the good manners, depending on how hard I am being on myself and others this Tuesday. Also, there are instances when one may reasonably conclude that she is not expected to play the role of the Reader, that an adequate reader might only partly fill the bill of particulars and would be allowed to enjoy the pretense of a role she might grow into. Is there not a possible flattery involved in John Trimble's allusions to the intellectual interests and concerns of his freshman readers? And again, I can be flattered or annoyed. In reading, nothing is forcing a decision on these points. Gibson is right, I think, in stressing the subjectivity of interpersonal response ("hearing voices" is his image), but wrong in focusing just on the extreme responses of irritation, annoyance, and breaking off the interaction. Put the other way around, Gibson seems to valorize a particular experience of reading—total immersion and possession by the text—in which the writtenness of writing is temporarily forgotten, and to hold that congruence with his personal self is a necessary condition of such immersion.

In a curious way, almost all literary discussions of readers tend to be normative and pedagogical in orientation, concerned with defining the ideal role and with bringing actual readers up to standard. Good, conscientious reading is work, and one might imagine these discussions arousing a certain amount of anxiety in readers as to whether they are reading in the right way, such anxiety leading, perhaps, to an effort to make themselves into the right sort of reader. Gibson's discussion often carries us in a different direction, however, toward an overly smart, or smarty-pants, reader. In part this is so because he often deals with texts from popular (or, as he says, middlebrow) culture; indeed, his sketches of the willful reader bring us close to the problematics of advice writing, which as surely occupies this cultural space as any of Gibson's magazine pieces or advertisements.

The interest in pop culture and in sophisticated or willful responses to it has been further developed by Umberto Eco in his *The Role of the Reader*, where it appears as the distinction between open and closed texts. Closed texts are those that appear to be written for a particular, concrete audience, to meet their needs and interests exactly, and hence to be used up and exhaustively experienced by their intended users. Eco's examples are drawn from the comic pages ("Superman") and detective and spy novels. Almost paradoxically, Eco argues, a consequence of this extreme determination of audience and response is that the reader is not engaged in a constructive, meaning-building endeavor of any complexity, and hence closed texts are susceptible of being read in any number of ways, of being used in any number of ways they do not anticipate. Thus they can be taken as a stimulus, treated as psychological or cultural symptom, example of prevailing ideology, archetypal fantasy, and so on. Open texts, however, resist such 'uses' because they entangle readers in a complexity in which all interpretations reinforce each other and lead to the same place. Just because one would not imagine a determinate audience, purpose, or set of responses for them, they must fashion a particular reader for themselves; the reader is as it were most at their mercy, must give himself over most obediently to evoking the complexity and plurality of their unique meanings. (Eco's example is Joyce's *Ulysses*.)

It does not seem to matter very much whether we regard the open/closed distinction as one of texts or one of modes of reading; the latter interpretation avoids the implication of essence and seems advisable inasmuch as texts do not come with 'open' or 'closed' printed beneath their titles. We could choose to read a text as open or closed with relative degrees of success or insight depending on the text. Reading can easily become normative in this framework, since one should presumably not read an open work as if it were closed (or vice versa). Eco actually mentions a third type of reading, which is the most arbitrary and willful. This involves taking the text "as an uncommitted stimulus for a personal hallucinatory experience, cutting out levels of meaning, placing upon the expression 'aberrant' codes. As Borges once suggested, why not read the *Odyssey* as written after the *Aeneid* or the *Imitation of Christ* as written by Céline?"[9] Questions have been raised about the sharpness and applicability of the open/closed dichotomy; for our purposes, the issue is whether advice books (or some advice books but not others) should be read as closed texts, which is to say, as encoding a Reader who is less sophisticated than the actual one (who may be a 'smart semiotician' or rhetorician). The actual reader, then, would be less immersed or engrossed, or written on by the text, than the hypothetical reader who receives and exhausts its effects, the completely unreflective automaton. Are we not, dear readers, very much in this position in relation to the many advice books we have looked at, the position roughly of Eco and his advanced students at various universities reading the James Bond "007" saga, or "Superman" comics? When we trace the workings of figuration in crisis books, for example, or Elbow's struggles with writing as aggression, or Harper and Ellis's combats with the reader, are we not using those books in a willful way, reflecting a complex attitude not intended by the writer? The very self-evidentness of the answer ought to give us pause. All of these tracings were at least not hallucinated; they develop themes and features raised in the text. The burden of proof, it seems to me, ought to be on those who would rule out a particular response as clearly not one a proper reader of the book would have. Eco himself raises a complexity in all of this: since reading Bond/Fleming, for example, in the context of the entire oeuvre and with a view towards the underlying ideology does yield some insight, as does reading "Superman" in relation to themes of myth and temporality, these 'smart' insights must be in some sense in the text; specifically, the Reader must be the smart one, not the naive one who reads them, e.g., as a child might (pp. 33, 122). And similarly with the various winks and excesses and self-commentaries that abound in advice writing—how can the reader be sure he is supposed to be dumber than he actually is? In any case, dumbness, in Eco's view, is not a virtue; the smart reading encompasses the dumb one—it receives the intended effect of the work as well as the dumb one does and in addition, sees more.

Common-sense seems to support Eco's notion that *some* readings are quite arbitrary and willful (and perhaps some just a little bit that way, and so on). But what is the theoretical basis for this distinction? Might it be possible to feel that someone is being arbitrary and willful without being able to say exactly what a perfectly unarbitrary and submissive reading would be? I think so—such things are not uncommon in daily life. Further, if we could specify a perfect reader and reading, we would seem to close the text—a conclusion that Eco would find un-appealing in the case of the *Odyssey*.

A leading feature of advice writing, we have seen, is that it typically characterizes its readers not just by implication or presupposition but by scripting him as well. Perhaps we should look a little more closely at the Reader actually inscribed in the book. For example, the passage cited above from Gibson (an example of the excessively Sweet voice) does inscribe a Reader ("You may be saying to yourself"), though the Stuffy texts never do, and the Tough texts only imply a Reader. Literary theorists reflecting on the inscribed Reader (IR) have noted that the IR is a part of the text, not the implied ideal receiver of it (i.e., the Reader), so that the IR is one of the things the Reader takes into account in reading. W. Daniel Wilson suggests that in fiction, as a rule, an IR is usually a negative foil in the work, a reader whose responses are less adequate than the Reader's should be, sometimes even an ironic counterpointing of them.[10] This line of thought points in the direction of a subtle slipperiness in the inscribing of Readers, a slip-periness that springs ultimately from the force of representation. An IR is a representation of a Reader—not us, but a sign of us, a gesture toward us that is always slightly deflected or deferred. The more vivid or 'immediate' the inscription (the extreme perhaps being the Whew!

of Bolles and the printer manual), the clearer it is that the reader's role is play: these inscriptions do not bear down on the reader, insisting on his assent; rather, they displace him with a foil, a representative, a mask that the reader may wear or not.[11] From this perspective, we could object to the passage Gibson annotates on the grounds of triviality and delay in getting to the point, or in establishing any interesting relation with the Reader, but not for inaccurately representing the real reader's actual responses.

It is now possible to explain why the personalization of advice is problematic, why it is not simply the abandonment of 'high' impersonality and a return to the common ground of real persons reading and writing. To represent oneself writing, or one's reader reading, is to make a self-reflexive motion, to point to the interaction rather than simply letting it happen. If inscribing the Reader is not the establishing of a foil but a lunge at capturing the reader, it is one that gives itself away; the reader always eludes the grasp and is more wary. When self-help advice books stipulate their own special morality of reading—that the reader read carefully and consecutively, reread, and do the exercises—it becomes an exhortation to the Reader. Leviathan will not be caught in that net, as they very well know.

It seems that specifying the reader, whether in the text or outside it, by the critic, involves a kind of doubling activity: we infer a Reader, and then infer a reader who would exist in some complex relation to this Reader but who, ideally, would enact the role of the Reader in an untroubled and unconscious fashion. And, beyond that, we can project a smart reader reading with one eye on the naive reader's response but with the other looking behind and around it, and finally (is it really finally?) a smarty-pants reader reading as if he were someone inappropriate reading the book, producing responses he believes the book most likely did not intend.

It thus appears from this discussion that the Reader/reader distinction (polarized and prejudicial as it is) is caught in the forces of writing. We have been silently assuming that the general principle "Writing writes the reader" means "Writing writes the Reader," and hence assuming the existence of real empirical/historical readers out there who come to texts and go away from them—as common-sense a notion as the audience going into and coming out of a theater. But the real reader proves to be an elusive creature once we try to specify him in terms of knowledge, attitudes, and interests. We can of course imagine alternative kinds of readers: fat/slender readers of weight-reduction books, freshmen/professors reading composition guides, and so on. But are those real readers? It is far from certain that they are anything more than an abstraction or projection, stereotypes, pieces of writing if there ever were. One can imagine a male editor reading as a teacher would read as a teenage girl would read a textbook on nutrition. People actually do this sort of thing, some of them for a living, but in doing so, they do not get down to earth, they do not get out there, or, if they do, it is a codified earth, a written 'out there' that they are writing.

Clearly, we have arrived at an altitude where the special qualities of advice merge with other kinds of writing. In a sense, the foregrounding of the interpersonal so characteristic of advice changes nothing, does not escape from the anonymity and impersonality of writing and reading. We may or may not believe in an author behind the text, originating it and providing an ultimate referent for *I*, or personally responsible for the advice she gives. But we do not have a personal encounter with her. That is the practical force of Derrida's axiom that began the prologue. But it seems that the pathos of nonpresence extends in both directions: we must equally adjust our thinking to the 'death' of the reader. It is not our own true selves that we bring to reading and enact there. At most it is a version, one role among several that we might play as we read, though it may be the serious role defined by orthodox stipulations of earnestness, innocence, and submissiveness. Like other orthodoxies, the attempts to specify the proper role of the reader is an attempt to stabilize, to govern the unruly, and to close down some of the play of signifying. The orthodox stance (in one of its several variants) defines a way of 'being serious' about reading and may particularly appeal when one wants to play that role. But unless we adopt some such orthodoxy, we cannot anchor the text in the experience of its proper reader any more than we can in its author. The reader is not the target of the text in a way that can be definitively specified any more than the author is its source.

None of this, however, should lead to the conclusion that rhetorical thinking is bunk, that there aren't any real authors or real readers or relationships between them, so why talk about fixing them clearly in mind. It merely clarifies the nature of this fixing in mind, which is not an act of copying or discovering an external reality, but of forming a clear conception, an imagination of what one is trying to do and who one is doing it with, in the act of writing or reading. This is the core of what it means to view rhetoric as social imagination.

EPILOGUE
ADVISING/WRITING

This study, like many tragedies, must be approaching its end, since both principal characters, author and reader, are dead. It remains the task of the epilogue to summarize the action and highlight its significance.

We have come a long way from Halliday and Hasan's sketch of the 'interpersonal component of language' cited in the introduction, and we can see how far we have departed from common sense in relation to it:

> The interpersonal component is concerned with the social, expressive and conative functions of language, with expressing the speaker's 'angle': his attitudes and judgements, his encoding of the role relationships into the situation, and his motive in saying anything at all. We can summarize these by saying that the ideational component represents the speaker in his role as observer, while the interpersonal component represents the speaker in his role as intruder.

Several points now leap out. Halliday and Hasan refer to the speaker while apparently meaning 'writer.' This is perhaps just a stylistic tic of linguists, since it is otherwise a little odd to think of the speaker as intruding. We can also see now how the opposition observer/intruder gets started: The 'speaker' could choose not to "encode" his own involvement and "the role relationships" into the situation; he could have chosen impersonality; hence, representing himself (and the reader) constitutes an intrusion or supplement. Clearly, the word *encode*, also a tic of linguists, is doing heavy duty here: if "the role relationships" already (inherently?) exist, then all writing has an interpersonal dimension, is imbued with sociality. By encoded, then, Halliday and Hasan must mean represented and scripted—foregrounded—after the fashion of advice books. But to *represent* these "role relationships" is to transform them, to bring into existence a new level. And what do they mean by "into the situation"? Does the situation have them in it already or not? It seems to mean 'situation as represented in the text.' And the writer is choosing to disclose himself, to reveal his angle . . . or do they mean *taking* an angle, intruding not a preformulated real self but a foil—the intruder as phantom? To encode: to write a meaning in a code, or to be inside codes? They seem to be trying to have it both ways, which is generally the case with writing, especially writing about writing.

Halliday and Hasan's passage seems designed to obscure what writing does, implying both that it puts on the page something that was not there before and also that that something was implicit already in the very communicative event itself. Similarly, attacks on impersonality as an evasion of responsibility imply that by writing oneself (and possibly one's reader) into the text, one has simply acknowledged what is— hence is being more honest, straightforward, unobfuscating. But to write is to commit oneself to a medium with its own laws and dynamics. Even when the text is the self—when it is full of I's—it drifts beyond the determination and control of the sayer. Even the act of identifying oneself becomes the fashioning of an image. The rhetoric of personal interaction is heavily codified, and the codes ('colloquial,' 'plain-spoken,' 'deferential,' 'aggressive') extend complexly in many directions. Among the forces of writing are gesture and displacement: scripting and foregrounding the first and second persons do not provide windows for the real, the personal, to flow into the text, but mirrors or screens where the Writer and Reader are seen interacting over a book. Just as the reader may never be certain he is engaging the real writer, so he cannot be sure it is his own image he is seeing. Scripted interaction may feel closer and more immediate, but that is because it is sustained by acts of the imagination, springing from a desire to be, and to be engaged with, another. The impulse underlying the intersubjectivity of writing may be as much erotic—or as narcissistic—as contentious.

Chapter 1 described five parameters along which the relationship of Writer and Reader varies in 'scenes' of advice writing and probably in much other writing as well, and provided some relatively neutral categories for analyzing tactics writers may employ. These tactics were then linked to and motivated by the larger conceptions of how relationships work, either in terms of dyadic 'interpersonal' encounters (in chapter 2) or (in chapter 3) in terms of even larger groups, parties, and forces held to be operating in the social world. The notion of 'person' and 'relationship' vary accordingly. Though it may be argued that all action and interaction is political or has political implications, these implications are certainly more evident in the rhetoric of 'us' and 'them,' and one might as well say that the act of writing/reading is articulated in pre-political terms when it is conducted on the level of 'I' and 'you,' as in the texts discussed in chapter 2. The difference is perhaps best illustrated in Dr. Spock's revisions of *Baby and Child Care*, which move from a view of child rearing as a personal, essentially private endeavor to one of it as an endeavor that must be understood and guided by its social and political context and consequences. The scene of writing/reading opens to a wider perspective, moving from the privacy of the study to the public meeting.

Implicit in the notion of a projected or imagined scene of writing is its relative independence of a simple semiotic or speech act model with the sender/speaker on one end and the receiver/hearer on the other. Such models fail to grasp the force and workings of writing, reducing it to an incidental matter of the medium in which the message is transmitted. Most writing posits a self and an other—so far the model is correct—but it does not address the way the sender and receiver are transformed by the 'medium' and its codes. Even in speech, as Jonathan Culler observes, the lover who says, "I love you" can suddenly be aware of the extraordinarily codified nature of what he is saying, its status as *gesture*. And when the lovers are not looking into each other's eyes, and indeed have never met, the code stands shorn of presence. If there is an erotics of writing/reading it is that of a romance-by-correspondence between lovers who may not leave their own countries: it is sustained by stupendous acts of imagination.

As is clear in chapters 4 and 6, however, not all writers and readers explore the potential complexities of their engagement; some write, and read, from securely preformulated selves and ignore the way they are made and remade by the text. Writers like Elbow and Lappé, or the Boston Women's Health Book Collective, do not entirely abandon attempts to master the play of language, but they recognize some of its wildness—its tendency, for example, to turn sincerity into 'image.'

But the force of writing need not always be felt as self-alienating, something to be struggled against. It is also fecund and can work even when not under deliberate mastery: there is a kind of gaiety associated with play in the writings of Ruff, Casey, Bolles, and again in Carnegie and Smith, an abandoning of the One True Self to the conscious playing out of the role that emerges in the writing. The lover who is too appalled at the codified nature of his declaration will either be a great poet or a bad lover.

In contemporary American culture, though, he would not become a great wit, for the lover's discourse is among those most tightly constrained by earnestness and sincerity. We have a number of bad names for playfulness, teasing, or fluctuating commitment in this domain. The role of such conventions has emerged very clearly in the later part of this study: we might even define 'important discourses' as those that conventionally bind the writer to commit herself to a determinate, consistent, reasoned meaning and to stand unswervingly behind it, and equally bind the reader to make himself over into the intended, responsible, informed Reader. Certain enterprises work on the edges of or sometimes even against this predominant norm of interaction, notably some psychotherapeutic discourse, religious writing, some literature and literary criticism, and, apparently, some secular advice writing.

In saying that the persons, their Footing and situation are imagined and projected in all writing, however, we are not saying that they are fictional. One could argue that they are imitations of personal, face-to-face exchanges and therefore as faked as the friendliness of the telephone solicitor who calls us by first name; that reader and writer have any personal relation is simply an illusion willingly indulged, perhaps because it involves no ulterior commitments. But then one must identify the true, authentically personal relationship, and, as the lover's declaration suggests, that might best be done outside of language. For it is language, not just writing, that introduces the forces of figuration, gesture, representation—in short, the difference between saying and being. Any utterance beyond the purely formulaic "'Morning" automatically uttered exceeds the situational determinants, the self-evident realities, and bravely launches forth into the connotations, the makings and remakings, of the codes.

APPENDIX:

SYSTEMATICS OF INTERACTION

In the last fifteen years has appeared a large amount of work describing the units and rules of conversational interaction. A number of writers have not remained content with basic descriptive endeavors, however, but have tried to explicate the systematic aspects of interaction in terms of rationales for speakers' behavior, constitutive rules of interaction, networks of contrasting strategies and options, and so on. It may be useful to assay five of these accounts for their strengths and weaknesses as approaches to verbal interaction generally. Speech Act Theory is the first of them historically and a base to which the others refer; I will take up Brown and Levinson's theory of politeness phenomena second, Geoffrey Leech's model of Interpersonal Rhetoric third, Robin Lakoff's parallelogram of goals and aims in conversation fourth, and William Stiles's taxonomy of Verbal Response Modes last. To be fair, it must be understood that none of these accounts is put forward as a complete systematics of interaction. Each was developed with particular uses in mind. Nonetheless, some of them have excited fairly ambitious, even grandiose hopes.

Speech Act Theory, associated with John Austin and his student John Searle (in the Anglo-Saxon world at least), begins with descriptions of illocutionary acts in terms of the conditions necessary for them to be performed. A Request, for example, requires that the Speaker want the Hearer to do something, that the Hearer be able to do it, and probably wouldn't do it unless requested. If these conditions (and perhaps a few others) are met, and the Speaker utters the appropriate words, he will have felicitously performed an act of requesting. A key concept, often misunderstood, is that if the situation is as described, all parties must agree that the act has been performed, regardless of ulterior motives or mental reservations either party may have. The term *perlocutionary intent* is used to refer to whatever the Speaker may be up to when he performs a particular illocutionary act—he might, for example, be trying to establish a pattern of compliance on the Hearer's part (e.g., "State your date and place of birth, and mother's maiden name," said by a police interrogator). Perlocutionary intents are open to a wide range of interpretation and dispute, but illocutionary acts are not; intention is only a factor in regard to the mutual recognition of Speaker and Hearer that Speaker means to be taken as having performed that particular illocutionary act. The exact number and name of the illocutionary acts have been much disputed; there are several taxonomies in print. Should one, for example, treat questions as requests (namely, for information) and if so, should one distinguish them from commands? It is also sometimes assumed that these acts are only the smallest units of interaction, and that one can proceed to analyze bigger stretches of discourse in terms of 'macro-speech acts' such as 'conversation' or 'praise-promise,'[1] but on higher levels the problems of naming become very severe; there are after all very many ways to characterize what is being done in an extended stretch of speech.

Speech Act Theory also develops the rudiments of a systematics of gesture via the notions of Indirect Speech Act and Conversational Implicature—principles, roughly, by which one can utter a sentence normally associated with one illocutionary force that is taken in the context to have a different force, either by regular tactics ("Would you like to go?" taken as an invitation, not a request for information) or by general maxims of conversational cooperativeness, such as relevance, informativeness, clarity, and accuracy (e.g., "Are the Joneses here?" being taken, when the Joneses plainly are, as a request that the Hearer take note of the fact or comment on it). Crucially in these accounts, the utterance must be perceived as a gesture counting normally for one thing and hence performing the other only indirectly; otherwise one has a conventionalized 'indirection' (or 'speech act idiom'), such as "can you" (for requests), and 'conventional implicatures,' such as "Is the Pope Catholic?"[2] The result of conventionalization is that no interpretive effort is required—these in effect are direct. The ways these 'secondary' forces are limited and related to contexts has been the topic of much discussion. Clearly, it is generally agreed, a particular utterance can mean many things, but not just anything. The question for the linguist is where the rule-governed properties stop. One practical constraint is that these discussions are always conducted in terms of basic illocutionary forces—i.e., one force replaces another on the same level of specificity. One might describe the remark about the Joneses as catty, alarmed, or admiring, and so on, but all of this leaps to a level of interaction between participants about which Speech Act Theory has almost nothing to say. Speech Act Theory is only in a very narrow and abstract way a theory of interaction.

Among the gaps in Speech Act Theory is that it provides no principled explanation of why people make indirect acts, and similarly, under what circumstances people do not converse 'cooperatively.' In an early paper, Robin Lakoff suggested that an explanation would be a theory of politeness in verbal interaction (perhaps made up of such maxims as 'Don't Impose' and 'Give Options'); these suggestions were developed by Penelope Brown and Stephen Levinson in their theory of universals of politeness. Politeness, they hold, is a system for mutual preservation of face (which operates principally, as one would expect, in face-to-face 'social' situations). Politeness is typically suspended in situations of intimacy, urgency, or indifference to face (due to disparities of power). Politeness is 'on' when "mutual vulnerability of face is at stake." Gestures of friendliness, under this condition, become "a kind of metaphorical extension of intimacy" and function precisely by being *gestures* of friendliness (p. 108). Brown and Levinson's model is an attempt to give the rationale of various tactics of politeness in terms of two strategies driving the system (preserve esteem and preserve autonomy). They assume that speakers often find it necessary to perform acts that count as threatening the esteem and autonomy either of themselves or the addressee; in such cases, politeness requires 'redressing' the threat to face. The kinds of face-threatening acts that Brown and Levinson mention, though numerous (criticizing, borrowing sugar, admitting fault, etc.) are assumed to be self-evident, and hence the politeness of the redressing tactic is patent. There are no interpretive difficulties.

Brown and Levinson claim that acts are intrinsically face-threatening, but there is a crucial lack of clarity in what they mean by 'act.' They hold that complimenting, for example, is intrinsically face-threatening, since it is one instance of acts that "predicate some desire of S toward H or H's goods, giving

H reason to think that he may have to take action to protect the object of S's desire, or give it to S" (p. 71). Surely, however, some compliments are less threatening than others—compare praising a neighbor's car and praising his extension ladder. If Brown and Levinson mean that only compliments that can be construed in context as potential bids for an offer are warnings of covetous designs, then it is not the act of complimenting in itself that is threatening, but particular, situated acts of complimenting that are interpreted in terms of the speaker's inferred plans and goals. At most, Brown and Levinson can say that complimenting can be tricky and trigger redressive action, but not that it always is, or is 'intrinsically' so.

In an apparently bold and often-cited passage, Brown and Levinson declare, that "Discovering the principles of language usage may be largely coincident with discovering the principles out of which social relationships, in their interactional aspect, are constructed: dimensions by which individuals manage to relate to others in particular ways" (p. 60). However, in relation to their own work, this claim looks more like a definition of 'social relationships'—i.e., those relationships that are governed by the preservation of face. Brown and Levinson acknowledge that there are doubtless personal motivations for making indirect moves, such as avoiding personal responsibility for having 'moved' (p. 100), and this acknowledgement opens up a huge area that would have to be integrated into a complete model of interaction. It also introduces a level at which interpretation becomes much richer and more problematic.

Brown and Levinson's notion that various displacements of language can be understood in terms of the two strategies of face preservation is ingenious and intellectually pleasing for the level and kind of interaction they focus on and has indeed inspired the attempts of chapters 2 and 3 to link up the language to larger, explicit axioms governing all interactions. The match up with the parameters in the Footings chapter is only partial, however. Solidary and informal can be seen as moves enhancing the Reader's esteem, oblique and equal similarly as respecting the desire for autonomy, but such an explanation is less clear for impersonal, and the confrontive and superior Footings would come out overwhelmingly rude—the simple suspension of all considerations of the reader's face wants. It seems clear that interactions between Writers and Readers cannot be fully and adequately accounted for in terms of face preservation, perhaps because these interactions are much more sustained and complex than the 'social' relationships they describe, because no response or negotiation is possible, and because 'mutual vulnerability of face' is not in fact at stake. Readers are perfectly capable of playing roles that violate face wants.

A point that is unfortunately blurred in Brown and Levinson's presentation of their model is that it is a systematic deduction of the rationale behind various 'displacements' in language use and not an account of the actual mental processes of Speakers and Hearers when they talk. The point of blurring arises from the nature of these displacements as tactics rather than verbal formulas— that is, speakers are presumed to select a strategy, not a fixed phraseology, in executing a face-threatening act in a particular situation; the tactic is, as it were, a stimulus for verbal inventiveness and in that sense operative in the speaker's mind at the time of utterance (or immediately before). Brown and Levinson suggest that it may well not be conscious and may be so routinized as to be automatic (p. 90), but that is not the real question. When someone addresses us with a lot of redressive foreplay and byplay—asking after our health, work, family, and beating around the bush—we may begin to suspect ulterior motives. The verbal stream begins to seem like a series of gestures that could be interpreted in a number of ways, some of them along the lines sketched by Brown and Levinson: we might suppose that the speaker is leading up to some fairly face-threatening act, such as criticism or imposition (or that he thinks it is threatening, or that he thinks we are likely to find it so, or that decorum requires him to build up to the point, and so on). But we are not limited by the assumption that the speaker is behaving 'rationally' according to Brown and Levinson's rationale. We can never be sure *why* the speaker is behaving as he does, what complex of attitudes and intentions his behavior signifies. He may be being polite, but he may also be being neurotic, testing the waters, acting on misconceptions or nonshared codes, indulging a personal tic, and so on. At most, Brown and Levinson's principles provide some possible lines for interpreting a speaker's address to us, just as the maxims of conversation do. They do not in general provide a grammar of motives.

Politeness is also a central concern of Geoffrey Leech in the model of Interpersonal Rhetoric sketched in his *Principles of Pragmatics* (Longman, 1983), particularly as it helps to account for the many occasions when speakers do not behave according to the maxims of Cooperation defined by Grice. Like Brown and Levinson, he regards politeness as a mode of avoiding friction and lowered self-esteem between individuals, but he does not treat it as always redressive of face-threatening acts. That is, politeness is at work whenever social values (comity, conviviality) are enacted (e.g., as in offers, greetings, thanks, congratulations—all of which are treated as face-threatening by Brown and Levinson). Thus he can refer to "sincere politeness"—a concept that makes no sense for Brown and Levinson. Leech's concept of politeness is explicated in terms of six submaxims of the Politeness Principle, many of which can be related more or less directly to the Brown and Levinson conceptions of either endorsing the other's wants (maxims of Approbation, Agreement, Sympathy) or minimizing the incursions on his autonomy (maxim of Tact). But the maxim of Generosity, which accounts for the relatively greater politeness of

Are there any more potatoes?

than

I would sure like some more potatoes

seems only indirectly derivable from the principle of autonomy (i.e., the addressee is less required to oblige the speaker because refusal does not deny his expressed wishes). Similarly, the maxim of Modesty does not directly follow from the face-preserving axioms unless we add a proviso that self-praise diminishes the other's esteem (i.e., a maxim of competition for value). Some of these differences may result from the fact that, as Leech notes, the force and relative ranking of his maxims varies cross-culturally (e.g., self-praise is less impolite in Mediterranean cultures than in 'ours' and even more impolite than in ours in Japanese culture). Brown and Levinson, however, are aiming at universals of politeness and countenance cross-cultural differences only in terms of the definition and relative weight of face-threatening acts.

Interpersonal Rhetoric, then, is guided by the Cooperative and Politeness Principles; in addition, Leech has two metaprinciples of politeness—irony and banter—and two further principles to account for exaggeration and understatement. Irony and banter are related to politeness because they exploit politeness or impoliteness to achieve a 'polite' goal. That is, irony in his view is always excessively (mock) polite (exaggerated praise or understated criticism); banter ('A fine friend YOU are!'), on the other hand, is mock rude and may even exploit irony, as in the example. It is worth noting in passing that 'banter' is an extremely complex phenomenon with a rich set of 'synonyms' (kidding, ribbing, teasing, joshing, needling) and does not lend itself easily to the sorts of inferential reversals that Leech employs. In keeping with his desire to link his conception of rhetoric with the classical tradition, Leech refers to understatement as litotes and overstatement as hyperbole. This amounts to defining the figures solely as violations of the maxims of Quality (say the truth) and Quantity (say as much as is needed). The rhetorical tradition also includes in the definition some specifications of effect, often ironic. Litotes, for example, is often described as understatement that intensifies—"he likes his wife not a little;"[3] hyperbole likewise is usually defined as bold exaggeration often promoting an ironic deflation. However, it is also conceded that hyperbole can be used to amplify (suggesting strong emotion), and litotes can be used to "secure emphasis" as well as irony.[4] Thus it might be said that litotes and hyperbole are special cases or uses of understatement and overstatement, and should not simply be substituted for the latter set of terms.

In addition to the Cooperative and Politeness Principles, Leech proposes two other principles of Interpersonal Rhetoric—the Interest Principle and the Pollyanna Principle. The first (Be Interesting) accounts for exaggeration that does not trigger the Irony submaxim—i.e., is not hyperbolic, as Lanham defines it ("Exaggerated or extravagant terms used for emphasis and not intended to be understood literally; self-conscious exaggeration"), but rather the source of embellishments and dramatization. The second (Accentuate the Positive) accounts for optimistic overstatement and euphemistic understatement (again not ironic). (Leech also mentions yet another use of understatement that counters the Interest Principle ["She's not a bad-looking girl"] by establishing the speaker's honesty. He does not name the principle involved here.) Both principles, like the Politeness Principle, are invoked to account for departures from Cooperativeness as defined by Grice. (Exaggeration for Brown and Levinson is a device of positive politeness—that is, of enhancing solidarity). The suspicion begins to cross the mind that there may be an indefinite number of these 'Principles.' As a systematic effort, Leech's model is weak.

The special purpose guiding Robin Lakoff's partitioning of interactional styles is the differentiating of men's and women's speech in contemporary white middle-class American culture.[5] Nonetheless, her categories for describing modes of interaction are intended to cover all kinds of verbal interaction— written, spoken, broadcast. She begins with a scale of degrees of relationship between speaker and addressee, specifically one of "increasing awareness of the addressee's presence as explicitly manifested by the speaker" (p. 63)— foregrounded or scripted, in our terms. On this scale are four modes defined in terms of the aim of the speaker. The first mode is Clarity and is the zero-degree of relationship. Indeed, it corresponds to the notion of objective or impersonal writing; in a sense, it doesn't belong on the scale at all. The second and third modes, exhibiting increasing relationship, are Distance and Deference, with Camaraderie anchoring down the fully related end. Lakoff's definitions of these modes are highly evaluative. Distance is defensive, antiemotional, formal, and evasive of responsibility (models are the politician, bureaucrat, academic delivering a paper). Deference too comes under suspicion: one leaves scope to the addressee as to the aims and outcome of the exchange, but is also thereby attempting to control by making the offer of autonomy—i.e., a gesture that can easily be seen as manipulative. These two intermediate terms are tainted by the sense of a power struggle with the addressee. Only the fourth term, Camaraderie, is wholly positive in evaluation: though it is directly confrontive, "Camaraderie is the level of direct expression of orders and desires, colloquialism and slang, first names and nicknames—much that is considered good and typical contemporary American behavior" (p. 65).

Rather surprisingly, Lakoff maintains that these modes can be mixed freely, so that a simple scale is not as clear as a parallelogram with each term at a corner and the "overall stylistic behavior" of speakers plotted at points within the parallelogram. Possibly she means that individual speakers/writers may employ linguistic features associated with different modes (e.g., passive voice at the same time as 'you'), so that the behavior would be positioned by opposing forces, some pulling in the direction of Distance, others toward Camaraderie. One senses in this whole scheme a yearning for unmediated, unedited, face-to-face having it out, and a view of all written, public uses of language as fallings away from this true norm of full presence. Lakoff does speak of the animating force behind the posture of Camaraderie as "establishing a personal relationship with others" (p. 60). Again, "personal relationship," like "rapport," is a privileged term here and given a very culture-specific definition. Is the relation of diplomat to diplomat, or salesman to target, inherently less personal?

Despite this undertow, Lakoff does recognize that the system she is describing is subject to the forces of gesture and conventionalization: a use of a strategy may be conventional or real. "The politician's apparent Clarity, the diplomat's Distance, the salesman's Camaraderie—all are conventional. And indeed, conventional application of all these rules is found to a less pronounced degree in all our behavior" (p. 70). Here the opposition conventional/real is one of simple 'sincere/insincere' that presumably can be gauged in all or most cases as something that stands behind or beneath the utterance. It is of course clear why the salesman and politician can confidently be judged as using those styles 'conventionally' (sometimes), but is the case so clear with the diplomat? Such a simple opposition gives the system very little gestural play; the move of making a gesture recognized as a gesture, for example, as with Brown and Levinson's 'friendliness,' is not even discussed.

Almost as comprehensive is William S. Stiles's model of Verbal Response Modes (VRMs). Originally developed to classify types of interactions between therapist and client in psychotherapy, it is now offered as a "classification of intersubjective illocutionary acts."[6] Stiles identifies for each utterance its source, frame, and focus. Source of experience has to do with whether the Speaker or the Other is the source of the thoughts, feelings, or behavior referred to in the utterance. The Speaker is the source of Disclosures, Advisements, Edifications, and Confirmations, while the Other is the source of Questions, Interpretations (that is, the Speaker interprets what the Other said), Acknowledgements, and Reflections (in the clinical sense—Speaker rephrases what Other said). Frame of reference is the point of view with respect to which the experience is expressed, whether exclusively the Speaker's (as in Disclosure, Advisement, Question, and Interpretation) or with respect to a point of view shared with the Other (as in Edification, Confirmation, Acknowledgement, and Reflection). Focus refers to whether "the speaker implicitly presumes to know what the other's experience or frame of reference should be"—if so, the utterance is Other-focused (as in Advisement, Confirmation, Interpretation, and Reflection.) Stiles describes three scales according to the orientation in each of the three parameters:

	Speaker-Oriented	Other-Oriented
Source	informative ------------------------------	attentive
Frame	controlling (directive) ------------------	acquiescent (nondirective)
Focus	unassuming -------------------------------	presumptuous

Speaker-focus confines itself to I-statements; it is presumptuous (confrontive) to tell the Other what his thoughts and feelings are. Thus we have three scales of I-orientation vs. you-orientation or what Stiles calls "role dimensions." Some of his other work, he says, demonstrates the validity of these dimensions as constructs. Doubtless it does, but how many other dimensions might one also find support for?

Stiles also allows for one level of gestural displacement exactly parallel to the notion of indirect speech acts: a Question, such as "Did you know that two-thirds of the known food plants originated in the New World?" can be used with the intent of an Edification (informing the Other). And, like speech act theorists, Stiles is not interested in pursuing further the question of over-arching motives and (perlocutionary) intentions in saying something. One of his principal and mildly interesting findings is that client-centered therapists use about 90 percent Other-oriented utterances, gestalt (directive) therapists use the speaker's frame of reference, and psychoanalytic therapists use the Other as source of experience—though clients use mainly Disclosure and Edification, regardless of the therapist. This finding certainly does highlight one way therapeutic discourse is unlike ordinary conversation! Although Stiles's method of simply summing the numbers of utterances in each cell of his grid to describe a style of speaking seems rather crude, his framework does suggest something about how a speaker's discourse might enact attitudes like those we have called solidarity, equality, and obliqueness (as well as their opposite values). Choices of personal/impersonal and formal/informal apparently do not arise in his corpus of therapeutic discourse, or at least have no reflection in his system.

In a sense, the problem posed by Stiles's system, and Lakoff's, and the others, is not that they don't work, are inadequate for some uses of language, or the like, but that they all work tolerably well, capturing certain intuitions and evaluations we may have, and all exhibit the same limitation of self-containedness on a certain level of analysis. The procedure followed in all of these sketches is to take some descriptive terms that may constitute an at least potential folk taxonomy of ordinary language (promises, orders, requests . . . , autonomy, esteem . . . , deference, presumption, and so on), collapse near-synonyms into the focal word and capitalize the word to yield a theoretical primitive. One should not be too hard on this procedure, since it is the one used in chapter 1. The relative arbitrariness and plurality of these systems of interaction are embarrassments only if one is trying to pursue a certain program of scientific investigation—the program that proceeds by reducing the multiplex of phenomena to a simplex set of underlying categories that are the determinants, the real structure, of the surface manifestations. The notion of the codes of connotation developed in this book assumes that our knowledge and responses in verbal interaction are not organized and do not operate in this way. Rather, we characterize and respond to writers with a very large, open set of categories with much overlapping and subtle difference as well. There are doubtless reasons for schematizing and simplifying along the lines sketched here, but it seems unlikely we will ever reach rock bottom, and there is a danger that in pursuing system and science we may lose insight and understanding.

ADVICE BOOKS CITED

Barzun, Jacques. *Simple and Direct: A Rhetoric for Writers*. New York: Harper and Row, 1975.

Bell, Ruth (for the Boston Women's Health Book Collective). *Changing Bodies, Changing Lives: A Book for Teens on Sex and Relationships*. New York: Random House, 1980.

Berthoff, Ann E., *Forming, Thinking, Writing*. Rochelle Park, N.J.: Hayden Book Company, 1978.

Bolles, Richard Nelson. *What Color is Your Parachute?* Berkeley: Ten Speed Press, 1982.

Boston Women's Health Book Collective. *Our Bodies, Ourselves*. New York: Simon and Schuster, 1973.

————. *Ourselves and Our Children*. New York: Random House, 1978.

Brazelton, T. Berry, M.D. *Toddlers and Parents*. New York: Dell Publishing, 1974.

Carnegie, Dale. *How to Win Friends and Influence People*. New York: Simon and Schuster, 1936.

Casey, Douglas R. *Crisis Investing: Opportunities and Profits in the Coming Great Depression*. New York: Pocket Books, 1980.

Coles, William E., Jr. *The Plural I: The Teaching of Writing*. New York: Holt, Rinehart, and Winston, 1978.

Elbow, Peter. *Writing without Teachers*. New York: Oxford University Press, 1973

————. *Writing with Power*. New York: Oxford University Press, 1981.

Ellis, Albert, Ph.D., and Robert A. Harper, Ph.D. *A New Guide to Rational Living*. North Hollywood, California: Wilshire Book Company, 1977.

Flesch, Rudolf. *The Art of Readable Writing*. New York: Collier Books, 1979. Orig. Pub. 1949.

Ginott, Haim G., M.D. *Between Parent and Child*. New York: Avon Books, 1969.

Glenn, Morton B., M.D. *How to Get Thinner Once and for All*. New York: Dutton, 1965.

Gordon, Thomas, M.D. *Parental Effectiveness Training: The "No-Lose" Program for Raising Responsible Children*. New York: Wyden, 1970.

Hamilton, Eleanor, Ph.D. *Sex with Love: A Guide for Young People*. Boston: Beacon Press, 1978.

Heffernan, James A. W., and John E. Lincoln. *Writing: A College Handbook*. New York: W. W. Norton, 1982. (Cited as HL in chapter 1)

Johnson, Eric W. *Love and Sex in Plain Language*. 3d rev. ed. New York: Bantam Books, 1981.

Kelly, Lou. *From Dialogue to Discourse*. Glenview, Ill.: Scott, Foresman, 1972.

Lappé, Frances Moore. *Diet for a Small Planet*. 10th anniversary edition. New York: Ballantine Books, 1982.

Leach, Penelope. *Your Baby and Child from Birth to Age Five*. New York: Alfred A. Knopf, 1981.

Lieberman, E. James, M.D., and Ellen Peck. *Sex and Birth Control: A Guide for the Young*. New York: Harper and Row, 1981.

Mitchell, Richard. *Less Than Words Can Say*. Boston: Little, Brown, 1979.

Ploeger, JoAnn. *Slim Living Day by Day*. Wheaton, Ill.: Tyndale House Publishers, 1977.

Quinn, Jim. *American Tongue and Cheek: A Populist Guide to Our Language*. New York: Penguin Books, 1980.

Reuben, David, M.D. *Everything You Always Wanted to Know About Sex, but Were Afraid to Ask*. New York: McKay, 1961.

————. *The Save Your Life Diet*. New York: Ballantine Books, 1976.

Ruff, Howard J. *How to Prosper during the Coming Bad Years*. New York: Warner Books, 1981.

Safire, William. *On Language*. New York: Avon Books, 1980.

Salk, Lee, M.D. *What Every Child Would Like His Parents to Know (To Help Him with the Emotional Problems of His Everyday Life)*. New York: Warner Paperback Library, 1973.

Simon, John. *Paradigms Lost*. New York: Penguin Books, 1980.

Smith, Manuel J., Ph.D. *When I Say No, I Feel Guilty*. New York: Bantam Books, 1975.

Spock, Benjamin, M.D. *Baby and Child Care*. New York: Pocket Books, 1976.

Trimble, John. *Writing with Style: Conversations on the Art of Writing*. Englewood Cliffs, N.J.: Prentice-Hall, 1975.

NOTES

Prologue

1. Jacques Derrida, "Freud and the Scene of Writing," in *Writing and Difference,* trans. Alan Bass (Chicago: University of Chicago Press, 1978), 227. For some pedagogical implications of the notion of writer as first reader, see Donald Murray, "Teaching the Other Self: The Writer's First Reader," *College Composition and Communication* 13 (1982): 140–147.

2. M. A. K. Halliday, *Language as Social Semiotic* (London: Edward Arnold, 1978), 4.

3. Wallace L. Chafe, "The Deployment of Consciousness in the Production of a Narrative," in *The Pear Stories,* ed. Wallace Chafe (Norwood, N.J.: Ablex Publishing Company, 1980), 36.

4. John J. Gumperz, *Discourse Strategies* (Cambridge: Cambridge University Press, 1982), 61.

Introduction

1. Wallace L. Chafe, "Integration and Involvement in Speaking, Writing, and Oral Literature," in *Spoken and Written Language,* ed. Deborah Tannen (Norwood, N.J.: Ablex Publishing Company, 1982), 45.

2. M. A. K. Halliday and Ruqaiya Hasan, *Cohesion in English* (London: Longman, 1975), 26–27.

3. For a brief survey of such distinctions, see Gillian Brown and George Yule, *Discourse Analysis* (Cambridge: Cambridge University Press, 1983), 1–4. See also Paul Watzlawick, J. H. Beavin, and D. D. Jackson, *Pragmatics of Human Communication* (New York: W. W. Norton, 1967); Roger Fowler, *Linguistics and the Novel* (London: Methuen, 1977), 42–44 et passim; Emile Benveniste, "The Correlations of Tense in the French Verb" in *Problems in General Linguistics,* trans. Mary Elizabeth Meek (Coral Gables: University of Miami Press, 1971), 205–216; Roland Barthes, "Textual Analysis of Poe's 'Valdemar,'" in *Untying the Text,* ed. Robert Young, (London: Routledge and Kegan Paul, 1981). John Lyons traces the closely related distinction of expression/content back to Karl Bühler in his "Deixis and Subjectivity: '*Loguor ergo sum?*'" in *Speech, Place, and Action,* ed. Robert Jarvella and William Klein (London: John Wiley and Sons: 1982), 101–124.

4. John Lyons, *Semantics,* vol. 2 (Cambridge: Cambridge University Press, 1977), 835–6, 846.

5. Roger Fowler has repeatedly charged that the impersonal style of official rules, regulations, and notices obfuscates the interpersonal meanings that he feels should be spelled out in terms of I or we and you. See for example his *Literature As Social Discourse* (London: Batsford, 1981), 29–32; also throughout in Roger Fowler et al., *Language and Control* (London: Routledge and Kegan Paul, 1979). Richard Lanham carries on the traditional diatribe against 'voice-

less' directive prose in his recent *Prose Analysis* (New York: Charles Scribner's Sons, 1983). The assumption here is that all uses of language are communicative and are speech acts implying a Speaker and an Addressee, hence an interpersonal dimension, however muted or denied (see also Gordon Wells, *Learning through Interaction* [Cambridge: Cambridge University Press, 1981], 244; and Watzlawick et al.). The first premise is open to considerable doubt (see Noam Chomsky's *Reflections on Language* [New York: Pantheon, 1975] and Ann Banfield, *Unspeakable Sentences* [London: Routledge and Kegan Paul, 1982]); the conclusion seems to follow tautologously from the implicit, commonsense definition of 'communication.'

6. Dwight MacDonald, "Howtoism," in *Against the American Grain* (New York: Random House, 1962), 360–392.

7. See for example E. D. Hirsch, Jr., *The Philosophy of Composition* (Chicago: University of Chicago Press, 1977), 21–32.

8. As for example in several of the pieces in *Spoken and Written Language*, ed. Deborah Tannen (Norwood, N.J.: Ablex Publishing Company, 1982).

9. Fowler, 180.

10. Texts vary in their dependence on extracultural knowledge on the part of the reader. This variation may lie behind some of the extreme differences of opinion on the question of dependence. Walter Ong's discussion in "The Writer's Audience Is Always a Fiction," (*PMLA* 90 [1975]: 9–21) maintains that the interpersonal nuances of a text (he is discussing Swift's *Journal to Stella*) become irretrievably lost with the passage of time. Against this should be weighed the observation of Graham Hough (who is discussing the fiction of Jane Austin) that the values to be assigned to various speech styles are contained in the work and do not require knowledge of contemporary norms of conversation—*Selected Essays* (Cambridge: Cambridge University Press, 1978), 63–69. But Swift's *Journal* was probably never intended for publication, whereas Austin's novels have 'manners' as their theme.

On this point, David Silverman and Brian Torode argue for a much more sweeping, heuristic assumption that "a text or message itself sufficiently constitutes the sense of the communicational context within which it circulates" in *The Material Word* (London: Routledge and Kegan Paul, 1980), 315.

11. Manfred Bierwisch, "Social Differentiation of Language Structure," in *An Integrated Theory of Linguistic Ability*, ed. Thomas G. Bever, Jerrold J. Katz, and D. Terence Langendoen (New York: Crowell, 1976), 286.

12. Roger Fowler et al., *Language and Control* (London: Routledge and Kegan Paul, 1979).

13. See for example Silverman and Torode, 8.

14. Robin Tolmach Lakoff, "Stylistic Strategies within a Grammar of Style," in *Language, Sex, and Gender*, ed. Judith Orasanu, Mariam K. Slater, and Leonore Loeb Adler (New York: New York Academy of Sciences, 1979), 66.

15. We touch here on the problem often referred to Durkheim: how can a statistically observed tendency take on the function of a norm? For a brief discussion, see Stephen Tyler, *The Said and the Unsaid* (New York: Academic Press, 1978), 9.

16. Barthes, "'Valdemar,'" 155.

17. John Sturrock, "Roland Barthes," in *Structuralism and Since*, ed. John Sturrock (Oxford: Oxford University Press, 1979), 75.

18. An introduction and illustration of some of these functions of schemata

can be found in my *Constructing Texts* (Bloomington: Indiana University Press, 1981), chapter 3.

19. Here I dissent sharply from Bierwisch, who maintains that connotation must be defined as the link between linguistic items and some piece of social reality as it is ultimately modeled in a materialistic account.

Chapter 1

1. Walker Gibson, *Tough, Sweet, and Stuffy* (Bloomington: Indiana University Press, 1966), 24.

2. The term "footing" is Erving Goffman's; see his chapter by that name in *Forms of Talk* (Philadelphia: University of Pennsylvania Press, 1981), 124–159.

3. Hans Robert Jauss, "Theses on the Transition from the Aesthetics of Literary Works to a Theory of Aesthetic Experience," in *Interpretation of Narrative*, ed. Mario J. Valdes and Owen J. Miller (Toronto: University of Toronto Press, 1978), 143.

4. Richard Lanham, *Style, An Anti-Textbook* (New Haven: Yale University Press, 1974), 133.

5. Penelope Brown and Stephen Levinson, "Universals in Language Use: Politeness Phenomena," in *Questions and Politeness*, ed. Esther N. Goody (Cambridge: Cambridge University Press, 1978), 66. Mutual validation is not the only bond of sociality ever proposed, of course. Rousseau proposed pity, and others have suggested the closely related sympathy/empathy.

6. See Martin Joos, *The Five Clocks* (New York: Harcourt, Brace, and World, 1967), 29–32.

7. A useful survey of *crosscultural* conflicts in interpersonal expectations can be found in Leo Loveday, "Conflicting Framing Patterns: The Sociosemantics of One Component in Cross-cultural Communication," *Text* 2(1982): 359–374. See also Linda Wai Ling Young, "Inscrutability Revisited," in *Language and Social Identity*, ed. John J. Gumperz (Cambridge: Cambridge University Press, 1982), 72–84.

8. Umberto Eco, *The Role of the Reader* (Bloomington: Indiana University Press, 1979), 10–11.

9. Wayne Booth, *Critical Understanding* (Chicago: Chicago University Press, 1980), 268–272.

10. Roland Barthes, "The Death of the Author," in *Image, Music, Text*, tr. Stephen Heath (London: Fontana, 1977), 145.

11. On deliberative questions, see John Lyons, *Semantics* vol. 2, 753–757. The definitions for the rhetorical terms are cited from Richard Lanham, *A Handlist of Rhetorical Terms* (Berkeley and Los Angeles: University of California Press, 1968).

12. Rudolf Flesch, *The Art of Readable Writing* (New York: Collier Books, 1979), 85.

13. See for example Jeanne Fahnestock and Marie Secor, *A Rhetoric of Argument* (New York: Random House, 1982), 305–311.

14. Howard J. Ruff, *How to Prosper during the Coming Bad Years*, (New York: Warner Books, 1981), 16. Douglas Casey comes in a close second in the prefatory "Urgent Message" to his *Crisis Investing* (New York: Pocket Books, 1980): "Remember, money is a good thing (morally as well as in other ways) for many reasons, not the least of which is that it can insulate you from the

unpleasant things in the world while making available to you what you want. And as far as you're concerned, that's what is most important" (p. xiii). This was added in the paperback edition.

15. Tyler, 144.

16. For example, William S. Stiles, "Classification of Intersubjective Illocutionary Acts," *Language in Society* 10 (1981): 227–249.

17. Wayne Booth, *A Rhetoric of Irony* (Chicago: University of Chicago Press, 1974), esp. 28 and 42.

18. Lou Kelly, *From Dialogue to Discourse* (Glenview, Ill.: Scott, Foresman, 1972), 14.

19. Though not an advice book, the *User's Manual* for the Epson MX-80 dot matrix printer, by Dr. David A. Lien (San Diego: Compusoft Publishing, 1980), is a very interesting, rather extreme piece of what is called 'user-friendly' prose. The line cited is from page 21.

20. Kenneth Burke, *A Rhetoric of Motives* (Prentice-Hall, 1950), 55.

21. See the compiled lists of means of identification in L. Virginia Holland's *Counterpoint: Kenneth Burke and Aristotle's Theories of Rhetoric* (New York: Philosophical Library, 1959), 29–30.

22. Joseph Williams, *Style: Ten Lessons in Clarity and Grace* (Glenview, Ill.: Scott, Foresman, 1981), 49.

23. John Lyons, *Semantics*, Chap. 17.

24. Lakoff, 65.

25. Malcolm Coulthard, Martin Montgomery, and David Brazil subdivide 'subsidiary discourse' in academic lectures into *glosses* and *asides* and divide glosses into *restatements, qualifys,* and *comments*—the last of which most closely resemble Safire's parentheses. As they say, "Comments are particularly significant because they are explicitly oriented towards the audience's reception of what is being said and indicate that the speaker is attempting to cope with possible audience reaction overtly in the discourse itself"—"Developing a Description of Spoken Discourse," in *Studies in Discourse Analysis*, ed. Malcolm Coulthard and Martin Montgomery (London: Routledge and Kegan Paul, 1981), 37.

26. Richard Lanham's recent discussion of the high style/low style opposition suggests that it defines by vague social analogy; i.e., its aplication is almost entirely governed by its connotations. This is the way all codes of interaction work, I would argue, especially if 'social' is taken broadly to include personal, ethical analogies. See his *Prose Analysis* (New York: Charles Scribner's Sons, 1983), 182.

27. Martin Joos, 16.

28. T. Berry Brazelton, M.D., *Toddlers and Parents* (New York: Dell Publishing, 1974), 45–46.

29. Benjamin Spock, M.D., *Baby and Child Care* (New York: Pocket Books, 1976), 391.

30. Eleanor Hamilton, Ph.D., *Sex with Love: A Guide for Young People* (Boston: Beacon Press, 1978), 36–37.

31. Eric W. Johnson, *Love and Sex in Plain Language* (New York: Bantam Books, 1981), 66.

32. John Trimble, *Writing with Style: Conversations on the Art of Writing* (Englewood Cliffs, N.J.: Prentice-Hall, 1975), 4–5.

33. James A. W. Heffernan and John E. Lincoln, *Writing: A College Handbook* (New York: W. W. Norton, 1982), 15.

Chapter 2

1. Walter Ong, *Rhetoric, Romance, and Technology* (Ithaca: Cornell University Press, 1971), 14–17, Chap. 5. See also his *Fighting for Life*.

2. Kenneth Burke, *Permanence and Change* (Indianapolis: Bobbs-Merrill, 1965), 262–272.

3. See for example Lakoff, 53–80, but cf. also the remarks by Jessie Bernard, p. 117 of the same work. The case of gender differences in *styles* of interaction is put by Daniel N. Maltz and Ruth A. Borker, "A Cultural Approach to Male-Female Miscommunication," in *Language and Social Identity*, ed. John J. Gumperz (Cambridge: Cambridge University Press, 1982), 195–216.

4. Carl Rogers, "Communication: Its Blocking and Its Facilitation," reprinted in Becker, Young, and Pike, 284–289; Anatol Rapaport, *Fights, Games, and Debates* (Ann Arbor: University of Michigan Press, 1960); Richard E. Young, Alton L. Becker, and Kenneth Pike, *Rhetoric: Discovery and Change* (New York: Harcourt Brace Jovanovich, 1970); for the criticism of manipulation, see James P. Zappan, "Carl R. Rogers and Political Rhetoric," *Pre/text* 1 (1980): 95–113.

5. Goffman, 153.

6. Donald Meyer points to Carnegie's silence on how to sincerely like and be interested in people as the crucial gap in his model. See his discussion of Carnegie in the context of American 'mind cure' writing in *The Positive Thinkers: Religion as Pop Psychology from Mary Baker Eddy to Oral Roberts* (New York: Pantheon Books, 1980), 180–188.

7. Carnegie is generally disdainful of organized religion and its writings as not tough-minded enough for the man of action. Such remarks are cut from the new, revised edition.

8. Preface to the revised edition of *How to Win Friends and Influence People* (New York: Pocket Books, 1982), xii.

9. Lanham, *Style: An Anti-Textbook*, 133.

10. See Elinor Ochs Keenan, "Norm-Makers, Norm-Breakers: Uses of Speech by Men and Women in a Malagasy Community," in *Explorations in the Ethnography of Speaking*, ed. Richard Bauman and Joel Sherzer (Cambridge: Cambridge University Press, 1974), 125–143

11. Penelope Brown and Stephen Levinson in *Questions and Politeness*, 99–103, 233–234.

12. I would thus question Wallace Chafe's claim that colloquial/oral always connotes 'involvement' of the speaker in the communicative situation. See his "Integration and Involvement in Speaking, Writing, and Oral Literature," in *Spoken and Written Language*, 35–54.

Chapter 3

1. Wilson Follett, *Modern American Usage: A Guide,* edited and completed by Jacques Barzun (New York: Hill and Wang, 1966); Kenneth Hudson, *The Dictionary of Diseased English* (New York: Harper and Row, 1977); Theodore Bernstein's numerous books including *Watch Your Language* (New York: Atheneum, 1958), *The Careful Writer: A Modern Guide to English Usage* (New York: Atheneum, 1965), and *Dos, Don'ts, and Maybes of English Usage* (New York: Times Books, 1977); William Safire, *On Language* (New York: Avon, 1980).

2. Arn and Charlene Tibbetts, *What's Happening to American English?* (New York: Charles Scribner's Sons, 1979), 5.

3. John Dryden, "A Discourse Concerning the Original and Progress of Satire," in *Of Dramatic Poesy and Other Critical Essays*, vol. 2, ed. George Watson (New York: Dutton, 1964), 136–137.

4. George Landow, "The Victorian Sage in Carlyle, Arnold, Ruskin, Didion, and Mailer," lecture given at the University of Maryland, April 1983.

5. Dan Sperber and Deirdre Wilson, "Irony and the Use-Mention Distinction," in *Radical Pragmatics*, ed. Peter Cole (New York: Academic Press, 1981), 295–318.

6. Wayne Booth, *A Rhetoric of Irony* (Chicago: University of Chicago Press, 1974), 28–29;.

Chapter 4

1. Roland Barthes, *The Pleasure of the Text*, trans. Richard Miller (New York: Hill and Wang, 1973), 27.

2. Michel Foucault, "What is an Author?" in *Language, Counter-Memory, Practice* (Ithaca: Cornell University Press, 1977); reprinted in *Textual Strategies*, ed. Josué Harari (Ithaca: Cornell University Press, 1979), 141–160.

3. Notice prefaced to Casey's *Crisis Investing*, vii.

4. See for example the reference to the work of Robert Bierstedt in Reinhard Bendix's *Max Weber: An Intellectual Portrait* (Garden City, N.Y.: Doubleday, 1962), 298 n.2.

5. See the "Open Letter to My Fellow Physicians" prefacing his *Save Your Life Diet* (New York: Ballantine Books, 1976); Reuben's case is even more complicated because he has yet a third basis of authority as the author of two best sellers on sex—which, to be sure, mixes rather equivocally with the other two, also incompatible, bases of authority.

6. Frances Moore Lappé, *Diet for a Small Planet*, 10th anniversary edition (New York: Ballantine Books, 1982), 21.

7. Lappé has coauthored other works, however. Occasionally a husband and wife team write of their own experience as if it were that of a single individual.

8. Morton B. Glenn, M.D., *How to Get Thinner Once and for All* (New York: Dutton, 1965), 14n.

Chapter 5

1. Maurice Sagoff, *ShrinkLits*, revised and expanded edition, (New York: Workman Publishing, 1980), 65.

2. One widely cited model of this type of analysis is Paul de Man's "Semiology and Rhetoric," which is chapter 1 of *Allegories of Reading* (New Haven: Yale University Press, 1979).

3. Casey, by the way, has a very similar figure, likening the rapid upward and downward movements of short-term interest rates in the last decade to the movements of an elevator with a lunatic at the controls (p. 94). So, if we could replace the lunatic with a sane person . . . .

4. More recently, Ruff engaged in political action, forming a PAC (Ruff-PAC, of course) to influence the 1980 elections, an activity he reports in his new book, *How to Survive and Win in the Inflationary Eighties* (New York: Warner Books, 1981, 1982).

5. This is part of the publisher's blurb for *How to Survive and Win.*

6. Casey does reverse himself on this point later on in the penultimate chapter ("Reversing the Tide"), which explicitly advocates the radical free-market platform—but even there he concludes that the platform is unlikely to be implemented and advises moving to Tristan da Cunha. His general allegiance to the right-wing cause is sufficient to get his approving forewords by Robert Ringer and Rev. Philip M. Crane.

Chapter 6

1. Jacques Derrida, *Dissemination*, trans. Barbara Johnson (Chicago: University of Chicago Press, 1981), 142–155. The citation from the *Phaedrus* is from the Huntington and Cairns edition.

2. Charles J. Fillmore, "Ideal Readers and Real Readers," in *Analyzing Discourse: Text and Talk* (GURT 1981), ed. Deborah Tannen (Washington, D.C.: Georgetown University Press, 1982), 248–270.

3. Peter J. Rabinowitz, "Truth in Fiction: A Reexamination of Audiences," *Critical Inquiry* 4(1977): 121–142.

4. Barthes, *The Pleasure of the Text*, 31–32. This chapter's epigraph is from page 4.

5. See for example his "The Breaking of Form," in *Deconstruction and Criticism*, ed. Harold Bloom et al. (New York: Seabury Press, 1979), 1–38.

6. Judith Fetterley, *The Resisting Reader* (Bloomington: Indiana University Press, 1978).

7. Walter J. Slatoff, *With Respect to Readers* (Ithaca: Cornell University Press, 1970), 54.

8. Wolfgang Iser's citation of Husserl, *The Act of Reading* (Baltimore: The Johns Hopkins University Press, 1978), 157.

9. Eco, 40.

10. W. Daniel Wilson, "Readers in Texts," *PMLA* 96 (1981): 848–863.

11. So also Iser, 153: since the text works to alter the reader's disposition, "clearly, the text cannot and will not merely reproduce it."

Appendix

1. See for example Teun A. van Dijk's *Text and Context* (London: Longman, 1977), 232–247.

2. These are usefully discussed by Jerry Morgan in "Two Types of Convention in Indirect Speech Acts," in *Syntax and Semantics*, vol. 9, *Pragmatics*, ed. Peter Cole (New York: Academic Press, 1978), 261–280.

3. Lanham, *A Handlist of Rhetorical Terms*, 63.

4. Alex Preminger, ed., *The Princeton Encyclopedia of Poetry and Poetics*, enlarged edition (Princeton: Princeton University Press, 1974), 459.

5. Lakoff, 53–80.

6. Stiles, 227–249.

INDEX

George L. Dillon, Professor of English, University of Maryland, is author of *Language Processing and the Reading of Literature* and *Constructing Texts*.